MODES OF PRESENTATION

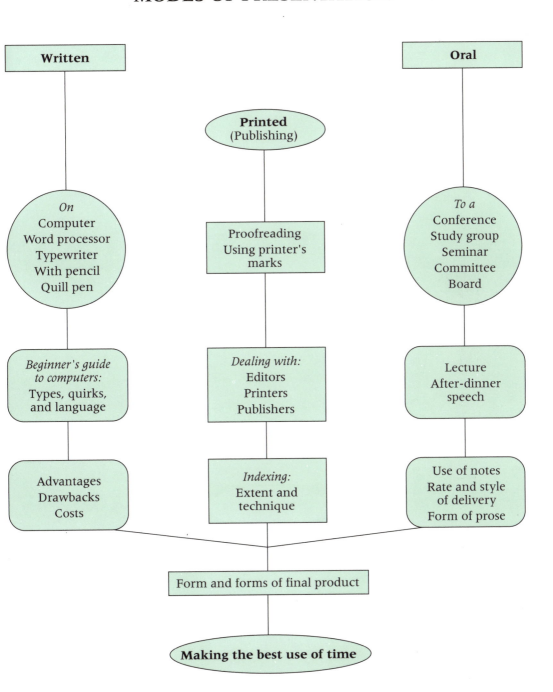

The Modern Researcher

Sixth Edition

Jacques Barzun and Henry F. Graff

WADSWORTH
CENGAGE Learning

Australia • Brazil • Japan • Korea • Mexico • Singapore • Spain • United Kingdom • United States

WADSWORTH
CENGAGE Learning

The Modern Researcher, Sixth Edition
Jacques Barzun, Henry F. Graff

Publisher: Clark Baxter
Assistant Editor: Stephanie Sandoval
Editorial Assistant: Richard Yoder
Technology Project Manager: Jennifer Ellis
Marketing Manager: Caroline Croley
Marketing Assistant: Mary Ho
Advertising Project Manager: Tami Strang
Project Manager, Editorial Production:
Kimberly Adams
Print/Media Buyer: Karen Hunt
Permissions Editor: Joohee Lee
Production Service: Shepherd, Inc.
Copy Editor: Jeannie Patterson
Cover Designer: Janet Wood
Cover Image: theispot.com/John S. Dykes
Compositor: Shepherd, Inc.

For product information and technology assistance,
contact us at
Cengage Learning Customer & Sales Support,
1-800-354-9706
For permission to use material from this text or product,
submit all requests online at
cengage.com/permissions
Further permissions questions can be emailed to
permissionrequest@cengage.com

Library of Congress Control Number: 2003107688
ISBN-13: 978-0-495-31870-5
ISBN-10: 0-495-31870-1

Wadsworth Cengage Learning
10 Davis Drive
Belmont, CA 94002-3098
USA

Cengage Learning is a leading provider of customized
learning solutions with office locations around the globe,
including Singapore, the United Kingdom, Australia, Mexico,
Brazil and Japan. Locate your local office at:
international.cengage.com/region

Cengage Learning products are represented in Canada by
Nelson Education, Ltd.

For your course and learning solutions, visit
academic.cengage.com

Purchase any of our products at your local college store or at
our preferred online store **www.ichapters.com**

Printed in the United States of America
4 5 6 7 11 10 09

ἱστορια (historia): knowledge or information obtained through inquiry.

—*Liddell and Scott,* Greek-English Dictionary *(24th ed., 1893)*

Assertions that everything is—or "soon" will be—accessible electronically often entail a dismaying ignorance of the abundance of material that is not, and never will be, included in any virtual library.

—*Thomas Mann (1998)*

The art of art, the glory of expression and the sunshine of the light of letters is simplicity. Nothing is better than simplicity.

—*Walt Whitman (1855)*

Preface to the Sixth Edition

From its first publication almost half a century ago, The *Modern Researcher* was designed to serve the needs not only of students in college or graduate school but also of professional men and women whose task is to "find the facts" and report on them in written or spoken form. The book is a guide to the necessary steps from inquiry to communication.

But since the edition of 1992, certain of these needs and steps have changed in character and the book has therefore been entirely reworked. It has been rewritten to make it more compact and to leave room for discussing the Internet and the Library in their latest configuration. The structure and coverage of the text remain the same. It is a *reading book,* not a collection of rules of thumb for solving isolated "problems." Through our analysis of actual cases and the reasons given for the instructions offered, the reader finds it easy to adjust the lesson to his or her undertaking.

After Research, Report and its components are treated at length and pointers given for putting the text through the press and for speaking it effectively. Such are the features that qualify the book for academic and professional use. In addition, on the strength of comments received over the years, it may be said that the amateur genealogist, the inditer of newsletters, the chronicler of local lore, and even the essayist or novelist will find in these pages suggestions and examples that they can turn to good account.

J. B. and **H. F. G.**
1 July 2003

Acknowledgments

We express our appreciation once again to Eileen McIlvaine, head reference librarian of Columbia University, for the benefit of her expertness and advice. We also thank Robert H. Scott, chief of the Library's electronic text service, for counsel and assistance. To Marguerite Barzun, Molly Morse, and Betsy Morse we are indebted for placing their specialized knowledge at our disposal. Treva Kelly, we hope, knows of our abiding gratitude for so patiently and good-humoredly word-processing the several drafts of the book. We are grateful too, for the superb editorial guidance of Judy Ludowitz and the attentiveness to detail of Kim Adams, the production project manager. Finally, Clark Baxter, our publisher, has shown uncommon care and enthusiasm for our undertaking this edition, and it has been an unalloyed pleasure to work with him and his associates.

The authors thank the following copyright holders for the privilege of quoting or reproducing selections from their works.

Figure 1 Cartoon © *The New Yorker* Collection 1989. Dana Fradon from cartoonbank.com. All Rights Reserved.

Figure 2 Left: *The Columbia-Viking Desk Encyclopedia,* copyright © 1953 published by Columbia University Press and reprinted with permission. **Right:** *Dictionary of Clocks and Watches* by Eric Bruton, copyright © 1963, published by Archer House.

Figure 7 Left: *Poole's Index to Periodical Literature* by William F. Poole and William I. Fletcher, published by Houghton Mifflin Company. **Right:** *Readers' Guide to Periodical Literature,* published by H. W. Wilson Company.

Figure 9 Left: *Uncommon Law* by A. P. Herbert, copyright © 1935, Methuen & Company Ltd., London, by permission of A.P. Watt, Ltd. on behalf of The Executors of the Estate of Jocelyn Hale and Teresa Elizabeth Perkins. **Right:** Column by Phyllis Battelle, reprinted with special permission of King Features Syndicate, Inc., copyright © 1975.

Figure 10 Cartoon © Bil Keene, Inc. Reprinted with Special Permission of King Features Syndicate.

Figure 16 Cartoon from *Basic Programming* by Donald Spencer, copyright © 1983 by Camelot Publishing Company. Reprinted with permission of Charles Scribner's Sons.

Figure 17 Cartoon reprinted with permission, Schwadron/ *Punch*/London.

Figure 19 *Moneysworth Magazine,* © 1987. Reprinted by permission of Avant-Garde Media, Inc.

Figure 24 Left: *Hubert Humphrey: A Political Biography* by Carl Solberg, © 1984, published by W. W. Norton & Company. **Right:** *A Stroll with William James* by Jacques Barzun, © 1983, published by Harper & Row and reprinted by permission of HarperCollins Publisher, Inc.

Figure 27 Proof sheet from Balzac's *Eugénie Grandet.* Reprinted courtesy of the J. Pierpont Morgan Library.

Figure 28 Cartoon reprinted with permission of *The Saturday Evening Post,* © 2002.

Page 170 Excerpt from *English Literature at the Close of the Middle Ages* by Edmund K. Chambers, © 1945, published by Oxford University Press, Clarendon Press. Reprinted by permission of the publisher.

Contents

PART II   Writing, Speaking, and Publishing

8   Organizing: Paragraph, Chapter, and Part 169

9   Plain Words: The War on Jargon and Clichés 193

10   Clear Sentences: Emphasis, Tone, and Rhythm 211

11   The Arts of Quoting and Translating 235

List of Figures

Part I

PRINCIPLES AND METHODS OF RESEARCH

CHAPTER 1

RESEARCH AND REPORT: CHARACTERISTICS

The Report: A Fundamental Form

In a once-famous book on the Middle East, the English archaeologist Layard printed a letter in which a Turkish official answered an Englishman's question. It begins:

My Illustrious Friend and Joy of My Liver!

The thing you asked of me is both difficult and useless. Although I have passed all my days in this place, I have neither counted the houses nor have I inquired into the number of the inhabitants; and as to what one person loads on his mules and the other stows away in the bottom of his ship, that is no business of mine. But, above all, as to the previous history of this city, God only knows the amount of dirt and confusion that the infidels may have eaten before the coming of the sword of Islam. It were unprofitable for us to inquire into it. O my soul! O my lamb! Seek not after the things which concern thee not. Thou camest unto us and we welcomed thee: go in peace.[1]

This public servant obviously made no annual report—those were the good old days. Note the three things he so courteously declined to provide: vital statistics, business reports, and history. Life today would stop if information of these three

---

[1]Austen H. Layard, *Discoveries in the Ruins of Nineveh and Babylon . . .* (London, 1853), 663.

kinds were not readily available on every sort of subject. All over the globe, every minute, someone is making a search so as to write a report on some state of fact, or else is reading and analyzing one, so that action may be taken. Reports are the means by which we try to substitute knowledge for guesswork. "The report" is fundamental in the conduct of affairs. It has become an accepted form, like the business letter or the sonnet.

Every report implies previous research, whether by the reporter or by someone else. Thousands of persons are thus turned into researchers, that is to say, into more or less able scholars. The Turkish official of today has dropped his hookah, leaped from his cushion, and is busy counting houses for the Ministry of the Interior. The figures he gathers are then published as government statistics, which other researchers will use for still other reports—from the university student writing a paper on modern Turkey to the foreign businessman who wants to trade in that country.

Among the many useful documents that may be classed as reports, there is no essential difference of outlook or method. The student writing a book report for a Freshman English course is doing on a small scale and with a single source the same thing as the president of a corporation who prepares his annual report to the stockholders, or as the President of the United States when he reports to the people on the state of the Union. The general form and the devices employed in preparation are identical in all three.

What is common to these tasks is the need to investigate and to write up findings, which means facing the problems of research and exposition. The writers of reports use the common tongue and draw upon the same vast reservoir of information. Apart from the fresh facts that, to pursue the examples above, the treasurer of a corporation or the Secretary of State supply to their respective presidents, the written sources for the millions of words uttered in reports are the familiar ones—newspapers, learned journals, histories, statistical abstracts, law cases, government documents, and the many categories of books found in large libraries—in addition to the vast amount of material on the Internet. The making of fresh surveys is another source, but its various techniques will not concern us here. The huge accumulation of gathered information is what the researcher must learn to use in any case to satisfy his or her particular need; and as the conditions of the search are the same for all who search and report, it is possible to discuss their tasks and methods apart from their occasion or subject.

The Historical Outlook Underlies Research *and* Report

The attitude and techniques of the report writer are derived directly from one of the great academic disciplines—History. Everything in a report is about what happened earlier. It is from historical scholarship that the world has taken the apparatus of footnotes, source references, and bibliography, which validate what is stated. It is from writers of history that others have learned to sift evidence, balance testimony, and supply verification.

It may seem as if, in spite of what has just been said, much difference separates the scholar's interest from that of other report writers. The former re-creates the past; the latter is concerned with what is still present, generally with a view to plotting the future; hence their outlooks must differ. True, but the difference does not affect method or change requirements. Take an article about foreign policy designed to change opinion and future action. It does so by discussing principles or personnel, and to do this the argument must lean on the evidence of what has been happening—on what is recorded and beyond the reach of change. It is in large part a piece of history.

Reporting History in Daily Life

Here, for example, is part of a bimonthly business report:

The International Monetary Fund created the SDR in 1968 as an asset that countries would hold and use in settling their international accounts.[2] The idea was that the stock of SDRs would be managed so that world reserves would grow in line with world commerce. The SDR was created in a world of fixed exchange rates that reflected fixed par values of currencies. . . . In early 1973, . . .

In science, which often seems timeless, and in social science, which makes comparisons through time series, dates are of fundamental importance. The scientist as weatherman reports on the recent and remote past: "Last April and May [1980] saw the driest weather in England and Wales since 1896, followed by the wettest June since 1879, but the year before suffered the wettest March to May since 1727."

One does not usually consider advertisers ardent champions of Fact, yet they too want to find out what's what. Here is a New York agency making known its philosophy. The heading runs, "First, Get the Facts":

More business mistakes are due to faulty facts than to faulty judgment. As used by us, research takes many forms: motivation studies, copy testing, leadership surveys, consumer opinion research, store audits, consumer panel surveys, and dealer surveys. . . . Research has provided a foundation for building a more efficient advertising program and taking the guesswork out of future planning.

One can imagine the endless reports arising from all these panels and surveys, the steady repetition of "It was found that . . ." with dates and percentages.

Like advertising, journalism has adopted the ways of historical research and popularized them. Magazines such as *Time* and *Newsweek* employ corps of persons who bear the title of Researcher and whose function is to verify every statement made in the stories turned in by those whose title is Reporter.

As a final example—this time on the geological scale—consider these few sentences from a journal of popular science:

The element uranium changes gradually, through a series of transition products—the most important of which is radium—into

[2]SDR stands for Special Drawing Rights.

its inactive end-product, the lead isotope with an atomic weight of 206. The transformation rate is extremely small; in any uranium mineral, only 1 percent of a given amount of uranium is transformed in 65 million years. . . .

The Past Is All-Inclusive

In short, every use of the past tense—"I was there"; "He did it"—is a bit of history. True, false, or mistaken, it expresses our historical habit of mind. We have newspapers to read the previous day's history. We call up our friends to tell them what has happened to us since the last time we spoke and to hear their story in return. People keep diaries to preserve their memories or to impart their doings to posterity; or again, they delve into their genealogies to nourish pride in their roots. The physician arrives at a diagnosis after asking for the patient's history—previous illnesses and those of the parents. Every institution, club, and committee keeps minutes and other records, as stores of experience: What did we do last year? How did we answer when the question first came up? Lawyers and judges think with the aid of precedents, and their research makes our law. All this remembering and recording is conveyed by the written word.

Out of what survives of these portions of history, the formal narratives of an age or of a person's life are fashioned. The letter that carried news or affection becomes a documentary source; the public official's diary, written for self-protection, throws light on governmental secrets; the broken pottery or the cave painting tells of a vanished people, as the modern novel and daily paper variously reveal the temper of the age. Thus does "history proper" intertwine with our speech, our beliefs, our passions, and our institutions.

For a whole society to lose its sense of history would be tantamount to giving up its civilization. We live and are moved by historical ideas and images, and our national existence goes on by reproducing them. We put the faces of our famous men and women on our stamps or coins;[3] we make symbols of historic places and objects—Monticello, Plymouth Rock, the Liberty Bell; and like banks, colleges, and married pairs, we celebrate anniversaries. Dates, too, trigger the historical memory; the president's budget director begins his report: "The events of 1989 [notably the collapse of the Soviet empire] and what they will have unleashed may one day rise to the place with those of 1688, 1776, or 1789."

We preserve anything that we think bears witness to something of past importance—not only presidential papers in separate libraries but also old houses protected by Landmarks Commissions. We want bits of old ships dredged up; details of what neighbors and friends thought of public figures. The result: fatter and fatter biographies. Thus in *The Day Lincoln Was Shot,* Jim Bishop, a newspaper reporter and not a professional historian, made the search into such details a formula. He read 7 million words of contemporary testimony to glean curious scraps; and he tells us: "I traveled the escape route of Booth in an Oldsmobile and checked it to the tenth of a mile."

The Turkish official we met earlier would say that we make a fetish of fact—and he would be right.

The Research Reporter and Scholar

This pervasiveness of factuality and history connects the researcher, whatever his or her purpose, with nearly every other branch of learning. For there is no telling what a report of world events may call for. Not only politics but geography, economics, military science, technology, and religion at any time become relevant. And now that business increasingly crosses international boundaries, the same array of topics will come into the report.

---

[3]Think of the ideas instantly raised in your mind by Mona Lisa and her smile. Books and advertising have frozen many characters into one significance each by one likeness familiarized through repetition. Who ever thinks of George Washington grinning or of Lincoln anything but sad?

FIGURE 1   *HISTORY AS VISUAL SYMBOLS*

"I like the concept if we can do it with no new taxes."

The viewer of this cartoon sees at once that it shows the Trojan horse used by the Greeks to smuggle their soldiers into the city of Troy and conquer it. The story is part of every educated person's memory, whether from repeated reference in the media or in books, and possibly from reading Homer's *Iliad*. Note the historic misnomer: the fabricated horse was Greek, not Trojan. Its use as a symbol makes the episode seem apposite to the current politics of defense procurement.

It is obvious that no report writer can know all subjects. But he or she must know how to use adequately the results supplied by others. What one adds to others' contributions is twofold. First, the special results of a search for facts as yet hidden or possibly ill handled by a previous worker.[4] Second, the organizing principles, narrative skill, and conclusions or explanations that make the disconnected facts intelligible.

To sum up, there is no difference between the historian's techniques and those of the researcher at large preparing a report. Both have recourse to the same infinite range of materials, find their way among documents by the same devices, gather and test facts according to the same rules, exhibit their results in the same order and spirit, and hope to impress others' minds by the same literary means.

Historical Writing: Its Origins and Demands

Researchers of all kinds are at one with the public in taking it for granted that to understand the state of a question or subject fully, something must be known about its antecedents. This is called the *genetic interpretation*. Every speech, report, inquiry, or application begins with "the background." This attitude affects the worker for the most part unconsciously. It guides his curiosity without one's being aware of it by making one look for answers to recurrent questions: Who is So-and-So? When did this happen? Why was that not done?

Assuming this cultural trait to be universal among us, we must go on to discuss the habits a researcher must acquire by attention and self-control, the impulses to be curbed or encouraged. No doubt, more qualities than the half-dozen about to be listed are called into play. But these are indispensable, and giving them names may help the worker along his paths.

1. The first virtue required is ACCURACY. No argument is needed to show why. If history is the story of past facts, and report, account, or news story is a piece of recent history, those facts must be *ascertained*. Making certain implies being accurate—steadily, religiously. To this end, train yourself to remember

---

[4]On this point, see p. 19.

names and dates and titles of books with precision. Never say to yourself or to another, "It's in that book—you know—I forgot the title, but it has a green cover." Being precise calls for *attending* to the object when you first examine it and noting small differences instead of skipping over them: "Here is a volume on the Lincoln Memorial in Washington. It is edited by Edward Concklin, and the author spells his name with an added *c* and no *g*." There is no profound significance in this fact, no imperative need to remember it, but if you do this kind of focusing repeatedly, regularly, you will avoid a multitude of mistakes. Some few you are bound to make. Everybody is liable to them almost in proportion to the length of one's work. But they can be kept to a minimum by the habit of unremitting attention. Do not fear that such details will clutter up your mind; they will lie dormant until needed and often will suggest important links with other matters you would not otherwise have thought of.

2. Next comes the LOVE OF ORDER. There is in any piece of research so much to be read, noted down, compared, verified, indexed, grouped, organized, and recopied that unless one is capable of adhering to a system, the chances of error grow alarming, while the task itself turns into a perpetual panicky emergency: What did I do with those bibliographic notes? In what notebook did I list the dates I have checked? Does this page belong to Draft 1 or Draft 2? And so on ad infinitum. Some people may overdo orderliness, but most of us underdo it, usually from groundless self-confidence. You may think you know what you are doing and have done. The fact is that as you get deeper into a subject you will know more and more about *it* and less and less about your own steps in mastering its details—hence the value of the system, which keeps order for you. Sticking to it is never a loss of time, though it calls for the union of three minor virtues: calm, patience, and pertinacity.

3. You may think that orderliness would also imply LOGIC. In practice, it seems to do so to a negligible extent; the one is

mechanical, the other intellectual. The logic considered here is not the formal art of the philosopher but its ready and practical application to the perplexities of the search for sources. As will appear, the researcher must quickly learn the schemes of innumerable reference books; if you are not adept at inference, you will bog down or make mistakes. For example, in the *Thesaurus* of ancient Latin authors, which offers to the eye under each entry an unappetizing block of print, the punctuation is faint and confusing. If you do not reason correctly from the first or last quotation in each block, you will infallibly connect the one you look for with the wrong author.

The physical arrangement of books in any given library may present the same kind of problem: if over here we are in the *G*s and over there in the *K*s, the intervening books (including the *H*s, which I want) must be in between, but where? Ah yes, in the lower part of this large reference table, which has shelves. If you run to the librarian for the solution of every puzzle, mental or physical, trivial or important, you will be an old but *in*experienced researcher before you have finished.

4. Elsewhere, HONESTY may be the best policy, but in research it is the only one. Unless you put down with complete candor what you find to be true, you are nullifying the very result you aim at, which is the discovery of whatever is in the records you are consulting. You may have a hypothesis which is shattered by the new fact, but that is what hypotheses are for—to be destroyed and remolded closer to the reality. The troublesome fact may go against your purpose or prejudice, but nothing is healthier for the mind than to have either challenged. You are a searcher after truth, which should reconcile you to every discovery. Even if you are pledged to support a cause, you had better know beforehand all the evidence your side will have to face. For if one fact is there obstructing your path, you may be fairly sure others to the same effect will be turned up by your adversary. It is the nature of reality to be

mixed, and the research scholar is the person on whom we rely to chart it. Accuracy about neutral details is of little worth compared to honesty about significant ones.

5. Some persons are honest as far as they can see, but they do not see far enough; in particular, they do not see around themselves. They lack the virtue of SELF-AWARENESS. You, the searcher, need it—first, to make sure that you are not unwittingly dishonest and, second, in order to lessen the influence of bias by making your standards of judgment plain to the reader. No one can be a perfectly clear reflector of what one finds. There is always some flaw in the glass, whose effect may be so uniform as not to disclose itself. The only protection against this source of constant error is for the writer to make all assumptions clear. To invent an *outré* example, a fanatical teetotaler might in a biographical sketch of General Grant assert that here was a man of revolting and immoral habits. Given nothing else, the reader is inclined to trust the conclusions of the writer. But if the accusation reads, "Anyone who habitually drinks whiskey is a person of revolting moral character; therefore General Grant, etc." The reader has a chance to dissent.

This simplified instance bears on two important realms of reporting: the description of cultures alien in time or space, and biography. In both, it is essential to control one's emotions as evidence turns up of behavior repugnant to either of them or to the standards of the age. In such cases, one must set forth (though more subtly than in the example) what one's criteria are before one passes judgment or describes by epithets. Failing this, the way is open to the meanest kind of libel and defamation of character, to say nothing of the caricature of a person who has been thought important enough to write about.

6. Everybody is always urging everybody else to have IMAGI-NATION, and this is indeed good advice. But perhaps the hint should suggest not so much laying in a stock as releasing what one has. Convention and laziness often exclude the

happy thought that, if let alone, would lead to the desired goal. In research, this goal is double—practical and abstract. The researcher must again and again imagine the kind of source needed before it can be found. To be sure, it may not exist; but if it does, its whereabouts must be presumed. By that ingenious balancing of wish and reason, which is true imagination, one make one's way from what one knows and possesses to what one must possess in order to know more. The two chapters following will give concrete instances.

The researcher must also perform these acrobatics of the mind around problems that are abstract. For example, working upon a critical study of Henry James and noticing the novelist's persistent attempts in later life to become a playwright—a determination shown also in the dramatic tone and structure of the later novels—the critic begins to wonder what theatrical influences could have formed this taste. Is it possible that James as a child or youth attended the New York theaters, then famous for melodrama? The dates coincide; and behold, autobiographical evidence when sought confirms the inspired guess. Of course, the historical imagination of a genius cannot be asked of every modest worker. The historical imagination that is insisted on here is an implement that none can do without.

CHAPTER 2

THE ABC OF TECHNIQUE

The Prime Difficulty: What Is My Subject?

Any account, report, or other piece of serious factual writing is intended to take effect on someone at some time. It must consequently meet that someone's demands. Those demands amount to this: Is the account true, reliable, complete? Is it clear, orderly, easy to grasp and remember? All the devices and methods that the researcher combines under the name of technique exist to satisfy these requirements.

This in turn means that the researcher must first ask the questions of himself, and not only at the end, but at many points between the beginning and the end. It is evident that in order to be able to answer Yes to each part of the questions, the writer must be sure of what his subject is. If he does not know, how can he tell whether the treatment is complete? If he does not know, how can he expect a reader to find his paper clear? If he does not know, what yardstick can he use for including and omitting, and how can he proceed in orderly fashion from opening to conclusion? If he does not know, how can he test reliability? For reliability only means "These words fairly represent certain things in the outside world (facts, events, ideas) that are naturally linked to form 'a subject.'"

Now writers always start with *some* idea of what the chosen subject is, even if that idea is contained in a single term—Blimps or Fish or Day of Infamy. But these terms apply to large, vague collections of facts. The discovery of the true, whittled-down subject that the article will present to the reader is a task that begins with the first steps of research and ends only when the last word has been written and revised.

The truth of this statement you will experience the moment you tackle *your* subject. Between the first notion of it and the final draft, you will probably modify your conception more than once. It does not matter if during your research you pick up facts or ideas that you later discard as irrelevant. But it is obvious that if you take time to collect nearly everything that somehow clings to any part of your topic, you will have a library on your hands, and not the materials with which to work up a report on "a subject." Fortunately, as you proceed, your judgment grows more and more assured about what belongs and what does not, and soon you begin to *see your subject*. From then on you must not take your eyes off it.

The reason for this constant attention is that a subject does not let itself be carved away from neighboring subjects as if by a butcher carving off one chop from the next. A subject is always trying to merge itself again into the great mass of associated facts and ideas. Take a small book like Rachel Carson's *The Sea Around Us*. Before starting, the author undoubtedly had the general notion of writing for laymen about certain facts relating to the sea. She could hardly have chosen a more difficult *notion* to turn into a *subject*. The sea is immense. Its action and effects, its form, substance, and inhabitants furnish matter for thousands of monographs. Yet the writer could not choose for her book a few of these matters at random and then stop. The result would have been the same as that produced by the amateur writer who called up a publisher and asked, "How long is the average novel nowadays?"

"Oh, between seventy-five and ninety thousand words."

"Well then, I've finished!"

The anecdote illustrates by a negative example the principle that to make any lasting impression on the mind, the piece must have unity and completeness. To perceive what is necessary to completeness, you must first know the projected size of its treatment. Suppose someone asks: "What does 'Roman Empire' mean?" You can answer in a sentence, in a paragraph, or in a page. You can refer the questioner to an essay, a book, or Gibbon's six volumes. All these forms determine by their scale what is and what is not part of the subject; for if you have but one sentence at your disposal, you will certainly not mention the geese that saved the Capitol, or even the three wars against Carthage; and if you have six volumes at your disposal, you will nowhere find it necessary to give a one-sentence definition of the whole.

In other words, your subject is defined by *that group of associated facts and ideas which, when clearly presented in a prescribed amount of space, leave no questions unanswered* WITHIN *the presentation, even though many questions could be asked* OUTSIDE *it*. For example, if you defined the Roman Empire as "an ancient power that sprang from a city-state in central Italy to cover ultimately both shores of the Mediterranean, and that between 100 B.C. and A.D. 476 transmitted to the West the cultures it had conquered to the East," you would have, not indeed a *perfect* definition but one that is complete as far as it goes. In any longer account, the added detail must sustain the impression of closeness to the central idea and its even distribution around it.

Without unity and completeness, details make, as we say, "no sense." Even a reader ignorant of your subject will notice something wrong if you give a page to the legend of the geese whose quacking saved the city and later on dispose of Caesar's murder in one sentence. Nor can you at the last page leave a dozen questions hanging in the air. The reader knows from experience that things written about exhibit a logical structure. Time, place, and meaning give things their connectedness, which must come out again in the report upon them. And once subjects have been made distinct by an appropriate treatment, they will not readily mix again. This is the point of Dickens's joke about Mr. Pott, the journalist in *Pickwick Papers,* whose colleague had written an article about Chinese Metaphysics, though he knew nothing of the subject. He used the encyclopedia, said Mr. Pott, and "read for metaphysics under the letter M, and for China under the letter C, and combined his information."

To test the relevance of any idea within a large subject and as it were to draw a circle around whatever should be in it, the researcher will find that an expanded title helps. This is one reason why reports of factual investigation generally carry long and explicit titles. Books used to be titled in this same descriptive fashion, for example, Malthus's *Essay on the Principle of Population, as it affects the future improvement of Society: with remarks on the Speculations of Mr. Godwin, M. Condorcet, and other writers* (1798). The title not only gives fair warning about the contents; it also sets limits. It makes a kind of contract with the reader as to what he or she will get, and the contract helps the writer to fulfill the bargain. In this regard, such a title is at the opposite extreme from the modern style shown in *The Sea Around Us,* which could encompass anything and everything.

Note that a seemingly clear, sharply defined subject like "The American presidency" actually conceals a multitude of separate subjects. Would a book on the presidents from 1789 to the present take up their private lives and their careers before election? If so, to what extent? And what about their characters, their wives, their illnesses? We can think at once of instances in which any of these topics would be immediately relevant to the central theme—if we knew what that theme was. *The American Presidency—The Conflicts between the Executive and Congress* is a different book from *The American Presidency—A Study in Personal Power.* Lengthening the title to narrow the limits has the effect of driving doubts into a corner. There your mind can grapple with them and decide the recurring issue of relevance: Is this particular incident a case of personal power, Yes or No? Does it duplicate or amplify a previous instance, Yes or No? and so on until you have finished deciding In or Out.

These difficulties are inseparable from research. They illustrate the general truth that reading, writing, and thinking are the three activities of research.

Though hard work, delimiting the subject has one advantage—and this is a thought in which the weary researcher, struggling with a mass of notes and ideas like someone filling a featherbed, can take comfort—a writer cannot "tell all." No one wants him to. The writer will often wonder, "Do I need to mention this?" And he must frequently answer: "They don't want to hear about *that*!"

I Have All My Material—But Have You?

The material for research is the mass of words bearing on the innumerable topics and subtopics within the subject.[1] The first step before starting to carve out what you need is to find out whether someone has already dealt with the subject in print. At this late date in the world's history very few subjects of research can be entirely original. Even the newest experiment in science has been led up to, and new findings usually come with a bibliography that points to previous findings.

The record of earlier work in any field—known as its "literature"—is accessible in many ways, of which more will be said in Chapter 3. The fact to note here is that, barring exceptional cases, leads to your material exist, probably in abundance. Discovering them is a question of skill and patience—of technique.

Technique begins with learning how to use a library. Whatever the system, printed cards or digital, it is only an expanded form of the alphabetical order of an encyclopedia. A ready knowledge of the two ways in which the order of letters in the alphabet may appear is therefore fundamental to all research.[2] (See Figure 2.)

---

[1]Field investigations and laboratory experiments are in part exceptions to this generality, though they too involve research into sources.

[2]This remark may sound obvious and unnecessary; it is deliberately made as a hint to those people (including college and graduate students) more numerous than one would suppose, who are crippled in research by an inability to follow quickly and accurately the alphabetic order beyond the first or second letter of the key words.

FIGURE **2** *THE ALPHABETICAL ORDER*

Gleizes, Albert Léon (älbĕr' lāŏ' glĕz'), 1881–, French cubist painter and illustrator.

Glencoe (glĕn'kō), residential village (pop. 6,980), NE Ill., N suburb of Chicago.

Glencoe (glĕnkō'), valley of Coe R., Argyllshire, Scotland, overhung by lofty mountains. Macdonald clan massacred here by the Campbells in 1692.

Glen Cove, city (pop. 15,130), SE N.Y., on N shore of Long Isl., in summer resort area; settled 1668. Mfg. of office supplies, clothing, and radios.

Glendale. 1 City (pop. 8,179), S central Ariz., NW of Phoenix. Agr. trade point in SALT RIVER VALLEY. **2** Suburban city (pop. 95,702), S Calif., N of Los Angeles; laid out 1886 on site of first Spanish land grant in Calif. Mfg. of petroleum products, aircraft, and glass. Has Forest Lawn Memorial Park, cemetery containing reproductions of great works of art.

Glendale, battle of: see SEVEN DAYS BATTLES.

Glendive (glen'dīv), city (pop. 5,254), E Mont., on Yellowstone R. and NE of Miles City. Center of farm, stock, and poultry area. Has railroad shops.

Frequency Comparison Meter Special meter used at electricity power stations to compare mains frequency with a MASTER CLOCK, so that SYNCHRONOUS CLOCKS are kept to MEAN TIME.

Friction Spring Spring acting as a clutch for hand setting; also one for taking up backlash of a CENTRE SECONDS HAND.

Frictional Rest Most ESCAPEMENTS release a tooth of the ESCAPE WHEEL for a fraction of a second and then hold it up. With some, like the CYLINDER ESCAPEMENT, the escape wheel tooth is held up by its resting against part of the moving BALANCE WHEEL. Such frictional rest interferes with the free swing of the balance wheel. The LEVER ESCAPEMENT locks an escape wheel tooth without touching the balance wheel, and is therefore free.

Fromanteel Famous family of clockmakers in London, which originated from Holland. They were named Ahasuerus, John and Abraham. John learned how to make HUYGENS pendulum clocks in Holland and the Fromanteels were the first to introduce them into England in 1658. Evelyn

---

Knowing the order of the letters of the alphabet is indispensable to anyone who wants to find or consult a book. Catalogues, indexes, and reference works are built on the alphabetical order. But within that order variations in the sequence of words will be encountered. The reason is this: single words can be arranged in only one way if the order of letters is followed: ab*a*cus, abb*o*t, ab*d*icate, abd*o*minal. But double or compounded words offer a choice. Suppose that an index includes the names *Glencoe, Glen Cove, Glendale, Glendale, battle of,* and *Glendive.* The author may have chosen to list first all the names in which *Glen* is separate before putting down the others. Or he may have chosen to arrange the names regardless of the break, and then *Glencoe* comes first, *Glendale* and *Glendale, battle of* next, and *Glendive* last, as in the entries to the left above. The right-hand entries (from a *Dictionary of Clocks and Watches* by Eric Bruton) illustrate the alternative form by putting *Friction S* . . . ahead of *Friction a(l).* Note also that almost all indexes give the proper names that begin *M', Mc,* and *Mac* ahead of those that begin *Ma.* This is done because of the difficulty of remembering which variant spelling of *Mac* belongs to the name sought.

But the listing must be used with alertness and imagination, for topics, ideas, and events often go by different names. For example, coin collecting is called Numismatics. More complicated is the way in which one who wants information about the theory of the divine right of kings arrives at the term "Monarch." One might conceivably have reached the same result by looking up "right, divine," or even possibly "Divine Right," if the library owns a book by that title or its catalogue is fully cross-indexed. What is certain is that there is little chance of success if one looks up *King* and no hope at all if one looks up *theory*. As for all computerized entries, one must first consult the classification set up by the Library of Congress. In other words, one must from the very beginning *play* with the subject—view it from various sides in order to seize on its outward connections.

Suppose that after some ingenuity and considerable effort you have found two articles and three books, all bearing on your topic; the temptation is now strong to consider that the search in research is pretty well over. You like to think that what remains is to read, take notes and arrange them, and write your essay. You probably announce that you "have all your material." In this error you are not far removed from Dickens's brash journalist who "combined his information." True, you may as well start reading, but research has not yet begun, for the chances are that you have scarcely read more than a few pages in the second article when you discover between it and the first a discrepancy in date or name, which the books, when appealed to, do not resolve. You consult the nearest encyclopedia: it offers you a third variant. You are perplexed, yet you should feel a certain elation; research—as against *re*-search—is about to begin.

How far it will take you, no one can predict. By the time you have tracked down all uncertainties, followed up side lines to their dead ends, filled in gaps in logical or chronological sequence, and reached solid conclusions of your own, you will have acquired a sizable amount of information, written matter, and technique. But you may still not be entitled to tell your inquiring friends, "I have all my material."

What you have done—to go back to our pair of fundamental questions—is to make sure that your report will be true and reliable. But there is one more test of completeness to be applied. Assuming that you have been working steadily with extant sources and that in your single-mindedness you have neglected your ordinary routines, you must now remember that while you were busy working, the world has been moving on, newspapers have continued to come out, people have died, other researchers' work has been published. You must therefore make a last survey. Recent issues of periodicals will not have been indexed nor death dates recorded; you have to rely on your wits to find this type of fact. To the very end of your work on the paper, you must keep an eye on events and publications for the latest reports. At the worst, to neglect them may mean that you have overlooked something that knocks the props from under your results; at best, it may mean that you will be disconcerted in public or private when someone brings up a fact that everybody seems to know but you.

The Practical Imagination at Work

The nucleus of two articles and three books on your subject has expanded by addition and verification into material for an article or report possibly twenty pages long. This report of yours will be no mere précis or résumé of what you have found. It should offer something not directly or fully treated in any one source. It will be a new arrangement consisting of tested facts and fresh thought. At the moment, the new arrangement does not exist, but only the materials for it. These so-called materials are scribbles you have made on pieces of paper—notes taken as you pursued the elusive dates, the missing middle name, the descriptive detail, or the clinching piece of testimony supporting a conclusion.

But it is not possible to write a report direct from the sum total of the gathered materials. You can *compose* only from what you deliberately select from your notes, which bulk much larger than your report will when done. It is obvious that this collection of notes can very soon become unmanageable. You must therefore adopt some system for creating order as you go, so that you may select intelligently later on. There is no one system to be preferred above all others, except that the system most congenial to you will probably give the best results.

What you want is a regular procedure that will enable you to turn to a given note without having to riffle through sheafs of stuff. At any time in research you may want to compare a quotation you took down a while ago with a new version you have just come across; or you may want to fill in a blank with a date that has turned up unexpectedly. Ultimately, you will need to sort your notes into bunches of related matters, as preparation to writing your first draft.

For all these purposes, experience shows that you must take notes in a uniform manner, on paper or cards of uniform size. Some researchers favor notebooks, bound or looseleaf;[3] others prefer ruled or blank index cards—3×5 inches, or 4×6, or 5×8— but one size only for the main materials. Those who use notebooks, large or small, copy out facts or quotations as they come, regardless of subject. They leave a wide margin straight down one side to permit a key word or phrase to be put opposite each note as a guide to the eye in finding and classifying that note. It is also possible to write in notebooks in such a way that each note will fill no more than a given amount of space on the page. Then, when the book is filled, the pages can be cut into slips of uniform size and shuffled into groups.

The same principle underlies the use of small cards. Those who favor them make a point of noting down only a single item on any one card. Room is left in an upper corner for the key word by which related cards are later assembled. Advocates of

---

[3]Many professionals throw up their hands in horror at the thought of notebooks, but great examples justify their use (Gibbon, Rhodes, A. F. Pollard, Oman). No doubt this older practice will continue to have its devotees. Certainly the researcher who has to travel is better off with notebooks than with stacks of cards.

the larger cards use them as do the users of notebooks. Other variations of these fundamental ways will suggest themselves. A distinguished English physician of the early twentieth century, Sir Clifford Allbutt, recommended using slips of paper the size of a check and leaving a wide left-hand margin, partly for keying, partly for gathering under a snap clip. The notes for each section being held together provides the researcher with a series of small booklets that he or she leafs through thoughtfully when about to write.

The common feature of all these devices is clear: the information is extracted from all sources as it comes and is set down on one kind of card or paper. Before the miscellaneous collection becomes unwieldy, it is roughly keyed or indexed for ready reference after sorting. The single-fact-to-a-card system gives the most thorough index. But it has the drawback of producing very quickly a large, discouraging pile of cards, bulky to carry around and clumsy to handle when the time comes for writing. The notebook system is much less cumbrous but also less strictly organized. Which to choose? You should consult your taste and decide whether your temperament makes you want to have everything just so, or whether you can stand a certain amount of extra leafing through pages for the sake of having your materials more compact and portable.

The nature of the subject may also dictate a choice. For very large statistical surveys, it may prove desirable—even necessary—to put your data into a computer, but that requires special training.[4] In deciding upon a note-taking method, there is no substitute for judgment. Yet no researcher, it goes without saying, should amass notes higgledy-piggledy on a variety of slips or notebook pages, leave them unkeyed, and then face the task of reducing the chaos to order. If at times you are unexpectedly forced to take down a reference on the back of an envelope or scrap of paper, you should as soon as possible transfer it in proper form to the regular file.

[4]See Chapter 14.

The only sensible irregularities are those that have a purpose. For example, users of notebooks often find it convenient to make out a 3×5 card for each book and article they encounter, alphabetizing them by author as they proceed. Similarly, users of cards may keep a small notebook in which to list queries as they arise—points to look up later in reference works or elsewhere. It is a saving of time to do these verifications in batches, rather than interrupt the train of thought while reading and note-taking. One can set aside for days of headache or indisposition the more mechanical tracking down of dates and the like, thus reserving one's best mind for real research.

Researchers find a laptop computer extremely useful for taking notes. For adepts at touch typing it is faster than writing by hand. (Some libraries have installed desktop computers for this purpose.) One can then e-mail the note or copied texts to one's desktop at home. A so-called tablet computer is also available and favored by some, because one can write on it by hand with a stylus. But the laptop is the preferred instrument. It accepts CD-ROMs and other "peripherals" and can be used nearly everywhere. Schools, libraries, hotels, business centers, and other public places have portals to plug in to a power source through a DSL, T1, cable modem, phone line, or other type of connection. The note-taker thus armed will at times find a station coupled with wireless Internet capability, so that if one's laptop is configured for it, one can reach the Internet without hooking up.[5] [N. B.: Very rarely will a laptop be held on the lap.]

If you use a laptop (as in any note-taking), do not simply copy from book to disk without rewording—except, of course, when you intend to quote. Any quasi-mechanical, absent-minded transcribing keeps you from learning what you should know about the topic at hand and hampers you at the stage of working up your material.

If you keep in mind the foreseeable uses to which you are going to put your notes and also observe your own preferences,

---

[5]Bear in mind that rare-book and manuscript libraries generally prohibit the use of anything but pencil for the taking of notes.

you can put together a system that will suit you. Once you adopt it, stick to it, for it will serve you best from the moment you no longer think about it but use it automatically.

Again, if you do not discipline yourself to the habit of always writing down author, title, and page number each time you note a fact or copy a quotation, you will lose endless hours later in an irritating search for the exact reference. The same holds for clippings you make from newspapers: write the date and year of the issue, for the dateline of the news story may be several days before and the year is never given. Finally, there is in research one absolute rule that suffers no exception: NEVER WRITE ON BOTH SIDES OF ANYTHING. If you violate the rule and do it once, you will do it again; and if you do it from time to time, you can never remember when you have done it; you thereby condemn yourself to a frequent frustrating hunt for "that note," which may be on the reverse side of some unidentifiable slip or card or page. You will turn over hundreds of pieces of papers to recover it.

A Note Is First a Thought

So much for the mechanical side of note-taking. The intellectual side cannot be as readily described or discussed. The advice "Don't take too many notes" is like the recipe in the cookbook that begins "Take enough butter." How much is "too many" or "enough"? Too many is tantamount to reproducing your printed source. If you find yourself approaching this limit, even over the stretch of one page, halt and take stock. You might conceivably need a full page verbatim, but this is seldom true, apart from the need to reproduce letters, diary entries, and the like; in that case it is safer, because more accurate, to make photocopies from the book.[6]

---

[6]Because photocopying machines are easily accessible, some students like to make them do the work of taking notes—as we said about the mindless use of laptops. But although the accuracy of quotations is increased thereby, the saving of time hoped for is an illusion. Putting the substance of the notes through the mind, as described in the paragraphs that follow, cannot be eliminated; it is only postponed.

Rather than try to gauge your note-taking skill by quantity, think of it in this way: am I simply doing clerk's work or am I assimilating new knowledge and putting down my own thoughts? To put down your own thoughts, you must use your own words, not the author's. Make a conscious, steady effort to do this until it becomes second nature. For example, here is what you read in your source:

On May 15, 1918, Franklin and Josephus Daniels waited with the President, the Postmaster General, and other dignitaries on the lawn of the White House for the ceremonial arrival of the very first airmail delivery from New York. Democratic politicians had begun to talk of Roosevelt for the New York governorship, and when the subject of Al Smith's candidacy for that office came up, he made a point of reminding the President that while Smith was undeniably able, he was also a Catholic and would therefore not run well upstate. Wilson said that such considerations should be ignored in wartime: "People are every day reading the casualty lists of American boys of every creed."[7]

The lazy person's note:

> While waiting with president and others for ceremonial arrival of first airmail from NY on May 15, 1918, Franklin Roosevelt being mentioned by Dem. politicians along with Al Smith for gov. of NY reminded Wilson that Smith a Catholic, would "not run well up-state" (author's words) Wilson said such a consideration should be ignored when youths of all faiths were suffering war casualties.
>   p. 381 +

[7]Geoffrey C. Ward, *A First-Class Temperament: The Emergence of Franklin Roosevelt*, New York, Harper & Row, 1989, pp. 381–2.

The *work* done on that passage is minimal. It is also negative, in that it merely cut out connectives and fullness of expression. Such note-taking soon becomes absentminded. You do it
while half thinking of other things; hence, what you read
leaves little trace in the memory. This will handicap you at the
writing stage and will not be compensated by the fact that your
notes will be a perpetual surprise to you—stranger's work.

A better form:

> FDR at 24th Hse 5/15/18 waiting with P et
> al for first airmail from NY Al
> Smith's name came up as Dy gov
> possibility. FDR said Smith being
> Catholic would have trouble upstate
> H. demurred—improper concern when
> youths of all faiths suffering war
> casualties.
>
> pp. 381-2

What has been accomplished here is threefold: an effort
of thought has imprinted the information on the note-taker's
mind; skill in writing has benefited by making a paraphrase;
and at the same time a step has been taken toward the first
draft, for those are usable words, not a piece of plagiarism thinly
veiled by a page reference. The researcher has done a piece of
précis writing.

When you are good at taking notes, you will see that the
samples just given show different amounts of compression.
Ten lines are reduced to nine in one version, seven and a quarter in the other. With a longer original, you can do even better
than that. Whole paragraphs or sections can be summed up in
a couple of sentences. This may be due to the original's being

diffuse or badly written, as will be illustrated later on, or it may be because extra detail in the source happens to be of no importance for your purpose. Here is where your grasp of the subject comes into play. You are aware that the book in front of you was written with a certain aim in view—say, to give the story of Woodrow Wilson's life—whereas you, the researcher, are working on a study of American domestic policy. The two aims intersect, and only at the points of intersection do you make a note. You make it with *your* purpose in mind, leaving out what would be essential to another. If the note taken shows signs of having passed through a mind, it is a good test of its relevance and adequacy.

You will have noticed that to make the note as short as possible, abbreviations were used. This is legitimate but subject to the general caution that abbreviating must not lead to confusion. If in your notes W stands for Wilson, it must not stand elsewhere for White House. You must not only know what you are doing, but also imagine trouble ahead. At the moment it is taken down the note speaks volumes and looks foolproof. But nothing grows colder more rapidly than notes. A week later, that beautifully condensed and abbreviated statement may be incomprehensible.

Even when the statement is clear and, at the time, pregnant with meaning, you may think it advisable to guide your later self by an additional remark—anything from "X says, but cf. [=compare] Z, *Hist. Mexico*" to a full-fledged comment that might find a place in the finished paper. When such asides are put, quite rightly, next to the fact they refer to, it is advisable to mark them off by a special sign. A pair of slashes (or brackets) around the remark is convenient; it means: [I, the note-taker, am saying this, not the author I am transcribing]. Once adopted, the symbols for this or any other device must be invariable.

After taking notes on a book or two, you begin to discern the large natural divisions of the subject, the main heads of your report. You are now ready to begin indexing the notes you have collected. If the report is to be of modest size—twenty to thirty pages—three or four divisions will suffice. If the work is to be a book, you should break the main heads down into subdivisions, giving each a provisional name or, if you like, a number. In a biography, for instance, there might be Youth and Education; Adult Beginnings; Success as Lawyer; Politics; Early Character and Avocations; Crisis in Middle Life; Voluntary Exile; Last Years and Death; Estimate of Career; Bibliography.

These working titles, or their initials, or else Roman numerals corresponding to an outline on which the headings appear, form the key or index. The appropriate word or sign is written in the margin of the notebook opposite each note, reference, or quotation. If cards have been used, the key word or sign is entered in the chosen corner. Misjudgments as to where a certain fact really belongs are bound to occur. For this reason, it is best not to scrawl a large key word in the available space. You may have to cross it out and substitute another. Or again, a given fact may have two or more uses and need as many key words. It is likely, for instance, that some fact under the mid-career crisis will come up again under Estimate of Career and be anticipated in Early Character.

This grouping of notes carries as yet no hint of detailed order and sequence, but it does show how much is still lacking for a balanced treatment. The category Politics may be bulging with notes while Youth and Education is thin and anemic. By contrast, since no relevant reference to other sources goes unnoted, the Bibliography group grows as fast as any and gives promise of supplying the lack of information disclosed by the indexing.

It should be unnecessary to point out that every one of the technical hints just given is adaptable to any subject. The last example has been taken from biography because the life of a public figure is a typical subject familiar to all. The sources can be manuscript letters or diaries, answers to questionnaires, a court record of testimony, or the books of a business firm. Wherever there is a multitude of facts and assertions to be selected, marshaled into kinds, and used as evidence of a state of affairs, the operations of the mind that guides the pen are fundamentally the same.

Knowledge for Whom?

The effort of research is so taxing and absorbing that whoever has gone through it feels a natural desire to exhibit the results. Sometimes the audience is ready-made: the report may have been commissioned and interested people are waiting for it. At other times the research has been entirely self-propelled. In either case the report maker never knows exactly whom he or she is addressing. But one does know the general category of persons. Even a college student writing "for" his or her instructor may find a term paper being read to the whole group, or learn that it has been used as an anonymous example in another class. Similarly in the world of published research, it is impossible for the writer to foresee into whose hands his work will eventually fall.

These circumstances impose a double duty. You must write so as to inform your immediate colleagues, employers, or other defined audience; and you must also discharge your obligation to the Unknown Reader. Though you may fondly expect your intimates or fellow workers to understand you regardless of your powers of expression, you know that you cannot hold other readers' attention unless you are clear, orderly, and, if possible, agreeable to read. In truth, the difference between the two groups is an illusion. Neither the close nor the distant readers can be expected to see through a brick wall, to strain their wits as they grope for meaning. Those steeped in your subject may manage to catch your drift; but they will not be grateful or admiring if they do it in spite of you. A writer who has some contribution to make must so put it that any interested reader will grasp it with only a normal effort of attention. The possibility of this result is what makes the report useful, what gives the measure of its value.

It follows that *the report maker must write always as if addressing the whole educated community*. The yardstick is: Can another willing mind, not expert in my subject, understand what I am saying?

In using this standard of self-criticism, technical terms are of course left out of account. The assumption is that they will be used correctly, and they generally are. But good readers need no knowledge of such terms to tell at a glance whether a report outside their field is intelligible. They see at once from the ordinary words whether they could understand the report if they took the trouble to learn the technical vocabulary. The failure of all "difficult" writing without exception lies elsewhere than in the technicalities.[8] In such writing it is the common words that are misused, the sentence structure that is ramshackle, and the organization that is wild or nonexistent. And as we shall see, every one of these faults goes back to a fault in thinking. It follows that a fault in expression is a flaw in the knowledge that is supposedly being conveyed.

Take a famous example. When the original polio vaccine was first introduced, its merits and defects were of urgent concern to all Americans: deaths had occurred following its use. The U.S. Public Health Service accordingly issued a report on the vaccine supplied by the Cutter Laboratories, which was suspected of having caused instead of prevented the disease. That report exactly fits our double specification: the investigating physicians had to address their colleagues on a professional matter

[8]This statement is borne out by the efforts of scientific and other professional journals to coach their contributors in the craft of producing clear prose. In medicine, Dr. Lois DeBakey has devoted her life to holding seminars all over the country for physicians who publish research papers, and she contributes columns and articles on the subject to a wide variety of periodicals. Similar attempts to improve legal writing have produced such books as David Mellinkoff's *Legal Writing: Sense and Nonsense* (1982); Tom Goldstein and Jethro K. Liberman's *The Lawyer's Guide to Writing Well* (1989, paperback, 1991); and Bryan A. Garner's *Elements of Legal Style* (2002) and *The Winning Brief* (1999).

and at the same time inform the lay public. From either point of view the report could hardly have been more clumsily framed.

The organization was logical, for scientists are trained to follow a set form, but they are seldom trained to express themselves clearly and accurately, apart from the use of technical words. Here is how the report in question dealt in Paragraph 11 with a point of importance to every family:

There were ninety cases of poliomyelitis in household contacts occurring within forty-nine days after vaccination of a household associate with Cutter vaccine. In seventy-one of these cases the occurrence of the disease could be associated with specific distribution lots of vaccine.

It is difficult enough, even on a second reading, to grasp this short fragment; when twenty-five paragraphs in this style follow hard on one another, the effect is very likely total bewilderment. Ordinary citizens modestly conclude that here is science too abstruse for them. They skip to the summary, and this is what they find:

The study produced nothing which pointed to contamination as a source of the live virus but it did produce data suggesting the combination of inadequacy of virus inactivation and failure of the safety tests as responsible for live virus remaining undetected in the finished vaccine.

This conclusion is as murky as what went before. Let us see what might have been said if pains had been taken to communicate with the public as intended. The first passage meant to say:

Ninety cases of poliomyelitis occurred within forty-nine days after another person in the same household had received the Cutter vaccine. In seventy-one of these cases a connection could be shown with particular lots of the vaccine.

Before going on to the "translation" of the second passage, the phrasing of the first is worth analyzing. In the original text the ninety cases occurred not in people but in "household contacts," an ambiguous phrase, which leaves unclear whether it was the disease or the contact that occurred "within forty-nine days." Throughout, phrases are run on in defiance of syntax, and the word "associate" is used in two senses oddly linked ("household associate with Cutter vaccine") ("associated with distribution lots"). The result is to destroy the plain connections of things: people associating with people, disease occurring in people, and investigation tracing the cause to a particular (*not* a "specific") group of substances. The report is confusing also by its continual repetition of "distribution lots," as if other lots of vaccine, undistributed, could have been involved.

In the summary the ideas presumably intended were these:

> The study brought out no facts to show that the live virus came into the vaccine by contamination. But the facts did suggest two reasons why the live virus was present in the finished vaccine. One was that the means used did not make the virus sufficiently inactive. The other was that the tests for safety failed to detect this.

When the meaning is brought out of the depths in this way, it is seen to be a good deal less imposing and perhaps even tautological: since there *was* dangerously live virus in the vaccine, it is clear that it had not been deactivated and clear also that the safety tests had failed. These two reasons follow from the one important fact, that the live virus had not got in by contamination but by a failure in the preparation.

In business reports, the same fault is often, regularly found at the end of the figures for the current year. It is the fault of saying the same thing two or three times: "Our examination was made in accordance with generally accepted auditing standards, and accordingly included such tests of the accounting records and such other auditing procedures as we considered necessary in the circumstances." That is to say: "We audited."

Hard Work Makes Royal Roads

The point of these quotations is not to hold up the writers to ridicule or show superiority. Any of us might under certain conditions have written those sentences. They show how the mind strings ideas together—in a confused, shapeless series. But having written such sentences, the person who is going to thrust a piece of prose on someone else's attention has a duty to make them clearer and more attractive. He or she must try to read them with the eyes of a stranger and see and correct their faults. This obligation defines one of our principles: except for those who compose slowly in their heads before setting down a word, *no one, however gifted, can produce a passable first draft. Writing means rewriting.*

But how does one go about it? Rewriting implies dissatisfaction with what was put down in the first grapple with an idea—dissatisfaction with diction (the choice of words), coherence (the linking of ideas), and logic (the validity of the reasoning). For your self-criticism to be rapid and effective, you must be alive to a great many distinct faults and master an equal number of corrective devices. The most important of these devices form the subject of Part II of this book.

What you must be persuaded of at this point is that care lavished on expression is not some optional embellishment bestowed upon your work; it is the means through which your work begins to exist. Your research turns up raw materials—very raw. Writing and rewriting make them into finished, usable products. Until brought out in full view by the best possible arrangement of words, your results remain incomplete, doubtful, hidden from every mind but your own. And your own, as your first draft shows, is none too clear.

Rewriting is analysis of thought. You are therefore thinking hardest and most searchingly about your subject when scanning successive drafts to find and remove nonsense. To develop the sharp editorial eye, it is best to let some days elapse between writing and revision. You will then find that you yourself cannot make out the meaning of a sentence that seemed satisfactory when it was fresh. You will notice repetitions, illogicalities, circular arguments, tautologies, backtrackings, and all the other causes of confusion, from the vagueness of clichés to the ambiguity of pronouns with multiple antecedents.

Students complain when they are assigned readings in poorly written books. They call the book "dry" or "dull" and imagine that the fault lies in the subject. But every subject can be made interesting, because every subject *is* interesting. It would never have aroused human curiosity if it were not. The uninteresting assignment makes for heavy going because the ideas do not flow, because the sentences are off balance, because the syntax gives false cues that compel rereading, because the words do not say what they mean.

CHAPTER 3

FINDING THE FACTS

The Detective and the Clues

What is tantalizing about the proverbial task of finding the needle in the haystack is that you are assured the needle is there. The space is restricted; the object is unique; it must be possible to find it. And no doubt, with enough care and patience, it could be found with just a pair of eyes and a pair of hands. Of course, if the hay were to be packed in small cubes and a large magnet brought to bear as the contents of each were spread out, then the task would be made much easier—it would almost turn into a game.

This fairy-tale problem has its analogue in the researcher's hunt for the facts. The probability is great that any one fact that is wanted is in some printed work and the work in some library.[1] To find it, one has to find the right cube of hay, and then use one's magnetic intelligence to draw out the needlelike fact.

That "the library"—as yet unspecified—is the storehouse of by far the largest part of our recorded knowledge needs no

[1] To avoid tedious repetition, the words *print, book, work, source* will in the appropriate contexts be taken to include microfilm, microfiche, tape, disk or Web site. Similarly, *library* will include *archive, museum, historical society,* or other body whose collection of materials is open to the public.

demonstration. The author of an article on West Africa who reports that the annual rainfall in Fernando Po is 100 inches found this information ready-made; he did not measure the rain himself. Aside from the direct knowledge of an event by an eyewitness, or a firsthand investigation on the scene through interviews, laboratory or field work, or the study of relics,[2] the shortest path to the facts is library research.

The library may be a small collection on a special subject, owned by a business firm and housed in a single room; it may be a college library designed to meet the needs of undergraduate courses; it may be a reference collection of moderate size for the researchers of a magazine such as *Forbes* or *American Heritage;* it may be an "encyclopedic" library—properly a research library—that owns millions of old books and has a standing order with leading book distributors for a great many new ones; or it may be any one of the collections listed in the Footnote on page 39.

We shall take up first the library that is a collection of printed books. Unless the one accessible to you is specialized, the chances are that it contains something you want—if not for itself, then as a lead. If this something does not furnish sufficient information, it may prove negatively useful by enabling you to cross off what looked like a lead. In either case, there is no choice: into the library you must go. It is the researcher's first port of call.

It is natural enough for beginners to feel disconcerted—lost and lonely—in a strange library. You can quickly overcome this feeling by making up your mind to learn "the" library. Regardless of size, all libraries have common features that the experienced researcher looks for at once. After you have conquered a few of these strongholds, you will realize that to master one is to master them all.

In the simple days of not so long ago, users of an unfamiliar library could step into the catalogue room with a fair degree of confidence. They would find cards in trays, and the cards would

---

[2]See Chapter 6 on the evidences of history.

bear a call number for each book according to one of three systems: the Dewey decimal; the Library of Congress; or a local one antedating these two. Now all this has changed. A few libraries continue to use a card catalogue. Some of these face the researcher with two sets of cards, separated by a cutoff date: all books published before 1972 are in one row of cases and bear Dewey numbers; after that date, the new Library of Congress cards are in another set of drawers. In still other libraries (often in colleges), the researcher finds a microfiche system. It consists of a collection of thin plastic cards, each containing the images of hundreds of printed library cards in alphabetical order. A special "reader" is used to magnify the entries. Finally, many libraries have installed a computerized catalogue.[3] Its use and its possibility of a link with the Internet bring the reader into the electronic realm, which calls for some preliminary words if it is to be navigated with confidence and to the best advantage.

Library and Internet

The mushroom growth of "databases" on the Internet has given the public at large the conviction that it is not *a* but *the* repository of knowledge—"if you want to know anything about anything,

---

[3]See Figure 4, p. 49. The types of catalogues go by various acronyms suggesting that each is tailored to the needs of the particular institution, although many of the systems are variants of the one known as NOTIS, developed at Northwestern University. Thus Columbia University has CLIO (Columbia Libraries Information Online); Yale, ORBIS (Online Retrieval Bibliographical Information Systems); Harvard, HOLLIS (Harvard OnLine Library Systems). Princeton, New York University, and the University of Washington rely on another system, GEAC (General Accounting And Computing). The New York Public Library uses the CATNYP (Catalogue of the New York Public Library) system. Many small local libraries are computerizing their collections, some of them on yet another system, PALS (Public Access Library Service). Whatever the system, it is necessary to use the *Library of Congress Subject Headings* list, not merely your own phrasing of the desired subject.

click online." This is a misconception. Many databases are extremely useful;[4] others may mislead; and in any case we must re-affirm that the modern researcher's first step should still be to the Library. This injunction is not to mark down a new resource that may profitably be tapped for information by wire or wireless from a computer. It is only to remind the seeker of two things: when knowledge is looked for, or an item of information that is reliable; neither raw data nor verified knowledge can be found in one place, no more now than in the past.

Whether in a library or working at home, a researcher therefore must be prepared to use a computer—and, if in a library, be prepared to wait in line when all the computers are in use. This is the price of progress; the card catalogue enabled a great many more readers to search simultaneously. But this loss is partly made up for in certain libraries that provide readers entry into their network by means of the laptop computers they bring with them. They can in the same way reach the Internet databases, as students do from their room in college. Four out of five students report that they rely on the Internet for doing their assignments; but these are rarely as demanding as professional work for publication or delivery at a meeting.

For all these purposes the Library is the place where search should begin, for the best of reasons: it will save time, by avoiding fruitless dead ends and by enlarging the range of sources to draw from. Libraries contain scholarly periodicals not ever likely to be put online, and the use of those that are is free at the Library, whereas one usually has to pay to consult them on the Internet. There, if a given article proves useless, one is out of pocket for nothing. A Web site, moreover, can disappear without

---

[4]See Figure 3 and consult the excellent guides to a vast variety of resources in American and European history on the Internet: Dennis A. Trinkle and Scott A. Merriman, *The U.S. History Highway* (2002) and *The History Highway 3.0* (3rd ed., 2000). Novices may find helpful Dave and Mary Campbell's *The Student's Guide to Doing Research on the Internet* (1995). For a judicious evaluation of Internet search engines, see Sean Carroll et al. "How to Find Anything On Line," *PC Magazine*, May 23, 2003, pp. 80–89.

notice; the World Wide Web is in a continual state of add-and-cancel. Again, the charge for photocopies of what is useful is generally high on the Internet and may well be nil in the Library. Lastly, the Library provides a valuable shortcut in human form, the *Reference Librarian*. Never neglect to make his or her acquaintance and take advantage of professional expertise.

Outtopping all other considerations is the fact that the Internet is notorious for its generous delivery of *mis*information; and it is the Library that contains the means of verification. Error on the Internet comes from careless transfer of printed material, misattribution of authorship, absent-minded plagiarism, one-sided reports, superficial digests, incomplete bibliographies, and plausible fabrications—as a joke or from worse motives. This is not to say that printed books all enshrine gospel truth, but they have at least been read by one or more editors at the publisher's and some by qualified scholars at university presses.

The dangers lurking in the Internet give no warning. It follows that a fact obtained online, unless it comes from a known reference work or a tested database (see Figure 3), must be verified. Surveys show that about half those college students who get their answers from the World Wide Web distrust what they receive. It is not known what they do next.

A further contrast between Library and Internet: sheer quantity. Libraries acquire new (and therefore copyright) materials that will never be transferred online because it is not legal to do so or because it is too special. The United States, Canada, and the United Kingdom publish 170,000 books a year; the Library of Congress receives 10,000 a day from all parts of the world. Not all books find a resting place in a public library, being judged trivial or useless, but enough do to keep the Library well ahead of the Internet.

The same disparity is heightened by all the older books that are out of copyright and by the files of newspapers long extinct. These are full of history caught at the moment and recorded nowhere else (see pp. 72, 74, 85). Think, too, of the manuscript collections—letters and diaries—that would not justify transfer and that are thus inaccessible by computer.

FIGURE 3   *DATABASES COMMONLY CONSULTED*[5]

Lexis-Nexis Academic Universe
full-text coverage of general news, business, legal, government, and other topics

Pro-Quest Direct
full-text, citations and abstracts from periodicals in many languages and major newspapers

MedLine
citations and abstracts in articles in biomedical journals

PsychINFO
citations and abstracts from publications about psychology and related disciplines

Dow Jones Interactive
full-text stories and latest data on companies and financial markets

JSTOR
full-text articles from more than 100 scholarly journals

WorldCat
interface to the OCLC (the online catalogue of the Library of Congress consisting of 30 million records)

ERIC
citations, abstracts, and full-text articles in educational and other periodicals

Science Citation Index
bibliographical information and chief references in articles in scientific and technical journals

Oxford English Dictionary
the largest dictionary and most complete historical record of the English language

Multext
full-text investment research reports

PsychArticles
full-text articles from 42 journals published by the American Psychological Association

MLA Bibliography
citations for articles in literature, linguistic, and folklore publications

Britannica Online
the online version of the Encyclopedia Britannica

Dissertation Abstracts
index to all U.S. and some foreign dissertations and selected masters' essays, going back to 1861

[5]Shown in rank order and based on usage in the Columbia University Libraries during 2001–02. The list does not include the use made of individual online catalogues of the major research libraries, including Columbia's.

This quantitative relation between the two research sources is hardly likely to change. The volume of things recorded in print, on tape, on CD-ROMS, and in photographs, microfilm, and microfiche keeps increasing. More and more collections of manuscripts get deposited in libraries—public, private, and presidential—to say nothing of paintings and other artifacts that bear witness to past realities. Besides, a research library imports foreign books and periodicals of scholarly caliber that one, not knowing that they exist, cannot look for online.

To put this constant difference of scope another way, the limits of Internet "search engines" are narrow, as an authority on journalism recently told his profession: "Tomorrow's journalists must learn that the Internet hasn't made other research skills obsolete. It has made them more valuable—and necessary."[6] Experience shows besides that thanks to its highly evolved form, the book held in the hand, with its preface, acknowledgments, appendices, bibliography, and index, supplies many clues to the quality of its contents, just as that form also renders extremely easy its consultation for a particular fact without reading the whole.

One more reason for the necessary survival of libraries and their books is the recent discovery that has panicked some institutions, especially research laboratories. They have relied altogether on the digital recording of their work, while the format of the software has changed or the decoding application has gone out of existence. So the disk or tape made but a few years ago is now unreadable. Efforts to reconstruct the means of recovery generally fail, and the few that have had some success for scientific records still cannot recapture certain details invisible to the naked eye. Commenting on these losses, the head of a research station has been quoted to the effect that whereas the English census survey called Domesday Book of 1086 can still be read, all the BBC's talks, photographs, and writings depicting

---

[6]Thomas Mann, *Oxford Guide to Library Research* (1998), p. 132. This manual ably discusses the Library by categories of books. For a journalist's confirmation of the point in the text, see John Lenger's "If a Tree Doesn't Fall on the Internet, Does It Really Exist?" *Columbia Journalism Review,* Sept.–Oct. 2002, 74.

life in 1986 are vanishing. He now has all computer work printed out on acid-free paper; he is, in fact, creating a "library."

To sum up, each of the two great storehouses has unique qualities, and they complement each other. The Internet has speed of access and it offers a certain type of fact in abundance—*information*. One goes to it to find a name, date, distance, current statistical number, and the like. The Library supplies these too, less readily, but it adds to them the elements needed for verifying and producing *knowledge*. It gives, besides, the answers to questions one does not know enough to ask.

The modes of search in the two differ. The Internet affords word search and quick counting and printing features; it is connected to the whole world, which includes multitudes of unknown persons with a passion for putting what they know or imagine on Web sites, and it affords on given subjects organized databases that may be "surfed" (i.e. browsed), for a price.

Particularly convenient is the access, directly and through databases, to the files (and in some cases, the indexes) of the *New York Times,* the *Wall Street Journal,* the *Los Angeles Times,* the *Washington Post,* and other major newspapers throughout the world. And because much research in American history centers upon political figures, diggers should be familiar with the authoritative publications of Congressional Quarterly, Inc., and for deep retrospective searching, the *Guide to Research Collections of Former United States Senators, 1789–1995.*

The Library has continuously chosen its materials for their quality and utility and has sometimes specialized in one or more vast subjects. It has moreover organized its holdings physically in groups and reflected these distinct and helpfully narrow categories in its catalogue under a common heading; for example, The Novel: French; or: Realistic; Economics: Mathematical; or: the Business Cycle; and so on. Browsing along such shelves makes for rapid selection and happy discoveries.

One last reminder: *Library* means, of course, many different institutions of uneven size and scope. Not all answer to the specifications here given, but all have a common system, and even school and college libraries are by and large sufficiently well equipped to provide the budding researcher good practice. Library work should soon become as familiar to writers of any sort as shopping in a supermarket. If the particular institution lacks the desired book, do not forget that it can be borrowed for you on Interlibrary Loan.

A Surfeit of Sources

Publishing has so greatly increased, the world over, that it is no longer possible simply to scan a few shelves and take down the works you need. The expansion of the resources is as alarming as it is gratifying.[7] We quoted some numbers earlier; here are more, to reinforce the sense of size: The number of books in some of the great research libraries of the institutions of learning doubles every sixteen to eighteen years. Columbia University acquired its one-millionth volume in 1925; the six-millionth arrived in 1990–91, and 7,400,000 were in the catalogue by July 1, 2002. The principal book-producing countries publish around 600,000 titles each year. Each annual harvest takes about eight miles to shelve. What library-building program will be forever adequate to the need? And what system of retrieval will be either convenient or affordable? The cost of buying, cataloguing, and storing books is now above $80 apiece.

One answer to these questions is to limit the quantity of what is saved. The national libraries that are known as "libraries of deposit" (in the United States this refers solely to the Library of Congress) receive a copy of every copyrighted book in the country, as well as many from outside. So far, the Library of Congress does

---

[7]The fax machine and e-mail are further complicating the work of the researcher. Many of the billions of communications passing from one user to another each year will never find their way into archival depositories and be sorted for research. But many others will. President George H. W. Bush in 1989, while flying from Wyoming to Nebraska aboard Air Force One, faxed to Congress the message that accompanied his veto of a minimum-wage bill—a presidential "first" and a portent of things to come. For every such scrap of paper, every tape or disk gets saved and winds up in a Presidential Library. There are already twenty of these and related sites, crammed full of official papers. President Clinton's holds 76,800,000 papers, 18,500,000 pictures, 17,000 tapes, and 75,000 "museum objects."

not discard what comes to it, but several of the great European depositories have turned selective, eliminating whole categories of publications they consider ephemeral. The risk, of course, is that this stringency will work against the needs of scholarship, for who can say for certain that this or that pamphlet this or that poster will not be the decisive document in an inquiry? The only comfort is that the world will still be better off than in earlier centuries when pure chance (or almost) determined what survived.

The rate of growth is not the only predicament. Another huge problem confronting libraries—and thereby civilization itself—is the disintegration of millions of books and other documents. The cause lies in the paper manufacture that became almost universal in the nineteenth century. That process leaves a residue of acid in the paper, which in the course of time destroys its cellulose fiber, turning it yellow, brittle, and flaky. If catalogues are not to become mere fossil records of books that once existed, heroic measures are required without delay, because tons of printed matter are now in danger of being lost. At the Library of Congress, about 77,000 of its 13 million volumes become each year too fragile to use. The number of imperilled books in the British Library is nearly 2 million, as are at least half a million at the Bibliothèque Nationale. No simple and cheap solution for restoring these books is at hand. To de-acidify a million books a year—50,000 at a time by a diethyl-zinc process—requires special funding at an increasing rate.[8]

Defining the Quarry

So much for the overwhelming supply and its vulnerable state. Whichever form of the source you seek, or whatever means you use for finding it, you should already have answered in your mind

---

[8]Microform reproduction has reached countless fields, even outside the realm of print—the monumental *Index of American Design,* for example, is on microfiche. The massive two-volume *Guide to Microforms in Print,* a cumulative annual listing published in Munich, provides international coverage of titles and sources. But these two substitutes for paper are also vulnerable to decay in about forty years.

the question, What am I hunting down? We shall make various suppositions to show that "knowing what you want" depends on "knowing what you don't want." Thus, suppose that you are looking for Benito Mussolini's early political ideas but not necessarily for a history of fascism; or you want a detailed explanation of the World Bank's operation but will not be sidetracked to a general history of international finance; or you want to know the origin of the use of firecrackers in patriotic celebrations but do not need a history of the Declaration of Independence.

If by luck or cunning you happen to know the name of the author of a work on your particular topic, you know what to do with the catalogue, on card or screen. But, if you cannot name an author, use the name of the subject in brief form: for somebody's *Origins of American Independence* or *Causes of the Revolutionary War,* the formula "American Revolution" is enough to bring a selection of titles on the screen. From then on, it is best to make a point of remembering books by their authors. It will help you to discriminate among the many books on the same subject; sometimes, indeed, their titles are identical: at least six books about New York have been called *East Side, West Side;* seven other books, on different subjects, are called *East of the Sun and West of the Moon.* Generally, a confusion of titles nearly alike is more difficult to straighten out than a garbled author's name, because librarians, like others who deal daily with books, tend to remember them by their author rather than title.

In looking up authors, it is sometimes necessary to know birth and death dates, at least approximately, because the catalogue contains more than one with the same name, for example, Samuel Butler.[9]

Quite often, to find a subject other than a person, you must use imagination. As was shown in Chapter 2 with regard to the divine

---

[9]First names are essential: there are two poets named Pope in English literature and two historians named Macaulay, one a woman. But there are not always first names to distinguish other pairs, e.g., the two famous Greeks named Thucydides; and there is a Sophocles in the *Dictionary of American Biography*: a Greek scholar who taught at Harvard. For these duplicated names, only dates will prevent confusion.

right of kings, you must guess under what word or words your subject has been catalogued. If it is "flying saucers," you are not likely to go astray even though books and articles call them UFOs—Unidentified Flying Objects. But for many topics you must know how a librarian thinks when classifying books. There is reason in their ways, yet small variations in wording can create puzzles. If you are studying the opening of Japan, for example, you discover that some of the pertinent books are listed under "Japan Expedition of the American Squadron, 1852–1854"; others as "U.S.–Japan Expedition of the American Squadron"; and still others as "United States Naval Expedition to Japan." Why the variation? Because books on the subject have been published for a century and a half, and rules and fashions in cataloguing, like other rules and fashions, have changed with the years.

Besides, new subjects are continually being created for which the old entries must still serve. For example, before 1954, the word "desegregation" was seldom used to describe the movement to end racial discrimination. The book hunter will have to try related words, such as "Negro," "Civil Rights," and "African-American". In many libraries, a list of subject headings may be consulted at the reference desk. Finding these cognate headings is the first skill a researcher must acquire.

Cross-Questioning the Book

There is yet more to be learned about catalogues. When from the list offered on the terminal screen, you choose by a click the book you think you want, its library card will appear, giving full details. Suppose the searcher has heard of a new book called *Supermoney* by Adam Smith, a writer who is obviously not the eighteenth-century Scottish philosopher who wrote *The Wealth of Nations*. The catalogue or its online equivalent will turn up "Smith, Adam, 1723–1790," with a dozen works by and about the Scotsman. Another "Smith, Adam," with no dates, is a librettist whose work is a comic opera in three acts called *Nectarine*, published in London in 1902. He is clearly not the author of *Supermoney*. It turns out that "Smith, Adam" is the pseudonym of Goodman, George J. W. (see Figure 4, p. 49).

FIGURE 4   *AN ONLINE CARD*

TALLONS

The Online Catalog of the Tarlton Law Library

(1) [AUTHOR ▾] [Goodman, George]   Search |

(2) Record 2 of 2

Call #	(3) HG 4910 G66
Author	Goodman, George J. W
Title	**Supermoney [by] Adam Smith** (4)
Edition	[1st ed.] (5)
Imprint	(6) New York, Random House [1972]

LOCATION	CALL NO.	STATUS
Stacks	HG 4910 G66	AVAILABLE

Location	Stacks (7)
Descript	(8) x, 301 p. 22 cm
Subject	Stock exchanges -- United States (9)
	Investments -- United States
ISSN/ISBN	0394479939 (10)

This catalogue card, accessible on the Internet, is from the Tarlton Law Library of the University of Texas, which calls its online system TALLONS. The first line (1) shows that the book was searched for by its author's name; Below (2) that the book was the second of two by him in the library's collection. Next (3) is the book's Library of Congress call number and, under it, the author's full name. Then comes the title (4) followed by Goodman's rather impudent pseudonym as it appears on the title page. Further, (5) shows that this is a first edition published (6) in 1972 by Random House in New York. All brackets indicate that the data they enclose were supplied by the cataloguers and not printed on the title page. The boxed matter tells at a glance where the book is shelved and that it has not been checked out. Location (7) indicates the stacks of the Tarlton Library. Description (8) gives the number of pages of introductory material, followed by the number of pages of text, and the book's height in centimeters. Subject (9) gives the names of other topics related to the theme so that they may be looked up in the catalogue. The long number (10) is the book's International Standard Book Number (ISBN), which makes the work identifiable worldwide. (Periodicals are assigned an International Standard Serial Number.)

Always scan carefully the information on the digital card of your tentatively chosen book; it may save you the trouble of going to the shelves or waiting at the delivery desk for a work that is of no use to you. From the wording of the title in full— for example, its "jazziness"—you know it is not what you are after. Suppose you want an account of the military history of the Civil War. Among the titles you find James Street's *The Civil War*. The entry gives you its subtitle: "An Unvarnished Account of the Late But Still Lively Hostilities." This suggests either a jocular handling of the subject or a narrative by a contemporary— though this is ruled out by the author's date of birth, 1903.

One can often size up a book by seeing the publisher's name. Is it an old-established house, known for its list of solid works? A privately printed work was probably unable to interest any established publisher; this need not prove it worthless: some volumes are privately printed to circulate family records or memorabilia among a small circle of readers; but the "vanity presses" will print anything an author pays for and never edits or recommends changes in what he wants set in type.

The classification used in large libraries today is that of the Library of Congress—although there are exceptions, as for instance, the Denver Public Library which sticks to the Dewey system. In the Library of Congress system, categories have fixed letters or letters and numbers. You quickly learn that the category of U.S. history runs from E to F 975 and European history from D to DR. Economics is in the range HB to HJ; books about pure science are under Q, and technology is under T. You need not memorize these and other designations; they will be posted in more than one place in any library, and frequent use will make them familiar.

The size of a work also tells us what to expect of the work itself. A book on the steel industry in 16mo size,[10] or one only sixty-four

---

[10]16mo = "sixteen-mo," a book size resulting from making four right-angle folds in a sheet and forming a thirty-two-page section. Each page is approximately 4-1/2″ × 6-3/4″. The standard book is 8vo (octavo), twice as large, in several slightly different page sizes.

pages long, is not likely to be the volume, rich in details, that you are looking for. The first may be a muckraking exposé, the other a piece of corporate promotion. In general, books issued by university presses are scholarly in form and treatment; books with indexes are more likely to be serious works than those without (though exceptions keep occurring); and books imported from England or translated from a foreign language may be supposed to justify this expense and effort. But all of this is only *presumable.*

The date of publication is a further sign to take note of. You need a biography of President Benjamin Harrison and the catalogue turns up one by Lew Wallace dated 1888. Since you once saw the movie of Wallace's *Ben Hur* on television, your first impulse may be to sample another of his works. But Harrison's having been elected President in 1888 alerts you: Wallace's book is a "campaign biography" for the voters rather than for you.

Next, is the book in its first or a later edition. When in 1945 Charles A. Beard brought out a new edition of his well-known work *The Economic Basis of Politics,* he added a chapter that put his view of the subject in an entirely new light. A researcher ascertains whether new editions were enlargements, abridgements, or some other form of revision. Depending on what is needed, he decides whether he must see all the editions for comparison or whether any one will do. For example, to know what Darwin's doctrine of the origin of species ultimately was, you must read all six editions of his great book—or find a copy of Morse Peckham's variorum text.

Professional Informants: Reference Books

Every aid to finding sources, other than a catalogue, is *a list.* And within any large grouping of items for convenience, the list follows the alphabetic order (see Figure 2). So the researcher is perpetually looking along some alphabetized set of words—names or titles: *List, catalogue, reference work* are different forms of one device.[11]

---

[11]For a quick rundown on types, see Figure 5.

FIGURE 5   *Types of Reference Books*

1. Encyclopedias (general, national, religious, and topical, e.g., the International Encyclopedia of the Social Sciences and the Morrises' Encyclopedia of American History)

2. Biographical Dictionaries (national in one or many volumes; regional; professional: topical, e.g., musical; contemporary, e.g., Who's Who; and current, e.g., Contemporary Authors), Dictionary of Contemporary American Philosophers

3. Indexes to Periodicals (retrospective and current, e.g., Poole's, the Readers' Guide; the Book Review Digest; Chemical Abstracts; the New York Times Index, and indexes to almost all journals, published annually in one of the issues)

4. Dictionaries of Quotations; Concordances (e.g., of the Bible and of famous authors)

5. Atlases and Gazetteers; some atlases are historical (e.g., Shepherd's, or refer to particular matters such as languages, treaties, etc.)

6. Chronologies or Books of Dates (many kinds)

7. Language Dictionaries (many kinds; note also: World Dictionaries in Print)

8. Handbooks and Source Books (dictionaries, manuals, and anthologies, e.g., the Oxford Classical Dictionary; Commager's Documents of American History; Twentieth Century Literary Criticism)

9. Bibliographies (national, topical, e.g., Arts in America [four volumes], of single authors: e.g., Bengesco, Bibliographie des Oeuvres de Voltaire (four volumes); Dan H. Laurence, G. B. Shaw (two volumes)

A mere glance at the offerings in the reference department of any well-supported library reveals a vast variety of works on almost every subject conceivable. No topic seems to have escaped the attention of compilers or failed of a willing publisher. A random selection turns up: *Major Events of the 20th Century as Reported in the Pages of the New York Times* (2000), *A Historical Guide to the U.S. Government* (1998), *The Baseball Encyclopedia: The Complete and Definitive Record of Major League Baseball* (1996), and the fifteenth edition of *Newsletters in Print* (2002). And among the latest works are: a new edition of the *Dictionary of American History* in twelve volumes, the twenty-first edition of *American Men and Women of Science,* the second edition of the *New Catholic Encyclopedia,* and the 2003–2004 edition of *Who's Who in the Arab World.*

Clearly, the reference shelves of the library are the real training ground of the researcher. The existence of so many compilations about facts, names, and books is fortunate, because the questions that come up in research are never all of one kind. Regardless of topic, the researcher must be a generalist. He may have to discover Bismarck's religious opinions as a young man; a specimen of Martin Van Buren's signature to compare with an A.L.S.;[12] what was in the *Lusitania*'s hold when she was sunk— gold or munitions or both; or who was the first American to win the Nobel Prize for Literature. To find reliable answers, only first-class reference books will serve. Whatever your field of study, you should begin with the most recently issued or revised.

Up-to-Date Reference Works

Every searcher should know about the rich variety of books put out by the Gale Group, a subsidiary of Cengage Learning. Gale is one of the world's leading publishers of research and educational material. Its extensive collection of reference series includes those established by the well-known firms of trade-book publishers: Macmillan and Schirmer. Among Gale's products available online is its *Biography Resource Center,* whose database contains 300,000 narrative biographies gathered from other Gale reference works. Subscribers to this treasury of names and lives also have access thereby to the *Complete Marquis Who's Who,* which adds a million more biographies to the collection. Every researcher will find it useful to consult the *Gale Print Catalog;* it can lead the way to just the right source that might otherwise escape notice among a library's crowded shelves.

Two other publishers offer the public each a sizable collection of works of reference of high merit: Scribner and Oxford University Press. Both have multivolume dictionaries of American biography, Oxford's the more recent but lacking Scribner's group of full-scale and unexcelled lives of the Founding Fathers and

---

[12]The abbreviation for "autograph letter signed."

other great Americans of the past. Oxford in its twenty-four volumes and Scribner in its periodic supplements have added new categories of subject: business men, sport figures, Indian chiefs, African-Americans, and more women than were formerly taken note of. The great Scribner *Dictionary of Scientific Biography* is alone in the field and superb in coverage and quality.

The other Scribner series—on Ancient, on European, and on American Writers—are less concerned with the subject's life. They are essays by authorities and thus fuller in assessment and opinion than the entries usual in dictionaries. Most of these sets are available on CD-ROM.

For an important part of American biography, *The Presidents* (ed. Henry F. Graff, 3rd ed., 2002) gives not only the latest views of their administrations and a history of the presidency as an institution, but also adds in very full appendices a wealth of detail not brought together elsewhere, chronological, bibliographic, and cultural, including articles about the White House, the makeup of the Executive Office, and the role of the First Lady as variously understood by the incumbents. For further details, including minutiae, see Joseph N. Kane, *Facts about the Presidents* (7th ed., 2001) and William A. DeGregorio, *The Complete Book of U.S. Presidents* (5th ed., 2001). One may also turn with assurance to the Congressional Quarterly's *Guide to the Presidency* (2nd ed., 1996). On Congress and federalism, *Atlas of American Politics* (2001) and *Politics in the American States* (7th ed., 1999) are indispensable.

Still other biographical dictionaries are: the familiar Chambers (7th ed., 2002), Merriam-Webster (1995 ed.), and the newest, the *Houghton Mifflin Dictionary of Biography* (2003), each in one volume. The fullest but not updated is the *New Century Cyclopedia of Names* (1977).[13] Two dictionaries of biographical quotations (Knopf, Routledge and Kegan Paul) contain statements by critics and others about notables and sometimes by themselves.

---

[13]For nineteenth-century French figures who flourished early in the century, the big work by Michaud, like that by Hoefer, is valuable, but they hardly go beyond the halfway mark. For later figures you must consult Larousse, Vapereau, or the encyclopedias and companions.

The Harper *Twentieth Century Culture* (1983) is another biographical companion; likewise, the Macmillan *Book of Saints;* the
Makers of Modern Culture (Routledge and Kegan Paul), and by reason of their subject, several of the works listed below. A prominent figure in the domain indicated is sure to have a biographical
entry. On American social and cultural history, nothing replaces
the classic *History of American Life* series edited by Schlesinger and
Fox. Some researchers may find adequate a one-volume abridgement of the series by Mark C. Carnes.

On religion, consult the *Oxford Dictionary of the Christian Church;*
the Scribner *Middle Ages* (twelve volumes); Hasting's *Encyclopedia
of Religion and Ethics* (Scribner), old and not biographical, but still
valuable; and the modern one-volume Scribner *Dictionary of
Comparative Religion.*[14]

On various phases and aspects of history, Scribner has published sets on American, on Diplomatic, and on European Social
History; as well as on the theories of Economics and of Sociology,
with their historical antecedents. The Oxford *Companion to Classical
Civilization* (illustr., 1998) and the Chambers *Dictionary of World
History* (2nd ed., 2000) are useful shortcuts to innumerable topics,
though "world history" is so vast a subject (if it is a subject at all)
that one must expect to find omissions not in the least the editors'
fault. *The Columbia History of the World* (one volume) is a series of
essays by specialists, uneven yet informative, but not a narrative
like the old multi-volume *Cambridge Modern History,* which is largely political. Oxford has brought out a third edition of the *American
Historical Association's Guide to Historical Literature* (two volumes,
1995). Also historical and biographical is the Harper *Encyclopedia of
the Modern World* (1970). *Mann's International Encyclopedia of Sociology*
is also part historical and part biographical.

For literature, consult the Oxford Press specialty, the *Companion.*
Each is a good-sized handbook to, among others, American,
African-American, English, French, German, Italian, and Canadian
literature. They contain biographical entries on authors, not only
the well-known, but the lesser figures down to about the third

---

[14]For *Who's Whos,* which are self-biographies, see p. 61.

rank. The works of the masters are described in separate entries, as are the notable movements and the main newspapers and periodicals, current or important in the past. Burke and Howe, *American Authors and Books: 1640 to the Present* (3rd ed., 1972) is an invaluable source. The *Columbia Dictionary of Modern European Literature*, especially the first of two editions, is recommended. The Princeton *Encyclopedia of Poetry and Poetics* is serviceably detailed, and *Women Philosophers* by Mary Warnock (Everyman, 2000) is an anthology and chronology alone of its kind.

In the quest for pictures, turn to: the *A.L.A. Portrait Index* (eds. W. C. Lane and N. E. Browne, 1960); Hilary and Mary Evans's *Picture Researcher's Handbook* (7th ed., 2001); the *Allgemeiner Porträt-Katalog* (1967) and its supplements, which locate 30,000 portraits covering the years 1600–1800; and Martha Kreisel's *Photography Books Index,* in two volumes (1980, 1985). Helpful also is the slim illustrated guide, *Library of Congress Prints and Photographs* (1995).

Another type of guide supplies nuggets of information on several subjects at once over a great span of time. It is organized by year and sometimes by month as well. The pioneer work, still useful, is Alfred Mayer's *Annals of European Civilization, 1501–1900.* It records the appearance of great works in the several arts. More comprehensive is the *Chronology of the Modern World, 800–1992* in three volumes (Macmillan Library Reference, publ. by Simon and Schuster). It enters by year political and military events on the left-hand pages and cultural ones on the right, with lists of notables' births and deaths.

On a different plan and extremely well done is James Trager's *The People's Chronology* (rev. ed., 1992). Year by year, after beginning in huge leaps of times with Prehistory, the work furnishes compact descriptions of every kind of important event, invention, movement, publication, and individual action down to 1991. The range of topics is not only large but also unconventional; it serves the needs of anyone who studies the past from any point of view.

Briefer references arranged in parallel columns to show simultaneous occurrence make up the *Time Tables of History* (rev. ed. transl. from the German, publ. by Simon and Schuster), which run from 4000 B.C. to A.D. 1978. Another repertory worthy of note

FIGURE **6**   *General and Specialized Encyclopedias*[15]

General

The Columbia Encyclopedia (6th ed., 2002, the best one-volume compendium)
The World Book Encyclopedia
Kodansha Encyclopedia of Japan (in English)
The Great Soviet Encyclopedia (in English)
Grand Larousse Encyclopédique (in French)
Encyclopaedia Universalis (in French)
Allgemeine Enzyklopädie der Wissenschaften und Künste (in German)
Enciclopedia Barsa (in Spanish and also in Portuguese)
Enciclopedia Italiana (in Italian)

Specialized

The Reader's Encyclopedia (literary and historical)
The Reader's Encyclopedia of American Literature
The Encyclopedia of Philosophy
The Encyclopedia of Education
The Catholic Encyclopedia
The Encyclopedia Judaica
The Encyclopedia of Islam
The Dictionary of Scientific Biography
McGraw-Hill Encyclopedia of Science and Technology
Grzimek's Animal Life Encyclopedia
Encyclopedia of the American Constitution
Encyclopedia of American Foreign Policy
An Encyclopedia of the Book
McGraw-Hill Encyclopedia of Russia and the Soviet Union
International Encyclopedia of the Social Sciences
The Encyclopedia of Religion
Encyclopaedia of Religion and Ethics
Halliwell's Filmgoer's Companion

[15]Consult *First Stop: The Master to Subject Encyclopedias,* Joe Ryan, ed. (1989).

is Mitchell's *European Historical Statistics, 1750–1970*. The Scribner *Atlas of American History* supplements the other atlases listed on p. 62f; and Jean-Claude Corbel's *Visual Dictionary* (illustr., publ. by *Facts on File*) comes in handy for identifying a word that refers to a mechanical device or describes it—the names and the pictures are mutually accessible. The Chambers *Book of Facts* (2002 ed.) is a very full collection of the World Almanac type and easy to use.

Dictionaries of technical terms are numerous, the most convenient being the one in four languages by W. J. Smith. Crispin's is illustrated. Similar works exist for special fields such as architecture, art, criticism, theatre, music, navigation, and so on. William Freeman's *Dictionary of Fictional Characters* in two editions misleads by its title: the characters are only from English fiction. For a wider view of literature, go to *Keller's Digest of Books,* which summarizes the plots of many masterpieces. For Shakespeare and the Bible, more than one concordance each is available; for Balzac and for Dickens there is a repertory of their respective fictional populations; and for Montaigne, Eva Marcu has inventoried his ideas at length.

Two valuable classics recently re-issued are those by the Cambridge scholar E. Cobham Brewer: *Reader's Handbook* and *Dictionary of Phrase and Fable*. The latter's scope is clear from the title; the former deals with a variety of literary subjects such as would fall within the range of interest of a reader in the last decade of the nineteenth century.

This brings us to dictionaries of quotations, a plentiful offering. The best-known, Bartlett's, has been frequently revised, but it must be noted that like several other kinds of reference work, earlier editions can be useful when some once important name or work is dismissed from the new edition in favor of later ones. Next to Bartlett, Hoyt (in two editions) is excellent and has the advantage of sections on classical and foreign quotations. For the rest, Oxford is the latest to be brought up to date (2001), but the remainder are still needed, because, fortunately, editors disagree about inclusions and only one collection has the statement you want while the others repeat a large identical core. Here are the older ones; the editor's name or his publisher's is enough to specify the work: Mencken, Benham, Flesch, Tripp, Dalbiac, Anna L. Ward (Prose), Simpson (Contemporary), Crofton (Art), Mackay (Scientific), Esar (Humorous), Readers Digest, Crown, Penguin. For the Greek and Latin authors' memorable sayings: Bohn, King, H. P. Jones, Ehrlich (and Hoyt cited above).

Contemporary Opinion Now and Earlier

We have stressed the importance of looking first at recently published works. The reason is obvious but it does not always apply. Older compilations contain names of persons, works, and events that have lost importance with the passage of time—which is why libraries keep earlier editions of certain reference books. The same consideration governs periodicals. The latest issue brings the latest views, but previous ones hold in reserve articles or correspondence that are of prime value for you if your subject is historical or biographical. Hence the existence of indexes such as are illustrated in Figure 7.

Although many libraries still rely on the six volumes of *Poole's Index to Periodical Literature* covering the years from 1802 to 1906, there is now available online a much richer resource— *19th Century Masterfile,* an electronic database (Paratext, Inc., Reston, VA, 1999). Organized in five series, it is available in institutions with a site license for its use.[16]

Finding One's Peers and One's Ancestors

For over a century the premier source for the biographies of living people of achievement has been the Marquis *Who's Who* volumes, originally based on the English *Who's Who.* The chief of the Marquis set are *Who's Who in America* and *Who's Who in the World.* The usefulness of the database underlying these annuals has been since extended through the *Who Was Who* and *Who's Who in 20th*

---

[16]See Figure 7 for the contents of the five series.

FIGURE **7**   *Types of Indexes to Periodicals*

Woman Question. Canad. Mo. **15**: 568. **16**: 80-620. —
(E. Archard) Radical, **2**: 715. — Victoria, **18**: 261-
449. — (J. Weiss) Chr. Exam. **56**: 1. — (E. C. Stan-
ton) Radical, **3**: 18. — (L. G. Noble) Scrib. **3**: 483.
—(E. Benson) Galaxy, **2**: 751. — (C. A. Bristed)
Galaxy, **9**: 841. — (C. Kingsley) Ev. Sat. **8**: 556. —
(O. A. Brownson) Cath. World, **9**: 145. — Brown-
son, **22**: 508. — Mo. Rel. M. **18**: 234, 399. **19**: 65.
20: 225. **21**: 179. — (H. James) Putnam, **1**: 279.
— Bushnell on. (E. L. Godkin) Nation, **8**: 496.
— Essays on. (O. B. Frothingham) Nation, **9**: 342.
— Hopkins on. (C. C. Nott) Nation, **9**: 193.
— in Berlin. Victoria, **8**: 291.
— Ladies' War. Victoria, **21**: 225.
— Latest Crusade. Victoria, **11**: 193.
— Men and Women. Victoria, **26**: 149.
— Modern Moated Grange. Victoria, **20**: 401.
— Neglected Side of. (E. L. Godkin) Nation, **7**: 434.
— Reply to Parkman on. No. Am. **129**: 413.
— The Revolt and the Revolters. (M. Taylor) Victoria,
17: 193.
— Sex in Politics. (E. L. Godkin) Nation, **12**: 270.
— Shall Womanhood be abolished? (C. W. Clapp) New
Eng. **36**: 541.
— Something on, from Germany. Victoria, **8**: 195.
— Various Aspects of. (F. Sheldon) Atlan. **18**: 425.
— A Woman's Protest. Mo. Rel. M. **32**: 213.
— A Working-Woman's Statement. (L. E. Chollet) Na-
tion, **4**: 155.
— Wrong and right. (G. H. Johnston) Mercersb. **25**: 524.
Woman Reformers. (J. R. Dennett) Nation, **9**: 479.
Womanhood. (H. T. Tuckerman) Chr. Exam. **68**: 157.
— and its Mission. Dub. Univ. **53**: 623, 696. Same art.
Ecl. M. **47**: 349, 492.
— Christian, French Study of. Dub. **88**: 288.
— Ideal. (S. B. Cooper) Overland, **6**: 453. **7**: 69-535.
— in America. Mo. Rel. M. **17**: 46.
— New Ideal of. (A. M. Machar) Canad. Mo. **15**: 659.
— Old, Two Pictures of. (C. Lushington) Good Words,
18: 476.
Womankind abroad. (W. L. Tiffany) Knick. **58**: 194, 487.
— in Western Europe. (T. Wright) Stud. & Intel. Obs.
1: 21-445. **2**: 15-448. **3**: 11-444. **4**: 32, 120, 187.
Womanliness. Knick. **63**: 227. — Sharpe, **43**: 151. —
N. Ecl. **7**: 451.

WOMEN as athletes
Barney, E. C. American sportswoman. Fortn
62(ns 56):263-77 Ag '94
Kenealy, A. Woman as an athlete. 19th Cent
45:636-45 Ap '99; Same. Liv Age 221:363-70
My 6 '99; Reply. L. O. D. Chant. 19th Cent
45:745-54 My '99; Same. Liv Age 221:799-806
Je 24 '99; Rejoinder. 19th Cent 45:915-29
Je '99; Same. Liv Age 222:201-13 Jl 22 '99
Sutphen, W. G. V. Golfing woman. il Out-
look 62:249-57 Je 3 '99
WOMEN as authors
Cone, H. G. Woman in American literature.
Cent 40(ns 18):921-30 O '90
DuBois, C. G. Femininity in literature. Critic
23(ns 20):310 N 11 '93
Gardener, H. H. Immoral influence of women
in literature. Arena 1:322-35 F '90
Green, A. S. A. S. Woman's place in the
world of letters. 19th Cent 41:964-74 Je '97;
Same. Liv Age 214:300-7 Jl 31 '97; Comment.
Spec 78:796-7 Je 5 '97
Lathrop, G. P. Audacity in women novelists.
No Am 150:609-17 My '90. Discussion. 151:
127-8 Jl '90
Noguchi, Y. Japanese women in literature.
Poet Lore 15 no3:88-91 Jl 1904
O'Hagan, T. Some Canadian women writers.
il Cath World 63:779-95 S '96
Rogers, A. Literary life of woman; does it
interfere with her domestic life? Outlook
52:666-7 O 26 '95
Sichel, E. H. Women as letter-writers. Corn-
hill 79(s3 6):53-67 Ja '99; Same. Liv Age
220:513-23 F 25 '99
Walford, L. B. Working women. Critic 16(ns
13):159 Mr 29 '90
Williams, A. M. Our early female novelists.
Cornhill 72(ns 25):588-600 D '95 (pub anon);
Same. Liv Age 207:804-12 D 28 '95
See also
Authors, Women
Women as journalists
Women as poets
WOMEN as farmers
Bradley, E. Agricultural brigade of the mon-
strous regiment of women. Fortn 69(ns 63):
334-7 F '98; Excerpt. R of Rs 17:346 Mr '98
Sykes, E. C. Simple life on a poultry-ranch
in British Columbia. Cornhill 111(s3 38):
214-22 F 1915
Women as stock-keepers. Spec 81:111-12 Jl
23 '98
WOMEN as inventors
Woman as an inventor and manufacturer;
review of O. T. Mason's Woman's share
in primitive culture. il Pop Sci 47:92-103 My
'95
Women inventors. Sci Am 81:123 Ag 19 '99

Contents of the 19th Century Masterfile of Periodicals:
Series 1 contains, in addition to Poole's Index, the following: Snead's Index to Periodicals (1890–1906) ; Jones & Chapman's Index to Legal Periodical Literature (1786–1922); and Richardson's Index to Periodical Articles in Religion (1890–1906). **Series 2** has 19th century book and periodical bibliographic records. **Series 3**, devoted to newspapers, contains the New York Times Index (1863–1905); the New York Daily Tribune Index (1875–1906); Palmer's Index to the Times (London) (1880–1890); Index to the Oregon Spectator (1846–1854). **Series 4**: indexes with full text links for Harper's Magazine (1850–1892); *Atlantic Monthly* (1857–1901); North American Review (1815–1877); and Library Journal (1876–1897). **Series 5**: patent and government document indexes: Subject Matter Index of Patents Issued by the United States (1790–1873); Descriptive Catalog of the Government Publications of the U.S. (1774–1881); Compilation of the Messages and Papers of the Presidents (1789–1897); Hansard's Index to Debates, House of Commons (1803–1830); Hansard's Index to Debates, House of Lords (1803–1830); Cobett's Parliamentary History of England (1066–1803).

Top left, part of a column from *Poole's Index;* to the right, a sample from the *Readers' Guide.* *Poole's* gives the title of the magazine, the volume number, and page. The lack of author entries was remedied at last by the publication of a cumulative author index in 1971. The *Readers' Guide* gives the title of the magazine, the volume number, and page; adds the month and year, and the date if appropriate. Beginning with the issue for 1983, the *Readers' Guide* was put online through the Wilsonline database and also on CD-ROM.

Century America, besides several regional listings and others covering the various professions. Some researchers may find need for *Who's Who on the Web,* touted as a "high-speed and searchable online database" that contains over one million entries. It is updated daily and can be used at any hour of the day.

The *Who's Who* that established both the title and the style was first published in England in 1849. Now in its 154th edition, its sketches contain information supplied by the subject and printed as received. This is true of all its clones, which tells the researcher at once to be on guard against distortions and omissions. Well-supplied libraries will own some of the 2000 other *Who's Whos* listed in the Library of Congress Catalogue; their titles vary from one country to another, and so do the criteria for inclusion. Specialists have produced such volumes as *Who's Who in Ancient Egypt* and *Who's Who in Ancient Rome,* and more recent additions include *Who's Who in American Quilting* and *Who's Who in Hell.*

Passing mention was made earlier of Genealogy as one specialized branch of History. Nowadays it attracts many persons eager to find what by analogy they call their "roots." To do so they often use firms that advertise—in fact guarantee—at considerable expense a copious and interesting ancestry. If one hints of a family tradition that suggests descent from Richard the Lion-Hearted, twelfth-century king of England, it miraculously turns out to be the "fact."

More sober persons prefer to do the searching themselves and, as virtual historians, deserve here a few indications of method. They should begin with the present and the recent past, that is, with birth certificates; church records of marriages, baptisms, and deaths; local cemetery records, back issues of local newspapers, and family letters and beliefs, however vague. Local libraries often have sections of genealogical books and other documents, also local, in addition to state and town histories, census rolls, and other data that have been collected state by state. This is where family tradition helps: great grandfather was said to come from . . . in another state. The national census rolls contain for over a century past much information about American households; and immigration records, also in libraries, are valuable sources too.

County courthouses and, in towns, the City Clerk's office keep track of land transfers and abstracts of deeds, also useful. State and national archives are sources about the military. The Civil War and two World Wars involved so many for so long that the veterans' and widows' pension records supply death dates and other details. Finally, the Mormon Church is the great repository; it holds the fullest collection of genealogical data in the United States. Its organized resources can be accessed through the Internet or by going to a local Mormon church, where one may find facilities for placing an order and consulting microfilm records. Besides this great collection, Ellis Island now makes available online the lists called "ship manifests" that contain the names of over 22 million immigrants.[17]

Facts and Numbers from Maps

The understanding of many subjects, even of literature, is often incomplete without the use of maps. They are found in atlases, which detail in print other things than geography. For American subjects, *The National Atlas of the United States of America* is without competitors. Originally published in 1970, it has been available online with printout capability since 1997. For the geography of the world, consult *The Times Atlas* and *The New International Atlas,* whose twenty-fifth anniversary edition appeared in 1994. It is published in English, French, German, Portuguese, and Spanish. Descriptive matter of many kinds on 165,000 geographical entities is found in *The Columbia Gazetteer of the World* (1998), likewise accessible online. Governmental information as well as geographical is found in the *Political Handbook of the World,* issued annually since 1975.

Any topic can call for the numerical and chronological detail that historical atlases provide. For instance, if you want to compare the distribution of the population of England in 1750 with that of

[17]Other online sources are Gale's *AncestorPlus,* which contains over a billion names, and *Passenger and Immigration Lists Index,* which covers arrivals to these shores from the seventeenth to the nineteenth century. As this book goes to press, Oxford will be publishing a *Dictionary of American Family Names* (three volumes), which should also be helpful to genealogists.

1850, or measure the distance between two points on the Oregon Trail, or look at the precise area of Africa into which European diplomats banned the import of arms and liquor in 1890, an historical atlas will give you that information. A variety of works supply by means of maps the answers to questions of military, economic, Biblical, literary, or other import. They also illustrate the salient facts about a stated region or period. For general use, the *Times Atlas of World History* (5th ed., 1999) is the most up to date of several good compendiums, including *The Harper Atlas of World History* (rev. ed., 1992) and *The Hammond Atlas of the World* (1997). For the United States, another attractive and comprehensive work is *The American Heritage Pictorial Atlas of United States History* (1966), and there is still value in the much older Paullin's *Atlas of the Historical Geography of the United States*. The most up to date is Carnes's *Historical Atlas of the United States* (2002). For American wars, one should consult the *West Point Military History* series published in 1986.

As for ascertaining dates when required by cross-cultural research, consult the diverse calendars in use. At times one must convert dates from one to another. Take note of G. S. P. Freeman-Grenville's *The Islamic and Christian Calendars: AD 622–2222 (AH 1–1650): A Complete Guide for Converting Christian and Islamic Dates and Dates of Festivals* (1995) and Arthur Spier, *The Comprehensive Hebrew Calendar: Twentieth to Twenty-second Century, 5660–5860, 1900–2100* (1986). For broader coverage use Shahabuddin Ansari's *A Compendium of Calendars: A Cyclopedia of the Christian (Julian and Gregorian) Calendars from 1 A.D. to 2600 A.D., the Indian National Calendar, from 1 S.E. to 2500 S.E., and the Muslim Calendar from 210 B.H. to 2730 B.H.* (New Delhi, 1999).[18]

What Else Do I Need?

Consider some out-of-the-way topics, such as certain domestic and social habits of modern American life. In the course of your narrative it occurs to you that you should mention the time, and

---

[18]To find the year in the Christian calendar when the day of the week and date of the month are given (or permutations of these), see Figure 8.

FIGURE 8 *Perpetual Calendar of the Christian Era* A.D. 1753–2020

COMMON YEARS

Years											Jan (31)	Feb (28)	March (31)	April (30)	May (31)	June (30)	July (31)	Aug (31)	Sept (30)	Oct (31)	Nov (30)	Dec (31)
1761 1767 1778	1789 1795	1801 1807 1818	1829 1835 1846	1857 1863 1874	1885 1891	1903 1914 1925	1931 1942 1953	1959 1970 1981	1987 1998	2009 2015	D	G	G	C	E	A	C	F	B	D	G	B
1762 1773 1779	1790 1802	1813 1819 1830	1841 1847 1858	1869 1875 1886	1897 1909	1915 1926 1937	1943 1954 1965	1971 1982	1993 1999	2010	E	A	A	D	F	B	D	G	C	E	A	C
1757 1763 1774	1785 1791	1803 1814 1825	1831 1842 1853	1859 1870 1881	1887 1898	1910 1921 1927	1938 1949 1955	1966 1977 1983	1994	2005 2011	F	B	B	E	G	C	E	A	D	F	B	D
1754 1765 1771	1782 1793 1799	1805 1811	1822 1839	1850 1861 1867	1878 1889 1895	1901 1907	1918 1929 1935	1946 1957 1963	1974 1985 1991	2002 2013 2019	B	E	E	A	C	F	A	D	G	B	E	G
1755 1766 1777	1783 1794	1800 1806 1817	1823 1834 1845	1851 1862 1873	1879 1890	1902 1913 1919	1930 1941 1947	1958 1969 1975	1986 1997	2003 2014	C	F	F	B	D	G	B	E	A	C	F	A
1758 1769 1775	1786 1797	1809 1815 1826	1837 1843 1854	1865 1871 1882	1893 1899	1905 1911 1922	1933 1939 1950	1961 1967 1978	1989 1995	2006 2017	G	C	C	F	A	D	F	B	E	G	C	E
1753 1759 1770	1781 1787 1798	1810 1821 1827	1838 1849 1855	1866 1877 1883	1894 1900	1906 1917 1923	1934 1945 1951	1962 1973 1979	1990	2001 2007 2018	A	D	D	G	B	E	G	C	F	A	D	F

LEAP YEARS

Years											Jan (31)	Feb (28)	March (31)	April (30)	May (31)	June (30)	July (31)	Aug (31)	Sept (30)	Oct (31)	Nov (30)	Dec (31)
1764	1792	1804	1832	1860	1888		1928	1956	1984	2012	G	C	D	G	B	E	G	C	F	A	D	F
1768	1796	1808	1836	1864	1892	1904	1932	1960	1988	2016	E	A	B	E	G	C	E	A	D	F	B	D
1772		1812	1840	1868	1896	1908	1936	1964	1992	2020	C	F	G	C	E	A	C	F	B	D	G	B
1776		1816	1844	1872		1912	1940	1968	1996		A	D	E	A	C	F	A	D	G	B	E	G
1780		1820	1848	1876		1916	1944	1972		2000	F	B	C	F	A	D	F	B	E	G	C	E
1756	1784	1824	1852	1880		1920	1948	1976		2004	D	G	A	D	F	B	D	G	C	E	A	C
1760	1788	1828	1856	1884		1924	1952	1980		2008	B	E	F	B	D	G	B	E	A	C	F	A

A

Sun	Mon	Tues	Wed	Thur	Fri	Sat
	1	2	3	4	5	6
7	8	9	10	11	12	13
14	15	16	17	18	19	20
21	22	23	24	25	26	27
28	29	30	31			

B

Sun	Mon	Tues	Wed	Thur	Fri	Sat
		1	2	3	4	5
6	7	8	9	10	11	12
13	14	15	16	17	18	19
20	21	22	23	24	25	26
27	28	29	30	31		

C

Sun	Mon	Tues	Wed	Thur	Fri	Sat
			1	2	3	4
5	6	7	8	9	10	11
12	13	14	15	16	17	18
19	20	21	22	23	24	25
26	27	28	29	30	31	

D

Sun	Mon	Tues	Wed	Thur	Fri	Sat
				1	2	3
4	5	6	7	8	9	10
11	12	13	14	15	16	17
18	19	20	21	22	23	24
25	26	27	28	29	30	31

E

Sun	Mon	Tues	Wed	Thur	Fri	Sat
					1	2
3	4	5	6	7	8	9
10	11	12	13	14	15	16
17	18	19	20	21	22	23
24/31	25	26	27	28	29	30

F

Sun	Mon	Tues	Wed	Thur	Fri	Sat
						1
2	3	4	5	6	7	8
9	10	11	12	13	14	15
16	17	18	19	20	21	22
23/30	24/31	25	26	27	28	29

G

Sun	Mon	Tues	Wed	Thur	Fri	Sat
1	2	3	4	5	6	7
8	9	10	11	12	13	14
15	16	17	18	19	20	21
22	23	24	25	26	27	28
29	30	31				

To find the day of the week for, say, July 4, 1776, first find the year in the two-part block at top left. Then go to July in the list of months at middle right. These two points are each on a "row." Where the rows meet is a letter—in this case A—which tells you which of the seven calendars to use below. There you find the fourth to have been a Thursday. In reverse, the process leads to more than one year. The right one is chosen with the aid of other known facts—century, life span, decade, etc.

preferably the date, when the supermarket became a familiar institution. Editor and Publisher's *Market Guide* is the work to consult. It chronicles the economic life of almost every community in the United States. From it you learn how many drugstores there are in Atlanta, the resources of the banks in Spokane, and the quality of the tap water in Cheyenne. Having once consulted this annual, you will know how helpful back issues can be for social history, long after they have ceased to interest the advertisers and salesmen for whom they are compiled. For inventions such as the binder-reaper, Kane's *First Facts,* largely based on patents, is comprehensive; but for other innovations such as the bicycle or the game of volleyball, one needs Patrick Robertson's *The Book of Firsts* (1974), which is indexed in great detail. If one knows the approximate date, *The People's Chronology* (see p. 56) will give information about phases of development.

In some searches of this kind, it may become important to know when the word *scientist* (replacing "natural philosopher") was first used in print and by whom; or to learn by what stages the meaning of the word *restive* was reversed; or to learn what *promove* or *Anschluss* means precisely. For these and their like, the researcher needs a dictionary—indeed, more than one: English, foreign, bilingual, technical. For English, Murray's *New English Dictionary,* commonly known as the *Oxford English Dictionary (OED)* will supply the lost meaning or the unfamiliar new, for the huge work has been steadily supplemented. Craigie and Hulbert's *Dictionary of American English on Historical Principles,* coupled with Mitford Mathews's *Dictionary of Americanisms,* corresponds to the great English model. For the slang and vulgarisms of all English-speaking peoples, Partridges's *Dictionary of Slang and Unconventional English* (and supplement) are standard, although students of American culture find value in Wentworth and Flexner's *Dictionary of American Slang* (2nd ed.).

Recourse to such works is imperative for writers of history. A correct idea of the French or American revolution and the political regimes that followed depends on knowing how the late eighteenth century used such words as "liberty" and "authority." American historians used to wonder whether Andrew Jackson was really the friend of labor; or was he rather a spokesman for the small entrepreneur? It is a matter of words: what did "workingman" mean at the time? Some argue that it meant "proletarian"; others insist it meant a small businessman. To settle the point, the first step is toward the historical dictionary.

Slogans, catchphrases and allusions, political and artistic nicknames are also signs of the times and call for attention. What is the connection of "twenty-three skidoo!" with the spirit of the 1890s? What is a "tandem" in the history of locomotion? What are "routs," "crushes," and "kettledrums," in the context of sociability? Who, exactly, belongs to the *demi-monde,* and when was the phrase first used? For phrases and allusions, consult the two Brewer volumes cited among the guides to literature on p. 58; for political and social nicknames, the sole repertory is George E. Shankle, *American Nicknames: Their Origin and Significance* (2nd ed., 1955).

With the works recommended and commented on in this chapter, anyone should feel equipped to begin the hunt for facts, whatever the field of one's inquiry. Even if the single item desired is not found in one of the books, it would be strange if the lead, the pointer to it were not there. Nor should one think that this sampling of resources is anywhere near the total at one's disposal. The current catalogues of the publishers mentioned contain many more titles in every category, as well as more new topics recently inventoried. The modern researcher need not feel at a loss.

CHAPTER 4

VERIFICATION

How the Mind Seeks Truth

Everybody daily faces the question: Is this true or false? Professional and private life are guided by the answer, which often falls short of certainty. The question then takes the form: is this likely, doubtful, or unlikely? The conclusions rest on a combination of knowledge, skepticism, faith, common sense, and intelligent guessing. In one way or another, we decide whether the road to town is too icy for going by car, whether the child is telling the truth about seeing a burglar upstairs, whether the threatened layoff at the local plant will take place after all. All adults have acquired techniques for verifying a rumor or report so that they can take appropriate action. They supplement their experience and learning by recourse to special sources or items of information—the broadcast weather report on the state of the road, the child's known habit of fantasy, or the word of the plant manager who has access to firsthand knowledge.

Few of those who run their lives in this way stop to think that in the first case they trusted a technical report which, though not infallible, is the only authority on the subject; that in the second case, the ground for judgment was prior observation and inference; and that in the third, resort was to a competent witness. It is sometimes possible to use all three kinds of aids to judgment, and others besides, such as the opinions of neighbors and friends. And then, too, there is trial and error. All but the most impulsive will stop and think before giving credence to others' say-so; they will try to collect evidence before trusting their own surmises. The intelligent newspaper reader, for example, daily encounters "incredible" stories and tries automatically to "verify" them, first by "reading between the lines" and drawing what seems at the moment an acceptable conclusion, and later by looking for further reports.

Limited as this effort is, one cannot always make it from an armchair. Take the once-shocking news story that appeared under the headline:

SPY AT LOS ALAMOS LAB

When ordinary readers encounter a story of this kind and carry their speculation as far as we have supposed, they end by doing one of several things: (1) they accept it because it appeared in a periodical they trust; (2) they reject it because it does not square with what they think likely; (3) they suspend judgment until more information comes out; or (4) they ignore the enigma altogether.

A judicious reader will adopt 3, although there is nothing downright foolish about the other choices. But the researcher or other kind of reporter has a greater responsibility, which denies him the right to any of the four solutions. He may indeed come to rest on 3, but not until he has done a great deal of work; and except under certain conditions, 1, 2, and 4 go against his professional training and obligations. As the student of events, past or recent, tries to answer the question, What *did* happen? he confronts the same uncertainties as the newspaper reader, but with this important difference: *the researcher must reach some decision and make it rationally convincing, not only to himself but to others.* The steps by which he performs this task constitute Verification.

Verification is required on a multitude of points—from getting an author's first name correct to proving that a document is both genuine and authentic.[1] Verification is conducted on many planes, and its technique is not fixed. It relies on attention to detail, on commonsense reasoning, on a developed "feel" for chronology and human affairs, and on ever-enlarging stores of information. Many a "catch question" current among schoolchildren calls forth these powers in rudimentary form—for instance the tale about the beautiful Greek coin just discovered and "bearing the date 500 B.C." Here a second's reflection is enough for verification: the "fact" is speedily rejected.

The first sort of verification consists in clearing up the obscurities that arise from one's own or somebody else's carelessness. A good example is found in the following account of a copy editor's search, as reported by the publishing house where she worked:

In the bibliography of a manuscript there appeared this item: "Landsborous, A., and Thompson, H. F. G., *Problems of Bird Migration.*" In the line of duty, the editor queried the spelling of Landsborous, but it was returned by the author without change or comment. Not satisfied, she searched in various bibliographies and in two history catalogues for the name. She could find neither it nor the title of the book. Then she began to look for "Thompson, H. F. G." but without success. Under the subject "Birds—Migration," she was referred to "Aves—Migration." There she found that an A. L. Thomson (without the "p") had written *Bird-Migration* (2nd ed.). Further research in the subject index of the British Museum Catalogue revealed that the first edition had indeed been entitled *Problems of Bird-Migration.* The proper entry then proved to be: "Thomson, Arthur Landsborough, *Problems of Bird-Migration.*" The initials following the name "Thompson" in the original

---

[1]The two adjectives may seem synonymous but they are not: that is genuine which is not forged, and that is authentic which truthfully reports on its ostensible subject. Thus an art critic might write an account of an exhibition he had never visited; his manuscript would be genuine but not authentic. Conversely, an authentic report of an event by X might be copied by a forger and passed off as his own work. It would then be authentic but not genuine.

version continued to puzzle the editor until someone suggested that they might indicate an Honorary Fellowship in Geography. . . . [2]

Not all uncertainties can be grappled with in this 1-2-3 order. Some are like prickly fruit: one does not know how to take hold of them. Others are plain enough but require enormous patience and tireless legwork. No interesting or important mystery can be settled without knowledge, judgment, imagination, and persistence. How to do it is learned by practice; to enumerate rules (if there were any) would be endless and of little use. The only way to show in what the practice consists is to describe in some detail a variety of typical operations that were gone through in actual research.

Collation, or Matching Copy with Source

One of the fundamental ways of verifying facts is known as collation. This simply means "bringing together." Thus when a scholar has found a manuscript and prepares it for the press, he or she must collate the successive proofsheets with the original before passing them for publication. Collating is best done with help: one person—the copyholder—reads the text, punctuation included, while the scholar—who is known in this role as the editor—follows the printed version.

Many rules govern the form in which this kind of transfer from manuscript to type is to be made. They need not concern us here. But the principle of collation should be what, on a small scale and apart from work with manuscripts, is called comparison. It is by rapid single-handed collation that you discover small discrepancies or oddities and can prevent error.

Among examples of the long survival of error through endless repetition in print, none could be more striking than the presence of a certain proper name in one of Edgar Allan Poe's best known stories. The name is La Bougive and it occurs in "The Purloined

---

[2]Columbia University Press (*The Pleasures of Publishing*, 14, June 30, 1947, 2). Thomson's names and titles appeared correctly in his obituary thirty years later (*New York Times*, June 11, 1977).

Letter," side by side with those of Machiavelli, La Rochefoucauld, and Campanella, all of whom Poe scorns for their shallow and specious notions of the human mind. La Bougive never existed; there is no use looking for him in any dictionaries of pseudonyms.[3] He is simply a misprint for La Bruyère, the French moralist and writer of maxims, who lived in the seventeenth century. Poe was fond of reading him, and in other stories and essays Poe spells the name correctly. But he missed the "typo" both in proof and in his own annotated copy of the *Tales* (1845). In the 1890s, the editors of the Chicago edition made the proper guess and put in La Bruyère; but down to the present, new anthologies, both the cheap paperback and the would-be scholarly, go on faithfully reproducing the error.[4] The basis of the necessary correction here is a knowledge of French literature and a sense of language in relation to proper names.

Rumor, Legend, and Fraud

It may seem more difficult to know when to be skeptical about small details in genuine documents than to doubt a legend or anecdote that sounds too pat to be true, but verification may be as laborious in the one case as in the other.

The doubtful anecdote you recognize immediately; it bears a family likeness common to the many that you know to be apocryphal. One such famous story has for its hero Stephen A. Douglas, the Illinois Senator contemporary with Lincoln. Tradition says that on the evening of Saturday, September 1, 1854, a few months after reopening the slavery question by introducing the Kansas-Nebraska Bill, the "Little Giant" stood before a hostile crowd in Chicago and attempted to justify his

---

[3]See p. 97f.

[4]One of the authors of the present book made a survey of all English and American editions available in print or on library shelves and found fewer than one in four with the correct reading. See Jacques Barzun, "A Note on the Inadequacy of Poe as a Proofreader and of His Editors as French Scholars" (*Romanic Review,* 61, February 1970, 23–26).

action. Booed, jeered, and hissed, Douglas held his ground for over two hours, determined that he would be listened to. Finally, so the story goes, he pulled out his watch, which showed a quarter after midnight, and shouted: "It is now Sunday morning—I'll go to church and you may go to Hell."

How does one verify one's doubts of a "good story" of this kind? The steps taken by one scholar to establish or destroy this legend were as follows.[5] First, he searched through the Chicago newspapers of late August and early September 1854 for some account of Douglas's return from Washington. This, he found, had been regarded as a great event, impatiently awaited by the public and fully covered in the press. Next, he scanned the accounts of the meeting itself, looking for any reference to the scornful remark. He found none. Neither the newspapers nor the first biography of the Senator, which was published in 1860, reported the incident. So far the results of a good deal of work, being negative, seemed to justify the doubt.

Yet on the main issue the search turned up some positive though indirect evidence. Two papers, one in Chicago and one in Detroit, stated that Douglas had left the platform at ten-thirty. Moreover, the meeting had taken place on a Friday, not a Saturday night. This is a fixed point: no doubt is possible that September 1, 1854 was a Friday. In the absence of a dated newspaper, a perpetual calendar (see Figure 8) will quickly establish the day of the week on which a date fell or will fall in any year of the Christian era.[6]

But considering the ways of press reporting in that age, another possibility remains: perhaps in the uproar no newspaper man heard Douglas's emphatic remark. Of course, if we suppose this in order to support the story, we must also assume that Douglas was so rattled by the heckling of the crowd that he could neither read his watch correctly nor remember what day

[5]Granville D. Davis, "Douglas and the Chicago Mob" (*American Historical Review*, 54, April 1949, 553–556). The definitive account of what actually happened is in Robert W. Johannsen, *Stephen A. Douglas* (1973), 453f.

[6]Researchers will find it advisable to have a perpetual calendar within reach, even when they are not neading source material.

of the week it was. When the researcher finds himself multiplying hypotheses in order to cling to a belief, he had better heed the signal and drop the belief.

"Good stories" will of course persist despite the efforts of historians. What fits character or the sound of a name acquires a life of its own that seems immortal.[7] The varieties of legend and counterfeit deserve the verifier's attention, so that he or she can develop a connoisseur's instinct for the genre. Consider a few more examples. Situations of chaos are likely to breed rumors. When Princess Diana was killed in an automobile accident, rumors flew that she had been assassinated on orders from Buckingham Palace. Again, a joke may unwittingly turn into a "fact." When the philosopher Diderot was visiting Catherine the Great in Russia, some disgruntled courtiers arranged an incident in which the French philosopher was challenged in aggressive words:

Sir, $\dfrac{a + b^n}{z} = x$. Therefore God exists. Reply.

Diderot, suspecting a put-up job and sensing the hostility to his presence, did not reply. Told and retold, this supposed dumbfounding of the learned man grew into the "fact" that to Diderot "all mathematics was Chinese."[8] The truth is that he published

---

[7]For example, Captain Kidd, Dr. Crippen, and Mata Hari stand in the popular imagination as, respectively, the archetypal pirate, murderer, and female spy. But James Kidd's pirating was brief and more a prospect than a success; Dr. Crippen was a physician, but not an M.D., who probably killed his wife unwittingly with the then untested soporific hyoscine; and Mata Hari, the promiscuous dancer, playacted the role of spy rather than carried it out. Yet she is the heroine of a recent musical as the greatest of her supposed kind. That the musical was chosen, rather strangely, for a charity benefit by the Association for Homemaker Service shows again the power of myth.

[8]Compare H. L. Mencken's famous "bathtub hoax," to the effect that President Fillmore on taking office in 1850 instructed his Secretary of War to invite tenders for the construction of a bathtub in the White House—as if it were a recent invention. Lives of Fillmore and even guidebooks to the White House were repeating the "fact" decades after Mencken admitted authorship, ten years after the hoax. His article was first printed in the New York *Evening Mail* for December 18, 1917, and reprinted in *The Bathtub Hoax and Other Blasts and Bravos* (1958).

mathematical papers which experts have called "competent and original." Yet the fabrication survives in serious books down to our day, the latest (1983), using the tale both in the preface and on the book jacket to show how important it is to know something of mathematics.

The type of *ben trovato*, or aptly made-up story, includes Galileo's experiment of dropping weights from the Leaning Tower of Pisa, Newton's observing the fall of an apple (a less strenuous "experiment"), and the remark "Let them eat cake," attributed to Marie Antoinette. Even such a mind as John Dewey, educated and exacting, seems to have believed that Columbus was the first man to think the earth was round.[9] All these are falsehoods. The Marie Antoinette tale was a commonplace of eighteenth-century hostility toward rulers and is mentioned by Rousseau and others before Marie Antoinette was born.

When it becomes necessary to test the accuracy of a story of this kind, whether because a broad conclusion depends on it or because the legend affects the character under discussion, the proof or denial presents uncommon difficulties. The first step is to try to trace the tale to its origin. But beginnings are notoriously hard to ascertain, unless someone happened to round up witnesses while memories are fresh and inconsistencies can be removed by questioning. Imagine trying to find out how the bikini swimsuit burst upon the unprepared universe. You might first consult fashion magazines or the family page of a great daily—provided you know roughly the date of the innovation. But has anything been written—article or book—on the subject by itself? There *is* a book entitled *Bikini Beach: The Wicked Riviera*, which gives a fairly complete history of the quasi garment. First designs of such a thing were made in 1945, but the real start was made in June 1946 when a Paris designer hit upon the now familiar name because of the publicity given to the island, just then the site of tests of the atomic bomb.

[9]*How We Think* (1910), 5.

As often happens, the original form was not what we now see, but simply a two-piece swimsuit that exposed only the navel. It took from ten to fifteen years for women in various parts of the world to accept the current style.[10]

If origins remain obscure, the search should establish the conditions that would have to be met if the suspected account were true. Thus it has been "well known" in French literary circles that Flaubert was the real father of Guy de Maupassant. The older novelist did encourage and coach the younger and showed and received from him warm affection: what more "obvious" than to explain these facts by the relation of father and son?

The biographer of both Flaubert and Maupassant, Francis Steegmuller, disposed of the story in the two ways mentioned above. He found the origin of the allegation in the *Journal* of the Brothers Goncourt (notorious gossips) under the date of October 1, 1893. The known relationship, other than literary between Flaubert and Maupassant is quite simple: Flaubert had a childhood friend whose sister married a Maupassant. Guy, the future writer and first son of that marriage, was born on August 5, 1850. What are the historical conditions required for Flaubert's paternity of that son?

Obviously, in late 1849 Flaubert, then aged twenty-eight, must have been in the same city as the Maupassant couple, who lived much of the time in Normandy. In the stated year, Flaubert was in Paris between October 25 and October 29, preparing for a trip to Egypt with his friend Maxime du Camp. He did not return to France until June 1851. The possibility of his paternity is thus limited to five days—unlikely, but not impossible. Flaubert kept a fairly full diary of those days and wrote at least once each day to his mother in the country. Nowhere does he mention seeing the childhood friend's sister Laure de Maupassant. For the rest, Flaubert was extremely busy and often accompanied by Du Camp.

[10]Geoffrey Bocca, *Bikini Beach* (1962), 132.

On the other side of the supposed affair, there is no evidence that Laure de Maupassant was in Paris, none that her husband or her son ever doubted the latter's legitimacy. It was not until Maupassant was seventeen that Flaubert met him, four years after a correspondence had begun between Flaubert and the young man's mother. Its tone makes it still more unlikely than the dates that the two ever had a love affair. So despite the reappearance from time to time of this old story, the conclusion must be that it is another legend made plausible by its aptness to literary purposes.

At the same time, not all discrepancies signalize fiction or fraud. In autobiographies, for instance, one must be prepared to find errors in dates and names without necessarily inferring that the account is false. Unless written with the aid of a diary or a full correspondence file, memoirs are likely to embody the unconscious tricks that memory plays in everyone, the "short-circuiting" of associations. Thus the first use of the block-signal system on a railroad in the United States is credited to Ashbel Welch, vice president of the Camden and Amboy. The installation was made in 1863. In memoirs written much later, Welch says that he was led to devise the system after a disastrous rear-end collision that killed many Civil War soldiers coming home on furlough. But that accident occurred on March 7, 1865. It would be absurd to disbelieve the main fact because the date is two years off. And the reason assigned is probably right, too— some rear-end collision that took lives, though not the one cited.

Falsification on the Increase

It should be borne in mind, however, that during the last fifty years, new modes of communication and entertainment have exploited in pseudo-historical fashion the recent and the remote past alike, and this popular (and profitable) enterprise has led to a noticeable weakening of the standards of evidence and truth-telling. In the so-called documentary film or broadcast and their more recent offshoot, the docudrama, a good deal of attention is paid to externals—the site, the costumes, the picturesque detail—but facts and their probability or even plausibility are steadily ignored. Thus in a British series about the life of the master spy Sidney Reilly, Sir Basil Zaharoff is shown shooting and killing one of his own aides with a revolver. Zaharoff, a millionaire arms dealer much valued (and decorated) by heads of state before and during the First World War, was called by his enemies a "merchant of death" and that label is apparently enough to justify depicting him as a cynical, indeed frivolous murderer.

For most people, seeing is believing and a strong image such as this becomes historical truth. The "researcher mind" will resist, of course, but it faces other pitfalls of a new kind. For example, in the interests of free speech, the libel laws in the United States have been notably modified in such a way that the press can without risk print fabrications—outright lies—provided no malice prompted the deed.[11] At the same time, the newspaper reporter is protected from having to disclose the dubious source. In these conditions, few public figures will venture to start a suit—indefinitely long and expensive—in order to clear their good name. The researcher dependent on reports published in reputable journals will therefore find no corrective to the lie, as might have happened when libel was still a serious matter.

To the same effect, it now appears that weekly journals, which employ researchers and thus guarantee factual if not intellectual accuracy, have been betrayed by some of their writers who—thinking of Thucydides, no doubt—invent speeches and persons and "telling" incidents. To make a splash in the endless flood of publications, authors have found that scandal, accusations, shocking discoveries are virtually de rigueur.

---

[11]The test is "reckless disregard of the truth." If a reporter sincerely believes the lie he or she has been told, there is no malice in printing it. This acts as an encouragement to print after superficial inquiry, the writer "sincerely believing" what one or two have said "in confidence."

Books are therefore cobbled together about the recently dead (or barely alive) to launch one of these "charges" and get noticed—never mind if no scrap of evidence is available.[12] The public has become used to this avalanche of gossip gathered from the subject's surviving neighbors, from schoolmates, second cousins, and friends and enemies at every stage of life. Unless authors can say they have conducted hundreds of interviews and traveled thousands of cassette miles, they are thought not to have done their homework. That work is inquisitorial and does not stop even before the unknowable: a reviewer complained not long ago, "We are not told exactly what went wrong between S—— and his second wife."

This frame of mind in both writer and reader destroys the proper taste for truth. It makes likelihood seem tame and bland. It tempts writers to throw the falsehoods into their text as interesting possibilities. They "take no responsibility" but gain credit for industry, thoroughness, and a sense of what is "important and exciting." In these conditions, a balanced estimate of a situation and a true portrait in biography become rarities. That superb writer and judicious critic Harold Nicolson pointed out long ago how by "telling all" one falsifies. In his life of Lord Curzon, he said, he refrained from dwelling on Curzon's obsessive parsimony and frequent bouts of temper, because these traits would have overimpressed the reader and distorted—not filled out—a true portrait of the man. Imagine the words of a stutterer reproduced throughout.

It should be clear that by definition, the whole human being, the interesting subject of the life, is the one who performed actions worth remembering and recording. Besides, some of the traits that can be gloated over are liable to grave misinterpretation. Thus Lyndon Johnson's habit of taking another person's elbow and drawing close for a conversation à deux was not "a sign of secretiveness"; it turns out the president was somewhat deaf.

---

[12]Reputable publishers have begun to ask authors for documentation when a thesis challenges probability too violently. See New York Times (August 2, 1984).

In sum, the increasing overlap between historical writing and journalism, both printed and broadcast, has led to much myth-making. Thus the threat to planes of "the Bermuda Triangle" becomes an accepted fact, and the demand for evidence grows weaker. A publisher was found for a book that says Pope John Paul I was murdered and that offered no proof; and a famous German magazine bought and published the "Hitler diaries" without verification and thereby gulled both journalists and scholars into accepting them.[13] It is a time for keeping your head when all about you are losing theirs.

Attribution: Putting a Name to a Document

The historian arrives at truth most often through probability. As will be shown, this does not mean "a doubtful kind of truth" but a firm reliance on the likelihood that evidence which has been examined and found solid is veracious. If you receive a letter from a relative that bears what looks like her signature, that refers to family matters you and she commonly discuss, and that was postmarked in the city where she lives, the probability is very great that she wrote it. The contrary hypothesis would need at least as many opposing signs of similar weight in order to take root in your mind—though the possibility of forgery,[14] tampering, and substitution is always present.

As everybody knows, the number of signs that point to genuineness reinforce one another and vastly increase the total probability. If their individual force could be measured, the total would be not their sum but their product. In other words, with each added particle of truthfulness, it becomes far less likely that deception has been practiced or an error committed. Hence in cases where no direct sign is available, a concurrence

[13]To see how publishers are taken in, read Charles Hamilton, *The Hitler Diaries: Fakes That Fooled the World* (1991).
[14]See pp. 99, 121n, 122 and n and 136.

of indirect signs will establish proof. The "circumstantial evidence" of the law courts is a familiar example of this type of mute testimony. It must always be received with caution and tested bit by bit; but when it survives analysis its probative value is fully as great as the testimony of witnesses—and often greater.

One type of difficulty that is overcome by looking for cumulative indirect proof is that of identifying unsigned contributions in periodicals. The problem is a frequent one, for until a little over a century ago nearly all journalism was anonymous. Sometimes an account book survives to tell us who was paid for writing what.[15] But usually no resource is in sight except the scholar's sharp wits. Here is how one researcher arrived at an important identification.[16] In the early 1830s, the young writer John Stuart Mill was greatly interested in the work of the Saint-Simonians, a French socialist group. He met some of their emissaries in England and studied their ideas. So much is clear. Now on April 18, 1832, there appeared in *Le Globe*, which was the newspaper of the French party, a long letter signed "J." that purported to give an Englishman's opinion of the Saint-Simonians doctrines. The mind naturally jumps to the possibility that this letter was a translation of something written by Mill. But jumping is not proving. How do we make sure?

- First, research discloses two earlier allusions by one of the editors of the paper to the effect that "one of the most powerful young thinkers in London" intended to write a series of open letters on the new ideas.

- Second, there exists a letter to that same editor announcing the visit of a third party who would bring him, among other things, "the work of your young friend M." With the published

---

[15]This was the method used by Daniel C. Haskell in producing volume 2 of his *Indexes of Titles and Contributors of* The Nation . . . *1865–1917,* (2 vols., 1951–1953).

[16]Hill Shine, "J. S. Mill and an Open Letter to the Saint-Simonian Society in 1832" (*Journal of the History of Ideas,* 6, January 1945, 102–108).

"J." the "M." makes out a *prima facie* case for identifying the writer as John Mill; yet it needs strengthening.

- Third, it was within three days of receiving the piece of news just recorded that the newspaper published the open letter of "an Englishman" who signed himself "J."

At this point the scholar whose researches we have followed remarks that "a cautious reader will still properly feel some reservations" about attributing the letter to Mill. He therefore continues the chase. "Two further bits of circumstantial evidence," he tells us, "seem decisive." They are, to pursue the enumeration:

- Fourth, a letter of May 30 from Mill to his Saint-Simonian friends refers to "my letter which appeared in *Le Globe*."
- Fifth, a footnote added to that private letter by the editor of Mill's correspondence, states that Mill's public letter appeared on April 18, 1832.

At this point no further doubt is possible and the researcher can exclaim, like Euclid at the end of a theorem: "Q.E.D."

Explication: Clearing Up Details in Manuscripts

Young researchers who want to obtain their professional license by earning the Ph.D. often believe that the best indication of merit is to find a packet of letters in an attic. The implication is that professionals value above all else a new primary source.[17] This is not so. The find may be valuable or trivial. Still, new evidence is generally interesting.

---

[17]A primary source is distinguished from a secondary by the fact that the former gives the words of the witnesses or first recorders of an event—for example, Victor Klemperer's diaries of life under the Nazis, *Ich will Zeugnis ablegen bis zum letzten* trans. as *I Will Bear Witness*, 2 vols, 1998. The researcher, using a number of such primary sources, produces a secondary source.

If it consists of manuscripts, it creates special problems for the verifier. Manuscripts often come in huge unsorted masses—the "papers" that are the bulky leftovers of busy lives.[18] Of such papers, letters are perhaps the most difficult to subdue: they must be forced, in spite of slips of the pen, bad handwriting, or allusions to unidentified persons, to tell the exact story that the author intended and that the recipient probably understood.

In this kind of decoding and classifying, no librarian can go very far in supplying help. It is an expert's job, and every expert is self-made. You learn your letter-writer's quirks and foibles from what he or she wrote and said; you date and interpret the documents by internal and external clues. To do these things, you go back and forth between clear and obscure, dated and undated pieces, acquiring information by which to pull yourself forward until many gaps are filled and some contradictions become intelligible. Dumas Malone, for instance, learned from long familiarity with Jefferson's papers that his subject's vocabulary grew more "radical" when writing to younger men. This was a sign not so much of Jefferson's eagerness for a new revolution as of his desire to awaken the coming generation to its responsibility for progress. This fact, once observed, becomes a test for the literalness of some of Jefferson's most advanced proposals. The point of this example is that only an expert—one might even say only *the* expert—is in a position to make sound inferences from a given letter.

Dealing with letters, then, is not a sinecure. It requires an agile mind, or one made such by repeated bafflement and discovery. Consider the simplest of questions: When was this written and to whom? Unless the writer was a regular "dater," or

[18]In making searches, the electronic resource, ArchivesUSA, available by subscription and on CD-ROM and updated periodically, is now the principal resource. It supersedes the *Directory of Archives and Manuscript Repositories in the United States* (DAMRUS), last published in 1988; the records from the *National Union Catalogue of Manuscript Collections* (NUMAC); and records from the major microfiche series, *National Inventory of Documentary Sources in the United States* (NIDS).

the post office stamped the letter itself (before the use of envelopes), or the dated envelope has been kept, or the recipient was a methodical person who endorsed each letter with the particulars of its date, author, and bearing, the precious piece of paper may raise more questions than it answers.

For a pair of representative puzzles we may turn to the letters of the composer Hector Berlioz (1803–1869). These letters kept appearing on the market when the publication of a new *Complete Correspondence* began several years ago. It became the editor's task to fit the new items among the hundreds already published. Place, date, and addressee's name had to be supplied. Two forms that this operation can take may be briefly illustrated. The A.L.S.[19] says, in French:

19 rue de Boursault
Thursday, June 23

Dear Sir:
Here is the Table of Contents of the book about which I had the honor of speaking to you. If you will kindly look it over, you will have a rough idea of the subjects dealt with and the general tone of the work. Till next Monday.

Yours faithfully,
HECTOR BERLIOZ

Now the address with which the note starts is in Paris, and it is one at which Berlioz resided from July 1849 till April 1856. (This knowledge comes from a table that the researcher has prepared for himself from a survey of the letters extant.[20]) So the piece to be identified falls within those seven years. The next step is to the perpetual calendar, which gives Thursday, June 23, as falling in 1853. This seems to settle the matter, except that the only book Berlioz had in hand during those years was ready by

---

[19]Autograph letter signed.
[20]For this table and examples of the dating techniques, see Jacques Barzun, *New Letters of Berlioz* (2nd ed., 1974), 304–305 and 273ff.

May 1852 and was published the same December. We are forced to conclude that despite the "Thursday June 23" the note was written not in 1853 but in 1852. This is at once confirmed by both the table of domiciles, which shows that in June 1853 Berlioz was in London, not Paris, and by the calendar. We know from other instances that he frequently mistook the day of the week. Moreover, in June 1852 the twenty-third falls on a Wednesday; so that, assuming a mistake, his dating would be only one day off. Combining the data and knowing also who published the book, we conclude that the note was sent to the well-known publisher, Michel Lévy. An inquiry at the present offices of the firm showed that no records of the period were preserved. Internal evidence is therefore our only guide.

Most researchers never use anything but printed sources. Yet these too are full of contradictions that have to be resolved, as are also the inferences from artifacts. Imagine, for instance, an observant student who has noticed that the words "In God We Trust" appear on some of our old coins but not on others, nor on old paper money. Imagine him further as writing a textbook on American history, for which he wants to verify his reasonable guess that the four words in question form the official, yet seemingly optional, motto of the United States.

His first step might be to find out how early in our history the slogan was used on our coins. Thumbing through *The Standard Catalogue of United States Coins*, he would learn that the phrase is not found before 1864. It first appeared on the bronze two-cent pieces and two years later on all gold and silver coins. The verifier would also observe that it disappeared from the five-cent piece in 1883 and did not return till 1938. What is more, it appeared on some of the gold coins struck in 1908 and not on others. Clearly, this "now-you-see-it, now-you-don't" suggests either fickleness or the probability that inscriptions on American money are not ruled by settled official policy.

Noticing that the picture of Secretary of the Treasury Salmon P. Chase adorns the greenbacks, or paper money, issued during the Civil War, when the motto was first used, the historian might conclude that Chase had a special interest in the design of our money.

The obvious course would be to seek more light in a biography of Chase. The surmise about Chase would be wrong, but the upshot would carry the researcher one step forward. He would find that although Chase took no interest in the numismatic art, he was a religious man. He put "In God We Trust" on the coins to satisfy a proselytizing clergyman who thought it imperative. Next, from the issuance of coins both with and without the motto in 1908, our researcher would correctly conclude that the choice lay within the discretion of the Secretary of the Treasury. No sooner would he be confident that the motto had no official standing than he would discover by further investigation a news report about the decision of Congress—ninety-two years after Chase's—to make the words official and inscribe them on all the currency, both metal and paper.[21]

Note by way of summary that before he could solve his puzzle this verifier had to consult a coin catalogue, one or more books about Chase, one or more about Theodore Roosevelt for the events of 1908, and a newspaper file.

Destroying Myths

The amount of verifying one does depends not only on one's own curiosity but also on the grasp of one's subject that one possesses at the start. The more one understands at the beginning, the more one finds to question and ascertain. It is expected, of course, that the researcher into any subject will approach it with a well-developed sense of time—whether the time be the few weeks or months of a particular crisis or the centuries separating St. Augustine from St. Thomas. Thus the narrator of the French Revolution or the First World War proceeds by days in

[21]Bill signed by President Eisenhower, July 30, 1956. Subsequently, a silver dollar memorializing Susan B. Anthony, the women's rights leader, was coined, bearing the motto. Her admirers objected that "she trusted no deity" and might have agreed with the Texas woman, head of an atheist group, who petitioned the Supreme Court to order the removal of the motto. The whole series of facts from 1864 on are indicators for the social and cultural historian.

those fateful summer and autumn months, whereas the historian of Rome must without stumbling move across a span of twenty generations.

But the investigator's original fund of knowledge must embrace even more than a well-populated chronology; it must include an understanding of how people in other eras lived and behaved, what they believed, and how they managed their institutions; and for contemporary research the same kind of knowledge is required about the present day.

The present day continues to believe in myths, some of which have been long regarded as well-known truths. Consider the sort of inquiry needed to discredit a belief accepted by the whole Western world about the Middle Ages. The importance of verifying or disproving such "facts" is that new beliefs are often based on them. Thus a modern psychiatrist's study of the states of mind of dying patients drew from his clinical researches conclusions he considered of practical value. Unfortunately, he buttressed them with historical statements, one of which is that:

When the first millennium after the birth of Christ approached its end, Occidental man was seized by the fear of and hope for the Lord's return. The end of the world was envisaged, which meant man's final end [sic] had arrived. With the approach of the second millennium, the conviction again has spread that the days of man are counted. . . . [22]

That this parallel is false in every respect will be clear if we retrace the path of the scholar who more than ninety years ago disposed of the legend about the end of the world coming in the year 1000.[23]

His first step was to discover when the tale originally came out in print. He found that this was in a 1690 edition of a late-fifteenth-century chronicle. Thus the first public record of the story dates from nearly seven centuries after the supposed date

---

[22]K. R. Eissler, *The Psychiatrist and the Dying Patient* (1955), 108.

[23]George L. Burr, "The Year 1000 and the Antecedents of the Crusades" (*American Historical Review*, 6, April 1901, 429–439).

of doom. Seven hundred years is a long time—twice the span since Shakespeare's death, or more than three times since the Declaration of Independence. In the eighteenth century, a period when the Middle Ages were in disrepute and instances of their superstition were gladly seized on, the published tale of 1690 was widely circulated. Indeed, it became usual to ascribe the launching of the Crusades to the sense of mercy and relief felt by the Christians when the end of the world did not come in A.D. 1000. This emotion was also said to account for the remarkable increase in church building. Although these explanations were abandoned by nineteenth-century historians, educated people have continued to believe the myth. The terror of the year 1000 has been the core of many a piece of moralizing. Said one confident writer of the 1880s about the people of A.D. 999:

Some squandered their substance in riotous living, others bestowed it for the salvation of their souls on churches and convents, bewailing multitudes lay by day and by night about the altars, many looked with terror, yet most with secret hope, for the conflagration of the earth and the falling of the heavens.[24]

In the face of such vivid reports, what could make a thoughtful scholar suspect the truth of the whole episode? The answer is: his intimate knowledge of the Middle Ages. George Burr knew, to begin with, that the end of the world had been foretold so often that only the ignorant in the year 1000 would seriously believe a new rumor. Moreover, long before that year, it had become orthodox belief and teaching that if the end of the world were really to come no one would know the time in advance.

Third, he knew that however impressive round numbers based on the decimal system are to us, they had no such hold on the imagination of medieval man. The numerals of that era were the Roman *Is*, *Vs*, *Xs*, *Ls*, *Cs*, *Ds*, and *Ms*. No special property would attach to "The Year M." Rather, mystery and significance

---

[24]H. V. Sybel, *Geschichte des ersten Kreuzzugs* (2nd and rev. ed., Leipzig, 1881), 150; quoted in Burr (op. cit), 429.

would have been connected with 3s, 7s, 12s, and their multiples; for these were the sacred numbers of the Jews, and the Christians had repeatedly used them for prophecy.

Fourth, our scholar knew that the Christian calendar did not come into general use until after 1000. And even then there was no agreement on dating. Nor was this the only difficulty arising from the calendar. When did the year 1000 begin? At Christmas, at Annunciation, at Easter, on the first of March (as in Venice), at the vernal equinox (as in Russia), on the first of September (as in the Greek Empire), or on the first of January (as in Spain)? In such a state of things the world obviously could not end everywhere on schedule.

Fifth, our medievalist knew that bare numerical dates meant little or nothing to the ordinary man and woman. They guided their life by the feast and fast days of the Church, not, as we do, by engagement books in which not only days, months, and years are marked, but also hours and half-hours, A.M. and P.M. We carry watches and consult them every few minutes. Medieval time, differently divided, was of a different texture, measured by the sun and by the church bell signaling morning and evening services.[25]

In short, it is unhistorical to read back our habits and behavior into a past era, and the conclusion is plain: taking the lack of any contemporaneous evidence of panic together with the facts of daily life and thought in the Middle Ages, the scholar demolishes a legend whose potent effects would continue to mislead researchers in cognate fields if his work had not enlightened at least a part of the educated public. One must say "a part," because a story that is dramatic and fits many contexts has a long life. Thus, the late Henry Focillon, a scholar highly respected in France and well known as a lecturer in the United States, acknowledges in his last, unfinished work, *The Year One Thousand* (1969), that historians doubt the "terrors" of that year.

[25]On this vast technological change, see David S. Landes, *Revolution in Time: Clocks and the Making of the Modern World* (1983).

But he finds it "convenient" to keep up the myth and he refers to "the approach of the fateful date."[26]

Again, like the year 1000, the capture of Constantinople by the Turks in 1453 has struck the general imagination and provided a convenient "cause" for Columbus's discovery of America: European traders, it was supposed, could no longer go east; they sought a westward passage. As late as 1967, this notion was used to introduce the visitor to a superb exhibition of "The Dutch in Manhattan" at the Museum of the City of New York. Professor A. H. Lybyer, who conclusively disproved the connection between the Turks and westward voyages, had published his study fifty-two years earlier.[27]

Even modern nations live by myths. Generations of children have taken to heart the story of George Washington and the cherry tree, even as Italian school children are told that Romulus and Remus, twin boys suckled by a she-wolf, founded the city of Rome. These two myths may be written off as ancient, but modern ones keep being created and believed in spite of debunking.

One myth made up in the twentieth century dies hard regardless of conclusive research: that Abner Doubleday invented baseball. He is credited with the diamond layout of the field and the rules of the game, an invention that sprang full-blown from his fertile mind in 1839 in Cooperstown, New York.[28] These "facts" are found in many of the older encyclopedias and

---

[26]The fiction appears to be perdurable. See the front-page review of Mario Varga Llosa's novel *The War of the End of the World* (1984) in the *New York Times Book Review* (August 12, 1984), and Chalmers M. Roberts, "To celebrate or not—*when* is the question" (*Smithsonian,* January 1990, 172). The endlessly fascinating subject of eschatology—the study of the end of things—is taken up by Cullen Murphy in "The Way the World Ends" (*The Wilson Quarterly,* Winter, 1990, 50–55).

[27]"The Ottoman Turks and the Routes of the Oriental Trade" *English Historical Review,* 120, (October 1915, 577–588).

[28]It is, incidentally, the town founded by the family of James Fenimore Cooper, the author of the world-famous *Leatherstocking Tales* dealing with the conflicts and friendships between the English colonists and the American Indians.

other reference books, including the authoritative *Dictionary of American Biography*. The battle of Gettysburg comes into the story. Doubleday was a career army officer who fought gallantly on that field, which makes him the perfect choice as creator of the national sport.

The truth is less glamorous: Doubleday was anointed baseball's originator by a commission formed in 1907 under the chairmanship of Albert G. Spalding, the sporting goods magnate, to find where and how the game began. Spalding was eager to have an American designated as the Father of Baseball, and somehow he chose a Civil War figure. He guided the commission into agreement. The myth is unusual in having its birth so clearly established. Sober inquiry shows that Doubleday makes no mention of the game in his diaries and that in 1839 he was not in Cooperstown. The site, then, is wrong.

Still, it is possible that the inventor's name is right. Further search shows that baseball began in the mists of time. It was first mentioned in Europe a thousand years ago. In England, it was referred to casually by Jane Austen in a novel before 1820. In America, John Adams and Daniel Webster seem to have played some kind of game involving bases and a ball. Perhaps it was what generations have known as "One Old Cat" (pronounced One o'cat) or another game called "rounders." As a boy, Ty Cobb, one of baseball's greatest players, developed his skill as batsman and base runner in yet another predecessor of baseball called *town ball*.

In spite of modern researchers, the Baseball Hall of Fame Museum is in Cooperstown. Wisely, the institution does not maintain that Doubleday was the brilliant originator, but his name lives in the memory of lovers of the game; it would be cruel to disillusion them.

Identification: Giving Due Credit for Authorship

Sometimes a problem of verification is solved by reaching behind your desk and taking down the reference book that contains the fact you need. But the researcher will soon discover that reference books frequently disagree. This does not always mean that

FIGURE 9   *FICTION INTO FACT*

XVII

BOARD OF INLAND REVENUE v. HADDOCK; REX v. HADDOCK

THE NEGOTIABLE COW

'WAS the cow crossed?'

'No, your worship, it was an open cow.'

These and similar passages provoked laughter at Bow Street to-day when the Negotiable Cow case was concluded.

Sir Joshua Hoot, K.C. (appearing for the Public Prosecutor): Sir Basil, these summonses, by leave of the Court, are being heard together, an unusual but convenient arrangement.

The defendant, Mr. Albert Haddock, has for many months, in spite of earnest endeavours on both sides, been unable to establish harmonious relations between himself and the Collector of Taxes. The Collector maintains that Mr. Haddock should make over a large part of his earnings to the Government. Mr. Haddock replies that the proportion demanded is excessive, in view of the inadequate services or consideration which he himself has received from that Government. After an exchange of endearing letters, telephone calls, and even cheques, the sum demanded was reduced to fifty-seven pounds; and about this sum the exchange of opinions continued.

 **PHYLLIS BATTELLE**

Write A Cow Check?

Imagine writing a check on a tobacco pouch, and telling the teller to stick that in his pipe and cash it. Fun? Boy!

Regulation J came to my attention a few weeks ago when the New York Public Library received a $20,000 check drafted on a specially-designed scarf from R. J. Reynolds Industries, which underwrote a fashion show for the benefit of the library. The idea for the scarf-check was to grab attention. It did. The First National City Bank in New York promptly cashed it.

Savvy people — especially when angry — have benefitted from the regulation. A Mr. and Mrs. Haldock, incensed at what they considered an unjust tax levy, presented their tax collector with a check written on the side of their cow. The collector said it was ridiculous, and took the case to court, where the judge looked into the law and ruled the bovine was negotiable. The assessor returned to his office with the cow's left hoofprint on the tax return.

An Elmira, N. Y., woman literally took the shirt off her husband's back and wrote a check on it for a creditor. A Charlottesville, Va., man paid his telephone bill with a check written on a coconut.

In a book published in 1935 (its parts having appeared serially in *Punch*), A. P. Herbert, the English wit, included one of his "Misleading Cases"— parodies of the law. His regular hero, the plaintiff Albert Haddock, attempts to bedevil the Revenue service by sending to it a check written on the side of a cow. Forty years later, in an American syndicated column, the same "fact" is related as having occurred in the United States. A couple reported as being a Mr. and Mrs. Haldock are credited with the use of the promissory cow. The change of name and venue strongly suggests that the original idea was transmitted by word of mouth through a great many storytellers. (A "crossed" check—see dialogue above—is one marked with two parallel lines across the front; it can then be cashed only by the payee.)

all are wrong except one; what happens is that one book in giving, say, the date of a treaty will give the year of its signing and another book the date of its ratification, months later. Similar disparities can and do occur about most events, so that the "right" date is frequently a conventional choice among several possibilities. Disagreement about authorship is less easily resolved.

On this point, whoever by research finds and publishes a reversal of common opinion must be prepared to see his discovery both accepted by some—not all—of his colleagues and neglected by the public. In proof of this truth, witness the literary detective work of Don Foster, professor of English at Vassar College. It is a lesson in at least three of the researcher's required techniques: tracking down sources, reconciling dates, and judging written text.

Professor Foster found reason to question the traditional view that Clement C. Moore, a New York clergyman, was the author of the well-loved "'Twas the Night Before Christmas." This slight classic has historical importance, because until its appearance and popularity, Santa Claus did not play the role in American life that he now serves. The original St. Nicholas was a bishop of that name, famous in Holland for his generosity to impoverished girls, and his reputation was brought to America by the early Dutch colonists. He was for some reason rejected as hero by the English and not welcome to the New England Puritans, for whom Christmas was for years forbidden as a pagan festival. He is now the familiar figure, certified by the press,[29] while being also the patron saint of pawnbrokers.

The publication of the poem in 1823 in the *Troy* (N.Y.) *Sentinel* opened the door on a new era. The unknown or misknown old St. Nicholas was metamorphosed into red-cheeked, jolly Santa Claus, loving toward all good children who had hung their stockings on the mantel to receive the goodies and gifts that he would deposit there during his midnight visit. The story, the

[29]In an editorial by Francis P. Church that appeared in the *New York Sun* on September 21, 1897, and was reprinted endlessly thereafter. Beginning "Yes, Virginia, there is a Santa Claus," it was a response to an inquiring letter from eight-year-old Virginia O'Hanlon, whose father had told her, "If you see it in *The Sun*, it's so."

vision of the poem, was unforgettable. Almanacs and magazines spread it wide, and when in the late 1820s it appeared in the *New York Morning Courier*, it was credited to Clement Clarke Moore, a professor of Bible at the General Theological Seminary in New York. He had also written verse of the same modest caliber. By the end of Moore's life—he died in 1863—he was famous everywhere as the father of the cherubic Santa Claus, inseparable from his reindeer also known by cozy names.

But strangely enough there was a striking difference between Moore's other versifying and the Christmas tale. Moore was a starchy, unbending man, given to decrying young people for preferring to carouse rather than pursue their duty—to work and to study. He seems to have had few diversions, indeed, never to have enjoyed himself. The fun-loving St. Nick was not his kind of companion, and hence, a very unlikely creation of his fancy.

So much was known but obviously not reflected upon. One day, a Boston lady who had learned of Professor Foster's ability as a research scholar telephoned him to say that her great-great-great-great-grandfather, Major Henry Livingston, Jr., whom she wanted to memorialize on a Web site, was the true author of "The Night Before Christmas." The notion caught Foster's imagination. He made himself acquainted with the Major's life and work. "He was an artist, journalist, and poet; a surveyor and cartographer; an archaeologist and anthropologist; a flute player and a fiddler; a free spirit and all-around merry old soul if ever there was one." He was, moreover, given to composing doggerel verses and poems for children, written in anapests—da-da-dum, da-da-dum—the meter used in "Christmas."

Foster then found that several earlier researchers had concluded in favor of Livingston as the author—among others the scholar Henry Noble MacCracken, long-time president of Vassar College. But the world clung to Moore by virtue of sacred tradition. To Foster, the evidence pointing to Livingston was overwhelming and it soon mounted:

1. Following up on a family tradition that "Christmas" had been published in a Poughkeepsie newspaper many years before it appeared in the *Troy Sentinel*, Foster went over microfilms in

the Vassar Library. He did not find what he was looking for, but he came upon something else as interesting: a poem called "Sante Claus," which explained to Americans who this strange being was. Thus, Poughkeepsie, not New York, seems to have been his entranceway into America.

2. Studying Moore's character and style, Foster found him to be a curmudgeon on a large scale. "In one early poem, Moore condemns the walk, talk, dancing, music, dress, and cosmetics of the girls of Manhattan ("Shame! Shame! Heart-rending thought! Deep-sinking stain! . . . Arts first taught by prostitutes of France!") Moore was waspish, cranky, and insensitive to everything but the sins of his fellow creatures. Moore also defended the institution of slavery, opposed public education, derided educated women, and dismissed Indians as "savages." Livingston, on the other hand, advocated educating all children regardless of sex; expressed friendship for the Indians; admired learned women; and loved music, dancing, and merriment generally. He argued for raising children without inflicting corporal punishment, whereas Moore was equally clear: "Withhold not correction from the child, for if thou beatest him with the rod, he will not die . . . "

3. Certain phrases in "Christmas" could not have come from Moore's pen. For example, in the poem Santa Claus is described as holding a pipe clenched in his teeth. This was surely not an image Moore would have thought of, for he abhorred tobacco, calling it "Virginia's weed, opium's treacherous aid."

Still, even though it began to strain credulity, the defense of Moore as the true author was keen. Tradition affirms that on December 24, 1822, during his first year as Professor of Biblical Learning at the General Theological Seminary, Clement Clarke Moore went shopping in Greenwich Village for a Christmas turkey. While riding in a one-horse open sleigh, he composed in his head the fifty-six lines of "A Visit from St. Nicholas." On arriving home, he wrote the poem down; and on Christmas Day

FIGURE 10   THE NIGHT BEFORE CHRISTMAS

"Nobody was using
the computer."

he read the verses to his family, just before sitting down to the turkey dinner.

Would Moore himself have made up such a story? He knew the awful price of fraud: a young brother-in-law of his had committed suicide rather than face the consequences of having forged the name "Clement C. Moore" to a banknote to discharge a gambling debt. The probability seems against his claiming authorship. But when in 1833 Moore published a volume of his poems, he included "Christmas" in it. The book was not a success, but that single poem continued to be reprinted year in and year out. Foster is convinced that it did not belong there. Examining the others in the collection, he found "Clement

Clarke Moore a learned man but not terribly original." Any number of phrases were lifted from other poems. Moore's work is "highly derivative—so much so that his reading can be tracked, and his poems dated by the dozens of phrases borrowed and recycled by his sticky-fingered Muse."

Drawing on his own knowledge of literature, Foster recalled two popular eigteenth-century poems in anapests that Livingston must have known; he shows their influence and favored that meter, whereas Moore wrote only one anapestic piece—"The Pig and the Rooster"—and it was modeled, according to Foster, "on the animal fables of Henry Livingston." Going deeper, Foster demonstrated that everywhere in "Christmas" were phrases that Livingston would use. More telling still, Foster caught Moore in a mistake: in writing out the poem and autographing it as a gift, he called two of the reindeers Donder and Blitzen. These were corruptions of words familiar to every Dutchburgher in the East, including Livingston, who was "three-quarters New York Dutch." It is the angry oath "Donder en Bliksem!" (Thunder and Lightning!)

Evidence mounted, but to a professional searcher the intriguing question remained: Would a religious man, who preached morality to his children and to the wide world in prose and rhyme, have published as his own a poem he had not written?

In the collections of the New-York Historical Society, the indefatigable Foster found two remarkable items. One was a manual entitled *A Complete Treatise on Merino and Other Sheep*, the translation of a work by an accomplished French veterinarian. Moore had donated it to the Society, inscribed "Translated from the French by Clement C. Moore." Moore, says Foster, should have read the book from cover to cover. Had he done so, he would have found on the last page that a Francis Durand was listed as "the sole translator."

The other item was a letter that Moore wrote early in 1844 to a Norman Tuttle, former owner of the *Troy Sentinel*, inquiring whether he knew the authorship of "Christmas," which his paper had published twenty-one years earlier. Tuttle recalled that the paper's editor had received the poem from a Troy resident, without attribution, and only later learned that it was Moore's. With this assurance, Moore no doubt felt safe enough to include "Christmas," an uncommon gem, among his collection, which was then about to go to press.

Foster's detective work was done.[30] Henry Livingston was the author of "'Twas the Night Before Christmas." Moore had lived a lie that the world accepted for almost two centuries—and the public at large will probably continue to do so. But for good scholars and readers of up-to-date reference works, the record has now been set straight. [31]

The Snare of Pseudonyms

Occasions arise when the contents of an otherwise acceptable book raise doubts in the ordinary reader's mind that prompt a desire to see it settled. For example, many books of the seventeenth and eighteenth centuries are attributed falsely and surprisingly to famous authors. And there is the matter of sequels: four were written after the great success of Voltaire's *Candide*, none of them by Voltaire.[32] The practice of using pseudonyms only heightens the confusion, and it is not generated only by forgers and imitators. Voltaire himself is said to have published under 160 pseudonyms and Franklin under 57. In the early nineteenth century, one L. A. C. Bombet published a book

[30]The full details of Don Foster's monumental search are in his *Author Unknown: Tales of a Literary Detective* (New York, Henry Holt, 2000), pp. 221–75.

[31]In the excellent book, *Inventing Christmas*, by Jock Elliott, the great collector of "Christmas Books" (small works about the holiday or published for the occasion), the author takes up the Livingston claim to the authorship of "The Night Before Christmas" and rejects it (p. 47). But in giving his reasons he fails to mention the two decisive proofs: Moore's other versifying and his pretending to have translated a book that was in fact done by another hand.

[32]For a long while, one of these sequels was regularly reprinted as Part 2 of *Candide* in a popular series of classic texts, giving the reader the false notion that Voltaire had had second thoughts about his "unhappy ending."

called *The Lives of Haydn, Mozart, and Metastasio*; it had had some currency in France and was translated into English. Copies of it occasionally appear in modern catalogues of second-hand books under that author's name. But you will not find Bombet in any French biographical dictionary; for he is in fact Henri Beyle, otherwise Stendhal, who wrote the famous novels *The Red and the Black* and *The Charterhouse of Parma*. To top it all, his *Lives* are largely copied from Carpani and five other writers—a mosaic of plagiarisms, though done with verve and genius.

How does one find one's way through such mazes of deliberate or accidental misdirection? For Voltaire, consult the bibliography by Bengesco in four volumes; for a contemporary, look for one that may have recently been compiled, such as G. B. Shaw's by Dan H. Laurence in two stout volumes.[33] For lesser and earlier writers, go to *The Bibliographical History of Anonyma and Pseudonyma* by Archer Taylor and Frederic J. Mosher, which lists many dictionaries and other reference works likely to afford help. Their discussion of the problems will by itself spur the imagination to find the path of discovery. For recent or contemporary writers, there are dictionaries, notably, *Pseudonyms and Nicknames Dictionary*, published by Gale (1980) and for anonyms a work by Ralph De Sola, *Abbreviations, Acronyms, Anonyms and Eponyms, etc.* (1908), as well as the more recent *International Authors and Writers Who's Who*, which gives lists of pseudonyms and which is regularly brought up to date. But take care! Not all lists are accurate, and they must be cross-checked, either by consulting a list in a more solid looking work or more simply by looking up the catalogue of the national library—British Library, Library of Congress, or other. Finally, the authenticity or genuineness of a text will prove relatively easy if there is a large, scholarly, so-called definitive biography of the (real) author, for these questions are bound to be taken up as part of the "life."

---

[33]Clarendon Press, Oxford, 1983.

Going through a search of this kind incidentally suggests that for scholarly work (as against recreation) it is important to get hold of an author's best text. This usually, but not invariably, means the latest. The preface will tell you what the author or editor may have changed; and if the edition is posthumous, the "apparatus"—footnotes and appendices—will show what kind of information has been gathered to help understanding. Judging the thing itself is the only guarantee, because even reputable publishers and "series" editors make mistakes. The *Candide* sequel is one example. The universally accepted text of James Joyce's *Ulysses* is another—a desperate case. Not until 1984—upwards of sixty years after the first publication during the author's lifetime—did someone discover that the transcriber of the manuscript had permitted himself omissions and transpositions amounting to some 5,000 misrepresentations of Joyce's work.

To look for evidence is something that one has come to take for granted in scientific research, but even there reports may falsify. After the exposure in 1991 of fabrication in an important scientific report, the principal researcher who put his name to the paper had to explain why he dismissed the first complaint, made by a graduate student who had found seventeen pages of notes showing discrepancies with the published text. The senior man, a Nobel Prize winner, declared to those investigating the fraud that "it did not occur to him at the time to look into the notebooks."

With the growth of interdisciplinary studies, the field of verification has widened and the difficulties multiplied. Consider the inquiry into the death of William Rufus, son of William the Conqueror and King of England. The event took place in August 1100, yet until a few years ago there was still something to be done about the how and the why of that variously interpreted death. The issue was: accident or murder. The missing effort was the investigation of the site itself, the New Forest, a partly wooded area north of Southampton Water.

The scholar who carried out this piece of detective work had no illusion that traces of the event would be left after nearly

900 years.[34] But he wanted to "see for himself," so as to understand the indications in the contemporary sources and carry away a picture of the conditions in which the king was killed. This the New Forest, set apart by William the Conqueror as a royal domain, might permit. William Rufus was shot by an arrow while hunting at dusk. Recreating the scene called for knowledge of the topography of the clearing and its cartography in recent centuries; for acquaintance with the arts of venery and archery and with the habits of deer and wind and weather in the Forest—all this in addition to the more traditional subjects of inquiry: who was there; why; and what were their characters, antecedents, and interests at the moment?

The report of this undertaking fills only a small volume, but the results are extensive and so rich in detail that they cannot be further summarized—to say nothing of spoiling a good detective story by giving away the solution. But it may be said that not just one but two kings and one nobleman come out with altered reputations, and that the arrogant nineteenth-century historian, Edward A. Freeman, whose work on William Rufus was first discredited by an earlier critic, appears conclusively as a prejudiced man pushing a thesis in the teeth of the evidence.[35]

No researcher can hope to unravel every mystery and contradiction or uncover every untruth, half-truth, or downright deception that lurks in the raw materials with which he or she must deal. But one's unceasing demand for accuracy must make one put to the test much of the material one uses. There is no substitute for well-placed skepticism.

[34]Duncan Grinnell-Milne, *The Killing of William Rufus: An Investigation in the New Forest* (Newton Abbot, 1968).

[35]This "revision" has further importance as a material point in the rehabilitation of James Anthony Froude, the historian of England, whom Freeman pursued with malicious hatred and succeeded in belittling on the strength of his own false reputation for faultlessness. See W. H. Dunn, *James Anthony Froude* (2 vols., 1961).

CHAPTER 5

HANDLING IDEAS

Fact and Idea: An Elusive Distinction

Daily speech encourages the belief that "a fact is a fact" and that it is useless to argue about it. And indeed it would be idle to dispute about pure fact. Yet we know that argument persists— in politics, science, the arts, family life, casual conversation, and the insides of books. A library is a sort of ammunition dump of unexploded arguments ready to burst forth the moment a live reader looks at a page. Why should this be, if we assume that most books—aside from fiction—honestly try to present verified facts?

The answer is that facts very rarely occur pure, free from interpretation or ideas. We all make the familiar distinction between "gathering facts" and "expressing ideas," but in reality most of the facts we gather come dripping with ideas. We may or may not be aware of these ideas as we move the facts about from the printed page to our minds, our notes, and our reports, but there they are, clinging together nevertheless. The only pure facts in any kind of reporting are those statements that express a conventional relation in conventional terms:

Thomas Jefferson was born on April 2, 1743.[1]

The Monroe Doctrine was promulgated on December 2, 1823.

President Garfield was shot by Charles J. Guiteau.

Through conventional phrasings like "born" and "was shot," conventional names like "Monroe Doctrine," and conventional terms for day, year, and length are expressed fixed relations of time, things, and persons. These relations may be said to be strictly factual, because each term is clear and distinct and remains so by tacit agreement. No one disputes the calendar, not even the Muslim, for whom the Christian year 1743 is the year 1156. Both calendars are conventions, and their numbers are convertible.[2]

But if in the Garfield example we add to "shot by Charles J. Guiteau" the words "a disappointed office seeker," we immediately pass from conventional fact into a different realm of discourse. True, it is a fact that Guiteau had sought a government post and had failed to get it. But putting these events into words next to the fact of Garfield's assassination introduces an idea. The effect is to say: "Guiteau's disappointment was the motive for the act." This is an inference, a hypothesis, an idea. And psychologists tell us that human beings act from a mixture motives.[3]

[1]Or April 13 according to the New Style calendar, which came into effect in 1752. See Chapter 4, p. 69.

[2]The Muslim year is computed from the Hejira, or Flight of Mohammed, in A.D. 622. Since it is a lunar year, it is shorter than ours, and this accounts for the fact that 622 plus 1156 equals more than 1743.

[3]The complexity of Guiteau's motives as they are now understood is examined by a medical historian, Charles E. Rosenberg, in *The Trial of the Assassin Guiteau: Psychiatry and the Law in the Gilded Age* (1968). See also the study "Symbolic Aspects of Presidential Assassination," by E. A. Weinstein and O. G. Lyerly (*Psychiatry,* 32, February 1969, 1–11), from which it appears that some of the assassins look upon the President as a substitute *mother*-figure. Another contribution to the subject is by Annalise Pontius, "Threats to Assassinate the King-President While Propitiating Mother" (*Journal of Analytical Psychology,* 19, January 1974, 38–53). For a curious classification of such violent persons, see Marshall Heyman, "A Study of Presidential Assassins" (*Behavioral Sciences and the Law,* vol. II, 1984, 131–149). On this melancholy subject the material is endless. There is now an *Encyclopedia of Assassinations,* Carl Sifakis, ed. (New York, 1990).

Historians, however, stress the disappointment and go on to say that, owing to this motive, the shooting of the President swung public opinion in favor of Civil Service reform—a further idea for which there is good evidence, but which, once again, is not a pure fact and is therefore disputable.

What then is an idea? In a large dictionary you may find upwards of forty definitions, which shows how indistinct the term is. Nor is this to be regretted, because ideas correspond to the substance of our inner life, which is also fluid, indefinite, and changeable. For our purposes as reporters of the past we may put it that an idea is *an image, inference, or suggestion that goes beyond the data namable in conventional terms.*

This definition is merely a useful one to keep in mind at this stage of our work; it may not be applicable elsewhere. The statement of a fact gives the impression of ending with itself, whereas an idea leads us on. Once you have ascertained that the Monroe Doctrine was promulgated in a presidential message to Congress on December 2, 1823, what then? Questions arise: Was the doctrine really the work of one man or the joint product of Monroe, Canning, and Adams's efforts? Is the doctrine of 1823 precisely the same as the one referred to under the same name since? Did the United States have the right to make such a declaration? Did it have the power to enforce it? These are ideas and they suggest doubts and possibilities. Before they can be answered they have to be narrowed down and studied in relation to "facts," as well as compared with other "ideas" that have occupied the minds of hundreds, living and dead. As a result, the authoritative work on the Monroe Doctrine by Dexter Perkins is in three volumes totaling over 1,300 pages.

It is obvious that any portion of the past consists of facts merged with ideas. The Monroe Doctrine's influence on the course of hemisphere history has derived from its being a powerful idea. From time to time this idea has been reinforced and also modified by such facts as the following:

Napoleon III is carrying out his designs on Mexico.

The Special Task Force has landed on Grenada.

The Soviet Union is installing missiles in Cuba.

Hence the importance of distinguishing clearly between the agreed-upon element of fact and the variable element of idea. Not that ideas are less certain but that the report maker goes to work differently on each. There is a technique to be learned for the handling of ideas.

With facts, as we saw in the last chapter, the reporter's effort is to be exact about the conventional terms—names, dates, titles, and other agreed-upon details. With ideas, the reporter's attitude must be no less exacting, though the same assurance of complete accuracy is not possible. Yet deftness and judgment make the report useful only insofar as it furnishes clear and precise ideas. For the "bare facts" generally are of little interest in themselves. Even the chronicler and the statistician hazard comments or conclusions, and these are ideas.

Before we take up the means by which special care about ideas is to be exercised, we have to consider still another aspect of ideas, whether in the past or the present.

Large Ideas as Facts of History

"Ideas" in the large, historic sense, ideas with a capital, Evolution; the idea "created equal" in the Declaration of Independence—these and many others have the property of being facts as well: they *occurred*. Like any other event, they have a place and a date. But their history is not easily reducible to conventional terms. For example, how would you date the idea of Evolution? Some textbooks say, "By his publication of *The Origin of Species* in 1859, Darwin established the idea of Evolution in Western thought." But research shows that similar ideas had made a stir in Western thought for a whole century before 1859. The contradiction would seem to hinge on the meaning of "established"—except that *The Origin of Species* did not immediately persuade mankind but set off a violent controversy that lasted twenty years. Faced with these complications, we may wonder what we mean by "a great idea," its date and destiny.

Obviously, when we speak of ideas on this scale we are talking about a changing entity. Evolution has not been one and the same idea from the beginning; Darwin himself was not putting forward Evolution but what he believed to be a means (not *the* means) of evolution, namely Natural Selection, and on the precise role of this means he himself varied his estimate in the six editions of his book. Ideas, in short, are neither single things nor simple. To illustrate this truth by another example, what are the so-called ideas of the Declaration of Independence? We know they were clear and governing ideas to Lincoln and presumably to his American contemporaries, but in his speeches he had to demonstrate their meaning and validity again and again. In his time and ours, those same ideas have been blamed as "glittering generalities," though without showing what is wrong with generalities or why they should not glitter.

The domain of ideas is thus full of pitfalls. And since ideas cling to every important fact and are what make it important and interesting, the reporters of events will unwittingly mislead if they are not adept at handling ideas. They must not only infer correct ideas from the evidence they have marshaled; they must also be critical about the previous reporters through whose minds the ideas have passed. In other words, the virtue of self-awareness must be acute, vigilant, and sustained.

Technical Terms: All or None

Many of the difficulties about ideas come down to the use of words. Unlike numbers, words have connotations, overtones—the power of suggesting more than they say. Their arrangement, too, conveys qualities and degrees of emphasis that strike the mind and affect meaning in subtle ways. We saw above how the mere putting of two statements about President Garfield side by side suggested an idea contained in neither of them. This happened because the reader brings something of his own to every act of reading, parts of his own experience and knowledge from previous reading. So unless the words in a report are mainly technical, he will readily think he understands it, even when what is said is confusing or adroitly tendentious. The whole power of propaganda lies in this human propensity to catch the drift, to make out a meaning, to believe what is in print. This being so, when your task is to report the findings of research you must turn into a professional critic of words and phrasing.

Compare three kinds of statements:

1. $(a + b)(a + b) = a^2 + 2ab + b^2$

2. Two molecules of common salt react with one of sulfuric acid to give one molecule of sodium sulfate plus two of hydrogen chloride.

3. "It is a just though trite observation that victorious Rome was itself subdued by the arts of Greece."

In 1, we have a statement in the most general terms used by man, and they are fixed terms. The statement gives no particulars. For any a or b the relation expressed by the equal sign will hold. Of course, the things symbolized must be units that are identical.

In 2, particular substances enter into the same relation of equivalence and a change in their form is described. This brings us closer to the tangible reality than No. 1 did. But the statement is general enough to be true of any amounts of sodium chloride (salt) and sulfuric acid, which are also fixed terms.

In 3, which is a sentence taken from Gibbon, we have again a broad generality and as exact as the other two; but in it none of the symbols is fixed. Each word is used with precision in a unique way, but the reader has to bring understanding and a knowledge of particulars to fill out the "equation." In some later sentence, perhaps, the same words—"observation," "victorious," "subdued," and "arts"—would have to be filled with somewhat different meanings, and "Greece" and "Rome" themselves might not indicate the same realities.

Everybody goes through these shifting operations all day long. We see at once that in Gibbon the word "observation" means simply "a remark." It differs from its meaning in "The patient was kept under observation." Again, "victorious" in

Gibbon does not refer to any particular war or battle but to the general domination of the Roman Empire over the Mediterranean world, time unspecified. As for "subdued," the arts subdue a people only when that people—or some of them—develop a taste for high culture. We know this was quite other than "the arts by which Cleopatra captivated Mark Antony"—no books or statues there. Lastly, "Greece" and "Rome" at different times refer to different areas, territories, power, forms of government, and degrees of civilization.

Now, let us ask, could not Gibbon have used other words to convey the same idea? We tend to think that he could. Suppose he had said, "It is an old story that when the Roman conquerors had seized all the wealth and power of the ancient world into their hands, their henchmen began buying up Greek ornaments and works of art and sank into self-indulgent luxury." The "general idea," as we loosely say, remains the same—but does it really? The same three facts do rattle around somewhere in the bottom of each remark: (1) Rome conquered the ancient world. (2) Romans came to enjoy the products of Greek art. (3) This is well known. But the idea, the precise, particular, all-important idea is utterly different in Gibbon and in the rewording. In each we are told many things between the lines, and the things differ in the two versions. Let us compare:

Gibbon reminds us (a) that Greece and Rome exemplify the connection between conquest and civilization, the conquerors being usually the "newer" people, who acquire a higher culture from contact with the "older" and defeated nation; (b) that Roman art was largely borrowed; (c) that Greece maintained its cultural supremacy after defeat; (d) that Gibbon regards the whole process as admirable and majestic. We also infer that his readers were educated people.

As against this, the rewritten version thrusts on the reader the conviction that (a) the remark to follow is only another sordid fact from the past; (b) the Roman Empire was the handiwork of a collection of greedy gangsters; (c) the upper class in Rome were merely the hangers-on of the conquerors; (d) these fellow brigands were philistines who bought Greek *objets d'art* mostly for show; (e) the cultivation of the arts is softening to the moral fiber.

The Technique of Self-Criticism

We are not concerned here with who is right—Gibbon or the Pseudo-Gibbon. We are concerned with the sizable difference of effect produced by different words purporting to relate the same facts. Now, it is bad enough when a willful or unconscious bias distorts by the phrasing what the researcher has discovered; it is far worse when verbal incompetence distorts without the guilt of bias. The truth is that the reader is always more sensitive to the *expressed meaning* than the writer, who has his *intended meaning* at the forefront of his mind so strongly that it hides from him the sense of the words he writes down.

The remedy is simple but painful—to scan every word, and not just once, until you are assured that it is *the* word corresponding to what you want to say. Bear in mind the idea that in reporting, every word becomes a technical word. For example, you would feel ashamed to call a general a captain or to write that B. was "executed" when he was only convicted. These distinctions are so familiar that failing to observe them is a blunder you will not forgive yourself for. But less glaring mistakes are often more important.[4] Here are illustrations of the lesson and hints for practice. The examples were not made up to be easily shown wrong; they are taken from students' work. The first is about Shelley's marital difficulties with his first wife, Harriet, who ultimately drowned herself:

> Had Shelley bided his time and talked over his problems, perhaps the couple might have found themselves incompatible and might have been legally separated. Had Shelley acted in this way he would not be the Shelley we know.

The trouble here begins with an unexpressed antihistorical idea, which is virtually acknowledged in the last sentence.

[4]See p. 277.

"Talked over his problems" is a piece of modern jargon. Vague enough now, it would have meant little or nothing in the early nineteenth century. Its effect now is to suggest falsely that Shelley refused to talk to his wife about their mismating. The very word *"problem"* is wrong, for it is a recent idea to regard all the accidents of life as *"problems."* The opening should perhaps read: "Had Shelley been more patient and helped his wife understand his character more fully. . . ."

The next remark as it stands is nonsense: "The couple might have found themselves incompatible. . . ." That is just what they did find. What the writer really meant appears next: "They might have been legally separated." But they *were* separated! One gathers the notion hovering in the writer's mind: had the couple proved their incompatibility before a court, they might have been divorced and Harriet might not have committed suicide. This is to flout historical probability and to misunderstand human emotions. Divorce was not and is not granted for incompatibility in England, nor is there any reason to suppose that Harriet would have been made happier by a divorce. All these loose remarks are contrary to fact and to good sense, and the confusion is admitted in the writer's last sentence declaring that if these so-called ideas had been carried out Shelley "would not be the Shelley we know." When the would-be biographer reaches such a conclusion, it is time to cross out and start again.

This example moreover shows that a passage which "anybody can understand" may well contain not an iota of sense and that the way to test for sense is to take each word or phrase, shake out its contents, and look at them with skepticism— almost with hostility: what in heaven's name *does* this mean? If the answer is satisfactory, let the phrase stand provisionally. How does it square with the next one? It may contradict or undermine. When you have done this, reconsider the order of your sentences until you are sure that the ideas they evoke in the reader's mind are your ideas at their most exact.

Language being metaphorical to start with, this close scrutiny of words should include a testing of images, figures of speech, and set expressions. It will not only disclose mixed metaphors, which are often ridiculous; but more important, it will show where you are missing the idea altogether as a result of loose coupling between images. Take an example from a book review: "This set of documents emphasizes the legal aspect of the United Nations." Can anything "emphasize an aspect"? An aspect is what one looks at. And then is it the documents that emphasize, or is it the editor who chose some documents and not others? Readers are in doubt, as they would not be if the reviewer had said simply: "Most of these documents [or, "The most important of these documents"] tell us about the legal history of the United Nations."

One more example, to suggest that, even in an acceptable statement, refining the thought adds strength at the same time as it sharpens the critical faculty. "We must not," says an author, "neglect the place of the individual in history." Good, but not quite good enough, for on reflection the remark raises a doubt, owing to the inevitable ambiguity of the word "history." The author may mean: "In writing history we must not neglect to make a place for the individual," that is, we must not write only about forces and factors. Or he may mean: "We must not neglect the *role* of the individual in *making* history," which is an entirely different idea.

Reporters' Fallacies: How to Avoid Them

In the handling of ideas we must also be on guard against fallacies that words mask or make attractive. There is no room here to discuss more than a few kinds of fallacy among those to which reporters of events are especially liable. Consulting an elementary textbook in logic will help detect the fundamental forms of bad reasoning, such as begging the question, *non sequitur,* denying the antecedent, and the like. But researchers or writers seldom encounter or produce fallacies in their pure form. They are apt, rather, to generalize beyond the facts. Bad generalizations are often the result of careless language: the author says "all" or "every" or "never" when the evidence goes but part way toward a universal proposition. Modifiers are called for: "almost," "nearly," "by and large," "in a manner of speaking," "hardly," and the ubiquitous "perhaps."

And yet, the reporter must avoid giving the impression of timidity or indecision. He will infallibly do so if every sentence he writes hedges with "often" and "almost." The account must be as precise as close research and guarded statement can make it, without losing vividness and impetus. An irritated reviewer was right to complain of a book in which "every sentence reads as if it had to be defended in court."

When overextended generalization does not come from the careless use of universals, it comes from the failure to think of negative instances. If after searching into the lives of Keats, Chopin, and Musset you are tempted to write "The Romantic artist is tubercular and dies young," you must at once test it by negative instances. Wordsworth, Hugo, Landor, Goethe are there to prove you wrong with their eighty years or more apiece. Four cases are more than enough to ruin your description of a type that is a crude abstraction to begin with. The corollary caution is to beware of what is new and striking in your research. It may be new only to you; and even if generally new, its effect must not overwhelm other impressions. Remember the anecdote about the English traveler who saw three red-headed girls at the inn where he stopped and who wrote in his diary: "All the women in this country have red hair."

Only the quite inexperienced researcher will generalize from a single instance or from too few. The danger that besets the more practiced is rather the opposite, called the reductive fallacy. As its name suggests, it reduces diversity to one thing: all this is nothing but *that*. Because of "nothing but" itself, it should be used only when you are absolutely sure of your ground and when that ground is limited in scope. For example, to make an event as vast as the French Revolution (no single event but a huge group of related events) result from a conspiracy is reductive in the extreme. Yet it has been maintained. So is ascribing war exclusively to "economics" or to the wirepulling of munitions makers. The study of history teaches the valuable lesson that all so-called events, like all human motives, are complex. A sound researcher shows the parts that make up the complexity, each part in its place and relation to the rest. Let the newspaper, which lacks time and room, enjoy the monopoly of reductivism.[5]

Between reducing and overstating lurks hidden repetition or Tautology. It is a frequent error in business reports, statistical analyses, and the like. Here is an example: "English aggressiveness spurred the nation to stimulate commerce on the seas and win the supremacy of trade routes." Here a thing called English aggressiveness works upon the nation (England), and England works upon English commerce in a stimulating manner. The three things are in fact one, as the writer would have seen if he had stepped out of his abstractions and visualized something concrete—not commerce but a merchant, a shipowner. *He* is English aggressiveness, and he is the nation, and he is the trader who wins the trade routes. Perhaps the writer's mind was visited by a fleeting idea of the English *government* acting independently of the trader, but this thought was unexpressed and it left three wordings of one thing acting on one another like separate powers.[6]

Another fallacy less easily discovered by the reader is Misplaced Literalism. It has many forms, and it is particularly insidious because the reporter must always *begin* by being literal. He must ascertain with all possible precision what his original text tells him. Lord Acton does *not* say, "Power corrupts and absolute power corrupts absolutely"; he says "Power tends to corrupt and absolute power corrupts absolutely."[7] Slight in wording but consequential in effect, the difference allows for

---

[5]See p. 615.

[6]In a textbook fortunately long out of use, one found listed among the causes that brought one or another party to power: (1) the strength of the party; (2) the weakness of the opposition. This is a truly convenient way to double the number of reasons for the outcome of any struggle.

[7]Letter to Bishop Creighton in Acton, *Historical Essays and Studies* (London, 1907), 504.

the possibility that a business executive or a public official will *not* be corrupted by wielding power.

By attending to an author's words, the reporter gradually acquires familiarity with the natural movement of the man's thought. It is at this point that Literalism would be misplaced if it re-entered. Its most obvious form would be to quote another remark such as Lord Acton's as if it had the same weight as the previous one. It may have more or less, depending on place and circumstance. Is the idea expressed the conclusion of a piece of reasoning? Or is it a notion struck off in a letter to a friend? Or, again, is it an improvised retort to an opponent? It is the critic's duty to judge importance and value by bringing to bear everything he or she knows. Critics must assess not only the tenor but the quality of the author's belief. If a researcher remains content to quote extracts, he ends by representing his human subject as a mass of contradictions.

The Scholar and the Great Ideas

Most professional thinkers are likely to use certain words in a peculiar sense. This individual usage must be ascertained. The American courts face the same task in interpreting a statute: they go back to the debates in the legislature and the known opinions of the proponents. This is research of the kind needed to answer the question: how should the Constitution be read in order to decide cases? The answer *strictly* means studying original meanings;[8] *broadly,* it means adapting the presumable intention of the Framers to modern conditions. The role of Research and Report in this situation is obvious: every judge turns historian. But most judges lack the time to go further down than the published records of the Constitutional Convention of 1787; none has thought to look into their validity.

This task was undertaken by James H. Hutson, Chief of Manuscripts at the Library of Congress, who reviewed what he

[8]Some legal minds oppose the practice: it reduces "flexibility."

called "the integrity of the documentary record."[9] The steps he took are a model of research. The Constitutional Convention sitting in Philadelphia held its sessions in secret and the participants maintained the secrecy enjoined upon them. The only sources of information are the journal of the Convention kept by the Secretary, William Jackson; Robert Yates's notes of the debates in the Convention; James Madison's notes; and Jonathan Elliot's collection of the debates in the state ratifying conventions. Until Jackson's *Journal of the Convention* was published in 1819, the public had almost no knowledge of the daily scrimmage at the historic convention.

The modern researcher Hutson found out that Jackson destroyed some sheets when he turned over the pertinent papers to George Washington, the President of the Convention. The Secretary of State, John Quincy Adams, inspected Jackson's work and said in his memoirs that he found it "loosely and imperfectly kept." This comment was a red flag to Hutson. But it turned out that Adams, a carping critic, was referring to only a few pages of the journal. Jackson's tallies of votes jibed with other records. At least the votes reported on the important resolutions were reliable.

Yates's work, Hutson quickly discovered, was another matter. A complicated family situation and its sequel brought into various hands the notes he had kept and led to their bowdlerization, perhaps for a political purpose. Moreover, they are incomplete; only two pages—not originals—are in the Library of Congress.

Hutson had to study the various shorthand systems, now defunct, of the men who worked at the state conventions. In Pennsylvania, Hutson concluded, the reporter was "technically unable to capture accurately most of what speakers said." Further probing revealed that some of the speeches that Elliot

---

[9]"The Creation of the Constitution . . ." (*Texas Law Review*, 65, November 1986, 1–39). A briefer version is in Hutson's *Supplement to Max Farrand's* The Records of the Federal Convention of 1787 (New Haven, CT, 1987), xx–xxvi. Farrand has long been the standard work.

included in his pages were of dubious authenticity. At least one was almost certainly written down long after it was alleged to have been delivered. So it went from state to state. Comments thirty years after the event are subject to being garbled by the work of memory; Hutson concluded that the reports of the debates in the state conventions must be regarded as unreliable.

Finally, Hutson turned to Madison's notes, the traditional source that the world has relied upon for over 150 years. The last of the Framers, Madison lived until 1836 and his invaluable document was published in 1840. It became at once a weapon in the controversy over slavery, which was then beginning to embitter party politics. It seemed to prove that the Constitution was indeed a "bundle of compromises."

Over the years, the accuracy of Madison's reporting has been questioned by some who alleged interpolations. The manuscript shows none, but perhaps Madison rewrote the entire document. Hutson therefore examined the paper on which it was written. The watermark shows it to be of British manufacture. From a book about the maker, Hutson picked up the choice fact that after 1794 British law required paper for export to include the year of manufacture in the watermark. Madison's notes bore no watermark date: hence it was of pre-1794 vintage. Letters that Madison wrote during the Convention were written on identical paper.

Hutson concluded that Madison's notes and the Convention Journal "do not suffer from [any editing] . . . disqualifying them as sources of information about the Convention." Nevertheless, he remained not fully satisfied. The Convention usually met for about five hours every day except Sunday (so George Washington says). Hutson experimented and found that an hour of discussion produces about 8,400 words. In the month when Madison's notes are the fullest, he recorded an average of 2,740 words a session, which would amount to ten percent of each hour's debates.

Hutson is also concerned about the large number of Madison's own words in the notes, since there are differences in contents between his text and those noted down by others. The conclusion is that although Madison did not distort significantly, what he reported cannot be taken as the whole account of the Great Convention. Hutson has demonstrated once again that "the mere fact that a record is in print does not make it reliable."

Shift now to textbooks and encyclopedia articles, which give starved accounts of the ideas ascribed to great thinkers responsible for great movements. Students who memorize the tags to pass examinations actually do not know what they are talking about. What meaning can they attach to the statement that Rousseau "wanted to go back to Nature"? It is a false attribution to begin with, but suppose it true, what beliefs or actions would the words cover?

These realities show what a writer must do whenever he raises the ghost of a great idea. He must avoid the fallacy of simplemindedness or misplaced convenience, either of which ignores the complexity of human affairs. For the same reason, automatic skepticism is as wrong as automatic belief. In sound reporting there is no need of bunking, debunking, or rebunking. The sole principle is as far as possible to present all things in their diversity.

CHAPTER 6

TRUTH, CAUSES, AND CONDITIONS

The Types of Evidence

The previous chapter has perhaps left the reader wondering how any account of past events can be trusted. If the only indisputable facts are those we have called conventional and if they are generally of little interest in themselves, then the veracity or truth-value of history seems slight indeed. The thoughtful reader's question to the historian contrasts the shifting uncertainty of history with the mathematical rigor of science and concludes that truth is absent from history because it lacks the form—and the formulas—of science.

This conclusion is plausible but false. To understand why, we must look at the kinds of evidence that are available for making historical assertions. They can for convenience be variously grouped. The first two kinds are the Verbal and Mute—the mute consisting of objects such as buildings, drawings, tools, fragments of pottery—any physical object bearing no words. A coin may belong to both kinds if it has an inscription on it. Verbal or speaking evidence need not, of course, be written: an oral tradition has validity under certain conditions and, with the growing use of tape recordings, oral testimony may once more regain its prehistoric prominence.[1] But as everyone knows, the bulk of what is commonly handled and offered as historical evidence is in written form.

Written evidence again falls into several subgroups: manuscript and printed, private and public, intentional and unpremeditated. The last distinction has diagnostic importance for arriving at truth. Intentional pieces of written evidence are such things as affidavits, court testimony, letters and diaries, and secret or published memoirs. The author of any of these meant to record a sequence of events and opinions, having presumably an interest in furthering his view of the facts.

By contrast, a receipt for the sale of a slave, jotted down in the second century on a bit of papyrus, is no premeditated piece of historical writing. Its sole intended use was commercial, and it is only as "unconscious evidence" that it becomes part of an historical narrative. The laws of states, ordinances of cities, charters of corporations, and the like are similarly unpremeditated evidence—as are the account books of a modern corporation or of a Florentine banker of the fifteenth century.

Yet, important as this difference is, the assumption that unconscious evidence is always sounder is by no means warranted; for with the widespread consciousness of history to which we drew attention earlier, there has been a general tendency to inject purposeful "historicity" into apparently unpremeditated documents. State papers nowadays frequently attempt to say more than is needed for their immediate use. They address the world and posterity.[2]

---

[1]In Oral History centers such as the first established, at Columbia University, the remarks of important persons who might not write memoirs are recorded electronically. The written word is still so compelling, however, that these recordings are transcribed and the typescripts filed like books. Catalogues of the available materials are published periodically.

[2]Consider the publication *Polish Acts of Atrocity against the German Minority in Poland,* issued by the German Library of Information, New York, 1940, 259 pp. Its internal terminology and arrangement are those of an historical monograph, but its apparent record of fact is but disguised argument. More deceptive because more roundabout are the carefully "planted" documents left by public figures; for instance, the so-called posterity letters that Theodore Roosevelt wrote to various correspondents. For examples see Elting E. Morison, ed., *The Letters of Theodore Roosevelt* (8 vols., Cambridge, MA, 1951–1954).

FIGURE 11   *TYPES OF EVIDENCE**

RECORDS
(intentional transmitters of fact)

Written
1. Chronicles, annals, biographies, genealogies
2. Memoirs, diaries
3. Certain kinds of inscriptions

Oral
4. Ballads, anecdotes, tales, sagas
5. Recordings in various forms (tape, disc, etc.)

Works of Art
6. Portraits, historical paintings, scenic sculpture, coins, and medals
7. Certain kinds of film, videotape, etc.

RELICS
(unpremeditated transmitters of fact)

8. Human remains, letters, literature, public documents, business records, and certain kinds of inscriptions
9. Language, customs, and institutions (as interpreted by contemporaries)
10. Tools and other artifacts

---

*Adapted from John Martin Vincent's *Historical Research* (1911).

And even business documents, such as reports to stockholders, contain statements of purpose and action that amount to propaganda. In other words, we have become so accustomed to the idea of "the record" that we are continually tempted to tamper with it. When we mean to be candid, we are careful to specify that our words must be "off the record."

This enumeration of the several kinds of historical evidence is enough to suggest the many difficulties arising from the materials. Figure 11 shows how the namable kinds of evidence can be grouped for quick review. Obviously not all kinds of evidence are available for every kind of report, history, or biography; and classifying them does not imply that there are fixed species with clear boundaries between them. Where, for example, would you place a television shot of a student riot? or the replay film of a crucial move in a football game? It seems like stretching terms to answer, as the table would suggest, "Works of Art."

No matter how it is described, *no piece of evidence can be used in the state in which it is found.* It must undergo the scrutiny of the researcher's mind according to the rules of the critical method. To appreciate this requirement, consider the taped interview that the cassette recorder has made so popular with biographers. They often seem to think that they have caught the living truth before it vanished. But the interview, whether for a news article or an archive of oral history, is a particularly treacherous source. The interviewer's questions no less than the answers he gets can introduce bias, purposely or not; and unlike the published reminiscence, the tape eludes the criticism—possibly the outcry—of other witnesses.[3]

When, therefore, a searcher for truth is faced with a piece of evidence in any form, the critical mind goes to work with the aid of a systematic interrogatory:

Is this object or piece of writing genuine?
Is its message trustworthy?
How do I know?

This leads to an unfolding series of subordinate questions:

1. What does it state or imply?
2. Who is its author or maker?
3. What is the relation in time and space between the author and the information, overt or implied, that is conveyed by the item?
4. How does the statement compare with other statements on the same point?
5. What do we know independently about the author and his credibility?

The point of these questions is readily grasped:

1. It is essential to ascertain, separately, what the document states and what may be inferred from it.

---

[3]For the theory and practice of safeguards in use among sociologists, see Robert K. Merton, *The Focused Interview: A Manual of Problems and Procedures* (2nd ed., New York, 1990).

2. If the document or the coin is not by the ostensible maker, it has no value as evidence. Gauging the truth of any statement is obviously assisted by a knowledge of who made it.[4]

3. The value of a piece of testimony usually increases in proportion to the nearness in time and space between the witness and the events about which he testifies.[5] An eyewitness has a good chance of knowing what happened; a reporter distant from the event by only a few years has a better chance than one separated by a century. (Recall the story of the Year 1000 in Chapter 4.)

4. A single witness may be quite accurate, but two witnesses, if independent, increase the chances of eliminating human fallibility. If a dozen reports already exist, a thirteenth just discovered is compared point for point with the others in an effort to resolve puzzling allusions or contradictions, to strengthen or destroy an interpretation. (Remember the debates about the Constitution.)

5. What can be learned about the author's life and character helps to make up our judgment on several of the previous points. If we know his life we can answer the queries: Was he there? Had he the expertness to appreciate the facts? Was he biased by partisan interest? Did he habitually tell the truth?

The principles contained in all these questions guide the researcher's mind and develop in him the temper of the assessor. Its operation becomes automatic, whether he is reading a president's inaugural or a rabid editorial in a tabloid. It is unlikely that the ordinary researcher will encounter problems requiring familiarity with the science of Diplomatics, which

---

[4]The truth or untruth of the presentment may also have value as evidence to convict the forger, or as evidence of his skill—witness the Van Meegeren forgeries of Vermeer paintings.

[5]This rule was doubtless hovering in the mind of the student who wrote in a comparison of Herodotus and Thucydides that Thucydides "had the advantage of being alive at the time he was writing."

teaches the technique of testing and dating documents, chiefly medieval. This takes special study of period penmanship, and much practice under tutelage, as does the reading of Greek papyri or the analysis of archaeological finds. If a point requiring such knowledge arises in your research, consult an expert, just as you would if you suspected forgery.[6] On ordinary printed matter no one can be critical for you. If you are so by nature, it can be guaranteed that this mental faculty will find much scope even when its exercise is limited to print.

Probability the Guide

When caution has been sustained and all safeguards taken, the historical method ascertains the truth by means of common sense. Systematically applied, common sense becomes a stronger and sharper instrument than what goes by that name in daily life. It shows the closest attention to detail and the tightest grip on consecutiveness and order. It includes both what is usually known by the well-educated and all the special information relevant to the question being studied; and to these bodies of fact and ideas it brings the habit of comparing and judging with a quizzical eye.

This point about *informed* common sense is most obvious in the writing of biography. The narrator of a life must become familiar with all the subject's activities and concerns, some of which may be special; and the common sense of these matters is not simply the ordinary knowledge we have of them today,

---

[6]Reading the Osbornes' *Questioned Document Problems* and Weller's *Die falschen und fingierten Druckorte* (on pretended publishing places) is, however, an instructive and entertaining use of spare time; valuable too is Hanna F. Sulner, *Disputed Documents: New Methods for Examining Questioned Documents* (1966). And persons interested will want to look up the methods of dating and testing by technical means—carbon 14 or the thorium-uranium technique, infrared and reflected light rays, aspartic acid racemization, and dendrology (interpreting tree rings).

but also the state of knowledge in the subject's lifetime. A life of Caesar presupposes a knowledge of Roman roads and Roman weapons in the first century B.C., to which must be added the awareness of incommensurables, such as Roman character, superstition, *gravitas,* and so on.

All these distinctions need only be stated to be understood. What is often ill understood and easily misconstrued is the role of this high common sense in matters that seem quite commonplace but are not so, matters that the plain man encounters daily in the newspaper and that the educated will come across again in their reading of books. For example, ever since the Warren Commission Report on the assassination of President Kennedy, many persons have attacked its conclusions, some in very elaborate works based on the published testimony. In a critique of several of these books, John Sparrow, an English scholar who was also trained as a lawyer, makes the point that concerns us here. It has no bearing on one's opinion about the Warren Report; its bearing is on common notions of evidence that unfortunately are lacking in "common" common sense. Sparrow shows what the denouncers of the Report all expect before they will accord belief: they trust only consistent and congruent witnesses. Yet, as he reminds us,

Every lawyer knows that a witness . . . while wrong on a number of points may yet be right on others, perhaps including the essential one. Every lawyer knows that honest and truthful witnesses may contradict themselves, particularly on questions concerning their own and others' motives and states of mind, without thereby forfeiting credibility. . . . Finally, every lawyer knows that in a big and complicated case there is always, at the end of it all, a residue of improbable, inexplicable fact. You do not invalidate a hypothesis by showing that the chances were against the occurrence of some of the events that it presupposes: many things that happen are actually improbable but they happen.[7]

[7]John Sparrow, *After the Assassination* (New York, 1968), 13–14.

Such is the higher common sense at work upon evidence when it comes from ordinary testimony, that is, the declarations of persons who are not expert, but who, by chance, witness some important event or part of an event.

Sparrow takes us still further along the road that historian and lawyer tread together when he says: "To make up its mind, if it can, what *must* have happened, in spite of incidental improbabilities—that is the task of a Commission of Inquiry."[8] The historian is in himself such a Commission, and when he has done his work it is no refutation of it to say that he has selected his facts to suit his case. Mr. Sparrow gives us the right view of that tiresome cliché also:

> What else should an investigator do? It is for the critics to show that they themselves have evaluated all the evidence, and can make a selection from it as reliable as [the other], and base upon that selection conclusions that compel acceptance. . . .[9]

So much for the lawyer's wisdom. There is a further step that the historian must often take, which is to seek expert opinion on technical matters. In the same attacks on the official view of the murder of President Kennedy, authors infer from the bullet wounds the number of assassins and the places where they stood. The fact is that rifle bullets do the most unexpected things, contrary to "common sense." Thus "if a high-velocity bullet is fired into soft clay it does not, as one might expect, pass through it. After tunneling in for a few inches it suddenly produces a cavity many times its own diameter, and quite frequently the bullet itself is smashed into fragments." The writer, long a medico-legal expert in Egypt and Scotland, goes on to give an account of the shooting of an official by a nervous sentry. The bullet passed through a car window and struck the victim on the chin, causing facial wounds of which he subsequently died. And when the car was examined,

> not one but a number of bullet marks were found. There were two holes in the license holder and the wind-screen under it, each of which

[8]Ibid., 14.
[9]Ibid., 15.

looked as if it had been caused by a separate bullet. The upper part of the left traffic-indicator had also been pierced, and there were several other marks apparently produced by the passage of projectiles. . . . On the back seat a portion of a .303 bullet was found, consisting of the aluminum tip and the cupro-nickel jacket. . . . It was thought that a number of shots had been fired. From the holes in the wind-screen alone, it seemed that two or three bullets must have struck the car. However, all the eye-witnesses spoke of only one shot being fired, and one cartridge case only was found on the scene; out of a clip of five bullets, the remaining four were still in the rifle. . . . Finally, a reconstruction of the affair . . . showed pretty conclusively that not more than one bullet had struck the car.[10]

It is in such cases that ordinary people are likely to display ignorant skepticism. They know better; they "use common sense": bullets fly in straight lines and make neat round holes.

To supply their readers with truths journalists daily profess to divine the wellsprings of high-level policy, though documentary evidence is rarely there. Later comers also must find plausible motives, but some events are never explained to general satisfaction and must remain anyone's guess. A persistent doubt of this sort attaches to Adolf Hitler's reason for declaring war on the United States in 1941. No treaty obligation required the German chancellor to join his ally, Japan. Yet only four days after the Japanese attack on Pearl Harbor, Hitler, to the surprise and dismay of even his closest advisers, entered the conflict against the United States.

Acting alone, he had reached his fateful decision the same week that his mighty *Wehrmacht,* standing before Moscow, was being hurled back in −35° temperature; while in North Africa General Rommel's vaunted *Afrika Korps* was retreating in the desert. Did Hitler feel that he had been put in an awkward situation by Japan's unexpected action and that "the point of honor" demanded his support? On this enigma, an exchange took place in 2000–2002 in the pages of the *Newsletter* published

---

[10]Sir Sydney Smith, *Mostly Murder* (London, 1959), 272–74.

by the Society of Historians of American Foreign Relations. One contributor argues that the Führer had a remarkable tendency to seek self-destruction. Whenever he faced reverses he immediately chose to go on the offensive regardless of cost.[11] Another historian insists that Hitler's action was simply in keeping with the man's irrational behavior generally.[12]

Yet another scholar takes a different tack, arguing that on December 12th, the day after Hitler's declaration, Germany officially denied it was at war with the United States, thus nullifying his words. And it is true that President Roosevelt did not regard them as the ground taken for American action against Germany. But according to this scholar, Roosevelt saw the assault on Pearl Harbor as due to Germany, Japan being one of Germany's "chessmen" moved by the master.[13]

Two prominent historians had earlier dealt with the subject; one of them, Ian Kershaw, a noted biographer of Hitler, pointed out that on November 22nd the German foreign minister, Ribbentrop, had laid down German policy: in the event of war between the United States and either Germany or Japan, the other country would not sign a separate peace; furthermore, it was a foregone conclusion that if Japan went to war against the United States, Germany would, as a matter of course, declare war. "No agreement compelled it."[14] Ribbentrop had simply proclaimed: "A great power doesn't let itself have war declared upon it, it declares war itself." That the United States was a great power, Hitler had acknowledged in a book which he dictated in 1928 but never published.[14a] In it he praises the United States for its

---

[11]Harvey Asher, "Hitler's Decision to Declare War on the United States Revisited," http//www.shafr.history.ohio-state.edu.Newsletter/2000/SEP/asher.html

[12]Letter from Michael Jonas, ibid. 2001/MAR/letters.html

[13]Richard Hill, "Hitler's Misunderstood Declaration of War on the U.S." ibid. 2002/JUN/hill.html

[14]Ian Kershaw, *Hitler: 1936–45. Nemesis* (New York, Norton, 2000), pp. 445–6.

[14a]It was published in an English translation in 1961 as *Hitler's Secret Book* and has come to public notice again through a new translation by Krista Smith to appear (Enigma Books) in October 2003.

"racial" unity and for its becoming a great power by joining in the First World War. With that status he says it is a threat, but he does not specify any object of possible American aggrandizement.

The other historian, Gordon Craig, a highly regarded student of German diplomacy, wrote that the declaration was such a surprise, even to the head of the plans division of the German army, that he was unprepared for it; he is reported to have said to the Army Chief of Staff, General Jodl, "We can hardly undertake this job just like that." "Well," said Jodl, "see what you can do." This conversation obviously does not square with Ribbentrop's defiance. Can it be that Germany was totally without plans for eventualities that its foreign secretary foresaw? Craig's view was that Hitler made his move as a gesture of friendship to Japan. Hitler might well think that the United States would be so occupied fighting in the Pacific that after the Germans had defeated Russia, the Americans would not be able to challenge the fatherland. By that time it would have become the most powerful nation in the world.[15]

After looking into these sources, what is a writer to believe? If one supposes that Roosevelt was a schemer and obfuscator, then one is likely to accept the notion that Germany *was* Japan's marionette handler. If one believes that hidden psychological factors determine all human actions, then the explanation of Hitler's step is the death wish. But that urge is still open to rival interpretations. Certainty is never possible; yet experience of life, wide reading, and close study of politics develop the power to form views that possess *plausibility*. One then casts up the points in evidence as tested by our list of questions and in many cases one reaches *probability*.

Clio and the Doctors

But that result entails work. The public tends to believe expert evidence, especially if it is of a familiar kind—not from the ballistics laboratory, but from the doctor. And today, when psychiatrists and physicians address the public on current

[15]Gordon A. Craig, *Germany: 1866–1945* (New York, Oxford, 1978), pp. 731–2.

issues, those among them who make an avocation of "diagnosing" contemporary and historical persons are credited with knowledge about things well outside the consulting room. Their evidence is usually slight, or confused, and sometimes the reasoning is circular.

For example, did the Romantic composer Robert Schumann's mental disorder come from syphilis? Recently examined, a sample of his hair showed traces of mercury, the substance used in his day to treat that disease. Yes, but (it is argued) his mental symptoms began in early youth, before sexual maturity. And at the very end of his life he produced well-conceived and well-crafted music. No, says another, the music is much inferior to his best, as it was bound to be in the third stage of syphilis. Ah, but remember: Schumann was a confirmed wearer of felt hats and these were commonly "blocked"—shaped and reshaped—with mercury. Let the reader decide a point of rather academic interest.

A case on which more important conclusions depend is that of Woodrow Wilson. His catastrophic stroke during the struggle over the ratification of the Treaty of Versailles in 1919 appears to have profoundly affected his effort to promote the League of Nations. Was his collapse a sudden "accident" or was it only the climax of a series of episodes long influential on his personality and public performance? In particular, was his fierce struggle with Senator Lodge over the Treaty foreshadowed earlier in his stormy encounter with Dean West at Princeton over a university issue? These events have become part of presidential history and are taken as signs of a stubborn man's devotion to principle, his refusal to yield to expediency. If, on the contrary, they are interpreted as morbid symptoms of a recurrent affliction, the stubbornness appears in another light.

In 1981, Edwin A. Weinstein, a distinguished neurologist, published the result of many years' search into Woodrow Wilson's medical history.[16] Weinstein concluded that Wilson

---

[16]*Woodrow Wilson: A Medical and Psychological Biography* (Princeton, 1981). He had foreshadowed his findings in an article in the *Journal of American History* (57, September 1970, 324–351).

had suffered a series of large-blood-vessel strokes during the productive years of his career, beginning in 1896, or possibly earlier. Partial loss of sight ten years later was the result of another stroke, and still other, less serious ones, occurred when Wilson was governor of New Jersey and during his White House years. Weinstein holds that Wilson's characteristic response to each was a burst of public activity, an expression of his resolve that the body be forced to serve the spirit.

Nor does Weinstein stop there. He speculates also that Wilson grew up suffering from what is nowadays called dyslexia, an impaired ability to read—hence the ignorant father's hectoring about young Wilson's "laziness," and the boy's shame and guilt. Step by step, the president's exhausting attempt to make something "good" come out of the war into which he took the United States emerges as atonement for "guilt" about the loss of thousands of American lives.

These assertions and conjectures have naturally been questioned. An ophthalmologist at Stanford University, Michael F. Marmor,[17] argues that what Wilson suffered from in early years was not strokes but "writer's cramp" or neuritis. The temporary blindness in 1906, which Weinstein diagnosed as a "major stroke," is held by Marmor to have been an "interocular hemorrhage." Repeated strokes must cause changes in personality, and "to find substantial changes in personality without a loss of cognitive power or the development of dementia would be unusual." Marmor is confident that there is little in Wilson's performance up to his breakdown in 1919 to suggest cognitive loss. A neurosurgeon at the University of Pennsylvania, Bert T. Park, is a late entrant into the fray. He argues that both Weinstein and Marmor are

---

[17]"Wilson, Strokes, and Zebras" (*New England Journal of Medicine,* 307, August 26, 1982, 528–535); a follow-up (308, January 20, 1983, 163f); and "The Eyes of Woodrow Wilson" (*Ophthalmology,* 92, March 1985, 454f). Next came an exchange between Marmor and his supporters, Alexander and Juliette George, on one side, and Weinstein and Arthur S. Link on the other, in the *Journal of American History* (70, 1984, 845–853, 945–955).

wrong, that Wilson was a victim of "small-vessel lacunar infarctions," which produced progressive dementia over a long period of time, evidenced in the president's marked personality changes.[18]

Which expert to believe? The historian who reads the record of Wilson's cordial and imaginative relations with Congress over his legislative program in 1913 asks himself whether the same personality was at work in the struggle over the Treaty and the League in 1919. The contrast makes Wilson's irritability and stubbornness seem excessive, quite apart from "principle" and the strains of conducting the First World War. Meanwhile, a close study by each of two independent German historians of Wilson's negotiations of the Treaty in Paris, against the master strategists Lloyd George and Clemenceau, shows Wilson as flexible, expedient, not at all a stubborn idealist.[19]

The physical well-being of presidents as a factor in their performance increasingly draws the attention not only of the general public but also of historians. Noteworthy are Robert H. Ferrell's two books, *Ill-advised: Presidential Health and Public Trust* (1992) and *The Dying President: Franklin D. Roosevelt, 1944–1945* (1998), and Robert Dallek, *An Unfinished Life: John F. Kennedy, 1917–1963* (2003).

Of course, the mystery of human personality remains. And in any case—which means in every case—explanations by

---

[18]*The Impact of Illness on World Leaders* (Philadelphia, 1986). Consult in volume 64 (published in 1991) of Link's monumental *Papers of Woodrow Wilson* (Princeton, 1966–1994, 69 vols.). Park's evaluation of all the reported symptoms (p. 506). Kenneth Crispell, a professor emeritus of medicine at the University of Virginia, and Carlos F. Gomez in their *Hidden Illness in the White House* (Durham, NC, 1988) accept the Weinstein-Link thesis and do not cite Park's book. For the latest and most balanced one-volume account of Wilson's character and lifelong modes of behavior, see August Heckscher, *Woodrow Wilson* (New York, 1991).

[19]The principal one is Klaus Schwabe, *Deutsche Revolution und Wilson Frieden: die Amerikanische und deutsche Friedens-strategie zwischen Ideologie und Machtpolitik, 1918–19* (Düsseldorf, 1971); trans. by Rita and Robert Kimber as *Revolutionary Germany and Peacemaking: 1918–19* (Chapel Hill, 1985). See also the *Journal of Modern History* (45, September 1973, 536f).

means of a single cause, hidden, startling, "scientific," is to be distrusted, if not on the face of it disallowed. The concatenation of acts, motives, and results can only be understood and described by the intuitive skill of the historian as artist. He will see Wilson or any other figure not as victim, but as doer. If before his breakdown the president was ever handicapped by a defective circulatory system, his abilities and his determination were all the more remarkable.

Assertion versus Suggestion

At no time should a reporter take a holiday from discipline. Fine scholars sometimes repeat campus gossip that they would scorn to accept as evidence in one of their monographs, a lapse that shows the importance of method: it is a safeguard, a means of protecting one's mind from oneself. One of the worst temptations of the gossip kind is to state a hypothesis—often a mere suggestion of possibility—and in the course of a longish book turn it gradually into a thing proved. A typical instance occurs in an English biography of Wordsworth, where it is suggested that the poet married because he found himself in love with his sister. Nowhere in the book is any evidence presented except that of the well-known close companionship of brother and sister and some doubtful allusions in poems and letters. The new "truth" rests solely on the author's repeated "it is clear enough," "undoubtedly," and the like. Upon this a scholarly critic wrote a definitive paragraph:

> If Mr. Bateson suggested that there was a morbid strain in her attachment to her brother, we would perhaps agree—with the proviso that she was probably in love with Coleridge. If Mr. Bateson fancied that she and her brother might have been consciously alarmed by mutual and illicit desires, he would be entitled to air his suspicion, wildly improbable as we might think it. To present their alarm not as a hypothesis but as an undoubted fact strikes me as inexcusable.[20]

[20]Raymond Mortimer in the *Sunday Times* (London, October 17, 1954).

Inexcusable it is, because the rule of "Give evidence" is imperative. No matter how possible or plausible an author's conjecture, it cannot be accepted as truth if he has only his hunch to support it.

When a hypothesis is deliberately offered as such, another common error is to think it proved when it appears consistent with the facts gathered. Proof demands *decisive* evidence, which means evidence *that not only confirms one view but also excludes its rivals.* Consistency is not enough. Neither is plausibility, for both can apply to a wide variety of hypotheses. This commandment about decisiveness leads to a second fundamental rule: *truth rests not on possibility nor on plausibility but on probability.*

Probability is used here in a strict sense. It means the balance of chances that, given such and such evidence, the event it records happened in a certain way; or, in other cases, that a supposed event did not in fact take place. This balance is not computable in figures unless statistical evidence, also reliable, supplies them; but it can be no less reliably weighed and judged. Judgment is the historian's form of genius, and he himself is judged by the amount of it he can muster. The grounds on which he passes judgment are, again, the common grounds derived from life: general truths, personal and vicarious experience (which includes a knowledge of previous history), and any other kind of special or particular knowledge that may be relevant.

Here, for example, is an improbable set of facts that are nonetheless not to be doubted, the local records and testimony being evidence of the most solid kind. In Liverpool, nearly a century ago, a long unsolved murder took place in a small and shabby back street never before brought by any event to the world's attention. Thirty-four small red-brick houses made up the whole of Wolverton Street, yet the frequency of sudden death along that double row exceeds plausibility and invites disbelief, though the facts are on record: within about a year, three persons had committed suicide and five other residents were widows of men who had just died in unusual circumstances. Then came the killing of Julia Wallace, the inoffensive wife of an insurance-premium collector.[21] Since it was only the strange puzzle of her murder that made the street an object of interest lasting to this day, we may note how far coincidence has to go before it draws attention to itself and upsets our conventional ideas of what is likely or unlikely.

At many points, then, the estimate of probability made by the student will coincide with that of an ordinary citizen; but there is this difference, that the researcher will not have reached it off-hand; it will not be a correct snap judgment, but a correct critical judgment. Anyone would say, for example, that under the conditions prevailing in this country today it is not probable that a public official, such as the governor of a state, could be entirely misrepresented to posterity as regards appearance, actions, and character. Too many devices of publicity are continually playing on public figures; whereas the probability of successful misrepresentation—as an historian could show—was quite likely in fifteenth-century England. This judgment is what has enabled a number of scholars to believe that Richard III was not the murderer of his nephews, not crooked-backed, not the villain depicted in Shakespeare's play. They cannot fully prove their contention, for decisive evidence is lacking, but they win a hearing for it because it is not against probability that the Tudor kings could blacken Richard's character and sustain the "big lie."[22]

Note Qualifiers in All Conclusions

The point here is not the pros and cons of this particular question. The point is that the carefully assessed probability of a known situation must govern judgment. This is still true when

[21]Jonathan Goodman, *The Killing of Julia Wallace* (New York, 1976), 25. In a later edition of the work, the author furnished on the basis of further investigation a cast-iron proof that Wallace did not kill his wife and a convincing identification of the murderer.

[22]For the latest review of the evidence, see Paul Murray Kendall, *Richard III* (New York, 1956); and for a condensed account, V. B. Lamb, *The Betrayal of Richard III* (London, 1965). An entertaining piece of fiction on the subject is Josephine Tey's detective story *The Daughter of Time* (New York, 1951, repr. 1988).

a scientific test is applied.[23] A recent instance in which the public at large took sides is that of Thomas Jefferson: was he the father of a child with one of his slaves, Sally Hemings? The question is important, because upon the answer rests the reputation for candor and rectitude of a Founding Father of the Republic, who is the author of the Declaration of Independence.

The question is asked because historians studying Jefferson's time have re-awakened attention to a political journalist, James T. Callender, who had once been an ally of Jefferson's and who turned against him in anger for the president's failing to appoint him Postmaster of Richmond, Virginia. In revenge, Callender in 1802 placed a piece in the Richmond *Record,* a newspaper of which he was co-owner, reporting "facts" he knew would be embarrassing: for many years Jefferson had "kept as his concubine, one of his own slaves"—and fathered "several children." Callender added the buttressing detail: "her name is Sally." In the tight-knit Virginia planter aristocracy, everyone knew that the woman in question was the attractive Sally Hemings. She was a half-sister of Jefferson's wife, now deceased. To this "revelation," Jefferson made no reply, even when the Federalist newspapers supporting his opponent for the presidency made the most of the charge during the campaign of 1804. Jefferson's dignified silence repaid: he was reelected.

The Jefferson-Hemings story continued to be whispered about, not only among Sally Hemings's descendants, but also in abolitionist circles in America and among critics of democracy elsewhere, the behavior of monarchs being conveniently forgotten. Most historians, however, dismissed the notion of Jefferson's liaison as unlikely.

A generation after the appearance of the "definitive" biography by Dumas Malone,[24] the advent of DNA testing made possible a

---

[23]See Richard D. Altick, "The Scholar and the Scientist," Chapter 7 of *The Scholar Adventurers* (New York, 1951), and Altick's *The Art of Literary Research* (4th ed., 1993). Consult also James L. Harner, *Literary Research Guide* (4th ed., New York, Modern Language Association of America, 2002).

[24]*Jefferson and His Time* (6 vols., 1948–81).

technical answer to the question, and so it became news once again. Using Y-chromosome analysis, Dr. Eugene Foster and a team of geneticists reported in 1998 finding a genetic link between the Jefferson and the Hemings descendants. Two years later, a newly-founded society formed another investigative group that included eminent historians, a political scientist, and a biophysicist. The probers spent a year examining the evidence afresh. Its report, with one dissent, declared that Jefferson's paternity "is by no means proven."

Faced with this pair of conscientious bodies offering the fruits of their inquiry and contradicting each other, the researcher has his job cut out for him, particularly because one of these sources is scientific. Of course, the word of a contemporary such as Callender is hardly to be trusted when we know why he hated Jefferson. But with the scientific evidence as given in the press, care must also be taken at several points. The researcher must ascertain by what team the study was conducted and make sure that their specialization is appropriate to the subject. If the issue rests on a comparison of DNA samples, the investigators must be microbiologists experienced in making genetic tests.

If possible, the original paper should be consulted, or a review of it in the periodical *Science* or another journal in the field; the news item in the *Cattycorner Gazette* is not a sufficient authority and it lacks necessary detail. In this case as in much else, the press reports are likely to emphasize one point and omit the precise qualifiers included by the men of science.[25] Thus the DNA finding that concerns Jefferson states that a *member* of the Jefferson family fathered the young woman's child,

---

[25]A distinguished newspaper editor has declared: "No week passes without someone prominent in politics, industry, labor or civic affairs complaining to me, always in virtually identical terms: 'Whenever I read a story about something in which I really know what's going on, I'm astonished at how little of what's important gets into the papers—and how often even that little is wrong.'" A. H. Raskin, "What's Wrong with American Newspapers?" (*New York Times Magazine*, June 11, 1967.)

whose present descendants may claim that offspring as ancestor. But not having taken in the exact wording, and encouraged by partisan propaganda, the public at large is doubtless convinced that Thomas is that ancestor. A few writers to the press have pointed out that he had a brother who would also qualify as father and is perhaps the more plausible candidate for the role, because he had a roving disposition. There is in fact no reason to choose one brother or the other.

What is the lesson here beyond resting in doubt? The researcher must bear in mind that scientific reports as such are not necessarily decisive. All must be judged by criteria that vary in each instance. Only a few years ago, a scientist (now deceased), who had served as medical examiner in two or three large cities, was found to have reported test results that were wrong or false in a number of criminal cases. Careless or fraudulent laboratory work comes to light from time to time, just like plagiarism and mendacity—and neglect of facts in the press.

We have repeatedly referred to "the situation." Some puzzles may be resolved by seeking well beyond the boundaries of a tight-knit story, enlarging "the situation" and finding in its purlieus resolving elements. Recourse to this device will on occasion uncover a puzzle where all seemed an open-and-shut affair resting on the solid base of a plain and genuine document. These words apply, for example, to the significance of Dr. Johnson's famous letter to Lord Chesterfield. The theme and style of the epistle are so splendid that even though it is an attack on Chesterfield, he himself relished it, and showed it to all his friends with evident admiration.

Now what the letter plainly says is that Chesterfield promised Johnson support in his enterprise of making a dictionary of the English language, failed to give that help, and now that the work is done is "encumbering" Johnson with public praise. So unmistakable is the statement that one might well think it a complete account of what happened, especially since Chesterfield did not rebut the charge and the well-wishers of each man kept silent. On the surface it is a clear-cut case of lordly indifference followed by an officious gesture of approval.

Yet a few additional facts change the whole scene. Chesterfield, busy with high office and many claimants for his patronage, had indeed forgotten the relatively unknown Johnson and his project of a dictionary. But shortly before the appearance of the work, the publisher Dodsley approached Chesterfield for a review that might help sales. Though old and ailing, Chesterfield did not refuse but wrote two "papers" of sincere praise in the weekly journal, *The World*, and these were widely reprinted.

Thereupon, Johnson felt bound to write to Chesterfield, not because of the long neglect—he would not complain of what is the common lot of authors until they "arrive"—but because of the misleading effect of Chesterfield's two articles. The original *Plan* of the Dictionary had announced to the public, correctly, that the project had won Chesterfield's patronage. Now Chesterfield praised the result. The obvious assumption would be that Johnson had enjoyed his lordship's help from first to last. Yet in the Preface to the great book that was about to appear, Johnson asserted, also correctly, that he had carried the burden unaided. Writing a protest to the noble lord was required by so complicated a series of events. The need for it was confirmed by one reviewer's hostile remark that Johnson had written a Preface (instead of reprinting the *Plan*) only that he might deny his debt to Chesterfield.

The happy postscript to the affair is that a message from the dying Chesterfield to Johnson earned the doctor's entire forgiveness. After his *faux pas* and the letter of rebuke, Chesterfield behaved magnanimously to Johnson, as Johnson did in reverse, never letting any copy of his stern letter out of his hands, though many asked to have one. Compare now the facts with the general opinion of the facts.[26]

[26]James H. Sledd and Gwin J. Kolb, *Dr. Johnson's Dictionary* (Chicago, 1955, 85–104). But old stories die hard, as we saw in the case of the year 1000. In a scholarly book by Allen Reddick, *The Making of Johnson's Dictionary* (New York, 1990), the simple (and erroneous) interpretation of Johnson's letter is repeated in three places, quotations from Sledd and Kolb's work being used out of context to validate the denigration of Chesterfield's mind and morals.

How soon biographies and reference-book entries about the two great characters will catch up with this rehabilitation, it is impossible to say. Meanwhile, the story contains another injunction for biographers. Their duty is not to their main subject alone; the lesser figures must also be represented in the proper light, and this may entail verification—and research. A striking instance that affected George Washington and the future government of the states is that concerning an immigrant and adventurer, Lewis Nicola.

A native of France, he came to Philadelphia around 1768 by way of Ireland, where he had been educated. Being in favor of American independence and a professional soldier, he sought service and in 1777, aged sixty, he was made colonel of an "invalid regiment," a unit of men still useful though not fit for combat. Ingratiating himself with Washington—so the story has run for over two centuries—he wrote to the general that after the war the country would thrive best under a monarchy. And he urged that Washington wear the crown. If there was some public sentiment in support of such a coup d'état, it was not widely shared. In the event, "as everybody knows," Washington vehemently brushed aside the suggestion, and Nicola apologized abjectly for his wicked idea.

The scholar who not long ago re-examined the documents found that Nicola was far from being a monarchist.[27] What he intended was to allay the continental Army's increasing discontent with their treatment by the Congress. He feared the situation would end in violence. Hence, his proposal to create a new state in the west for the benefit of ex-soldiers who could be induced to settle there. Nicola's goal was the precise opposite of monarchy: the removal of a threat to republican government.

He acknowledged his carelessness to Washington, saying that it owed more to "weakness of judgment than corruption of

---

[27]Robert F. Haggard, "The Nicola Affair: Lewis Nicola, George Washington, and American Military Discontent during the Revolutionary War" (*Proceedings of the American Philosophical Society*, Vol. 146, No. 2, June 2002, pp. 139–68).

heart." And still troubled by the thought that he had offended his general, he sent him a second letter deploring the step that led to "your thinking me capable of acting or abetting any villainy."

Skepticism under Control

The tale of misunderstanding just related is tenable, for History produced it. But we are entitled to feel even more confident when a set of events is public from the start and attested to by several independent witness. In such instances we *know*. Let us recapitulate the two reasons why: (1) we have abundant documentary evidence, and (2) a critical examination of it discloses a high probability of truth. "Well and good," says the skeptic, "but you were not there. All you know is what others choose to tell you—in memoirs, letters, newspapers, and your other vaunted evidences. How can you be sure? Most people are notoriously bad observers; some are deliberate or unconscious liars; there is no such thing as a perfect witness. And yet you naively trust any casual passerby, and on his say-so you proclaim: 'This is what happened.'"

Except for the words "naively trust," everything said above is correct. But in its effort to discredit history it proves too much. The key sentences are "You were not there" and "There is no such thing as a perfect witness." Granting the force of these two statements, what follows? It is that if any one of us had been there, there would simply have been one more imperfect witness on the scene. We might be convinced that *our* vision, *our* recollection, *our* interpretation was the right one, but other witnesses would still feel no less certain about theirs.

To put it differently, every observer's knowledge of an event doubtless contains some exact and some erroneous knowledge, and these two parts, multiplied by as many observers as may be, are all the knowledge there can be. Only a divine being would have perfect and complete knowledge of the event—"as it really happened." But outside our imperfect knowledge, the event has no independent existence; it is not hidden in some "repository of the real" where we can find it. Indeed, a notable

American historian of the Civil War and Reconstruction, William A. Dunning, was convinced that what the contemporaries of an event believed it to be is truer—more genuinely "the past"— than anything discovered later that the contemporaries did not know. Their views had consequences, whereas ours about their times played no part in the web of thought and action.[28]

In any case, comparisons with absolute knowledge or the substitution of a divine mind for the human ones that remember and write up the past are irrelevant. Far from disproving the truth of history, they lead to the conclusion that a capable researcher can know more about the past than did those contemporary with it, which is one reason why under the historian's hand the known past changes and grows clearer.

A typical illustration will show how. The story of D-Day, June 6, 1944, still fascinates historians no less than the general public, one of the debatable questions being the heavy pounding that some American troops experienced upon their landing. Eisenhower explained it by writing: "In the Omaha sector an alert enemy division, the 352d, which prisoners stated had been in the area on maneuvers and defense exercises, accounted for some of the intense fighting in that locality."[29] Writing more casually, Winston Churchill offered a slightly different explanation: "By an unlucky chance the enemy defences in this sector had recently been taken over by a complete German division in full strength and on the alert."[30]

[28]"Truth in History," in the volume of that name (New York, 1937), 3–20. For example, as Admiral Hyman G. Rickover has persuasively shown, if the United States had believed in 1898 that the *Maine* in Havana harbor had blown up "by an internal explosion or that the ship was destroyed by causes unknown . . . war might have been avoided." *How the Battleship* Maine *Was Destroyed* (Washington, DC, 1976), 104–105.

[29]Dwight D. Eisenhower, *Crusade in Europe* (New York, 1948), 253.

[30]Winston S. Churchill, *The Second World War: Triumph and Tragedy* (New York, 1953), 4. Similarly, on the Michelin map of the whole theater, issued in 1946 and reissued for the commemoration of 1984, the English translation does not match, on this key situation, the French explanatory text.

How does one decide between the word of the Supreme Commander four years after the event and of the Prime Minister of Britain, himself an accomplished historian, after the lapse of seven years? The researcher doubtless turns to the memoirs of the ground commander, General Omar Bradley, and finds confirmation of Eisenhower's statement, somewhat modified: "The 352d had been moved from St.-Lô to the assault beaches for a defense exercise."[31]

Obviously, one cannot stop here. A determined American student probed further. He could aver that "up to June 4 Allied intelligence had still placed the 352nd around St.-Lô, more than twenty miles away" from Omaha Beach.[32] The leading English authority asserts that some time before D-Day, British intelligence "suggested that the 352nd Division had been moved forward to the area below the elbow of the American beaches, although the evidence . . . circulated proved too uncertain to disturb the American planners."[33] So the researcher concludes that despite what Eisenhower and Churchill wrote, Allied intelligence gathering, which had otherwise succeeded in divining the enemy order of battle, failed at one critical point. Autobiographical accounts, even when not self-serving, can mislead. The authors, though competent witnesses on the spot, did not know the reality before them. Later-comers reconstruct it with the advantage of perspective and multiplicity of sources, but still without certitude.[34]

---

[31]Omar N. Bradley, *A Soldier's Story* (New York, 1951), 272.

[32]Cornelius Ryan, *The Longest Day* (New York, 1959), 162. See also the maps accompanying the U.S. Army publication, Omaha Beachhead (Washington, DC, 1945; reprinted, 1984).

[33]Max Hastings, *Operation Overlord: D-Day and the Battle for Normandy* (New York, 1984), 67. An American military expert, Carlo D'Este, states that the unnoticed German troops had been in Normandy three months before the invasion, *Eisenhower: A Soldier's Life* (New York, 2002), 533.

[34]The supposedly inveterate doubter, Voltaire, did not doubt history and was on the contrary an indefatigable historian. In 1769 he published a long essay answering Horace Walpole, in which he rejected equally "an extreme skepticism and a ridiculous credulity" (*Le Pyrrhonisme de l'histoire*, in *Oeuvres*, Kehl, 1785, 27: 9–10).

To the justly skeptical and comparing mind, history at its best is no more uncertain than the descriptive earth sciences whose assertions most people seem willing to take on faith.[35] Large parts of man's history are thoroughly well known and beyond dispute. True, the interpretations and the meanings attached to the parts are and will continue open to debate. But who has settled the interpretation or meaning of human life?

Subjective and Objective: The Right Meanings

Our cumulative reasons for trusting history are now four: we have documents; they are critically tested; the rule governing judgment is Probability; and the notion of an absolute past, which we might know if only writers did not produce faulty copies, is a delusion. Within the history we possess we can, of course, distinguish good and bad witnesses, good and bad judges of events. This conclusion brings up a question—or, rather, a usage often found in discussions of the present topic: on our own showing, all history, all reports, rest on "subjective (i.e. individual) impressions." All accounts of events must then be akin to images in a real reflection but all askew.

This is to mistake the meaning of "subjective." It is not the same as "biased," for which see the next chapter. "Subjective" originally was a technical term in a special brand of philosophy. It has come into the marketplace, where it often serves to mean: "this is only your opinion," probably mistaken; whereas "objective" is taken to mean "what everybody agrees on," the correct view.[36]

---

[35]The public is also docile about accepting radical revisions in the huge spans of time that geologists assign to the periods of prehistory including the age of man on earth. Note also the frequent changes in the reports of astrophysicists about the age, the components, and the current doings of the cosmos. On Revisionism in history see the next chapter.

[36]In colleges and universities the misusage has probably been encouraged by the term "objective examinations," which is a misnomer to describe multiple-choice questions. See Banesh Hoffmann's pioneering work, *The Tyranny of Testing* (New York, 1962).

"Subjective" and "objective" properly apply not to persons and opinions but to sensations and judgments. Every person, that is, every living subject, is necessarily subjective in *all* his sensations. But some of his subjective sensations are *of* objects, others of himself, or "subject." Your toothache is said to be subjective because it occurs within you as a feeling subject. It is not an object in the world for all to see and feel; it is yours alone. The tooth that the dentist extracts *is* an object and with its removal goes your subjective ache.

While the pain lasted, both tooth and ache were real. Now only the tooth is real—hence the tendency to believe that an object is somehow "more real," because more lasting, more public, than a *purely* subjective impression. But objects themselves are known only by subjects—persons—so the distinction is not clear-cut, much less a test of reality.[37] If this reasoning strains the ordinary faculties, get rid of the whole matter by dropping the jargon use of "objective" and "subjective" as synonyms for "true" and "false." To sum up, *an objective judgment is one made by testing in all ways possible one's subjective impressions, so as to arrive at a correct knowledge of an object.*

One more point about judgment: what is decisive is competence, and not majority opinion. There have been collective hallucinations that deceived large majorities. Now translate this into a researcher's challenging situation. From well-known writers who knew Henry James we have many reports on the novelist's appearance, manners, and speech. Most of them refer to him as either stuttering or hemming and hawing. One and only one entranced listener, herself trained in speech, has written down, with the aid of tempo marks, a characteristic sentence as James spoke it. From this it clearly appears that James was

---

[37]Another example for good measure: if you see spots before your eyes, they may be objective—a piece of material with polka dots—or subjective, a diseased condition of the body. Take quinine and you may hear a ringing in your ears—purely subjective, though real. But you have no difficulty ascertaining the absence of an objective bell that could account for the sensation.

not stammering or fumbling for words at all, but repeating himself in various emphatic ways as he went along, or—to quote his interpreter—"instinctively bringing out the perfect sentence the first time; repeating it [in bits] more deliberately to test every word the second time; accepting it as satisfactory the third time, and triumphantly sending it forth as produced by Henry James."[38] This extraordinary mode of speech needed an extraordinary witness to record it for posterity. Against her *objective* judgment and manifest competence, no "majority" of inattentive or inexact comments can prevail.

Knowledge of Fact and Knowledge of Causes

The wish to give an intelligible account of what happened, whether last week or 1000 years ago, poses the problem of causation. Whole libraries have been written about Causation. Only a sketch of the question can be given here. The chief difficulty lies in what is meant by Cause. In the mid-eighteenth century, the philosopher David Hume showed that the conception of Cause as a compelling push that produces an effect is an illusion. Man has no direct sense of the necessity that makes one billiard ball propel another after striking it; he has only an expectation of the event, an expectation bred by habitual experience. Ever since Hume, all that has been agreed upon is that where Cause is, there is Effect, but all we observe is Regularity.

When we speak of causes in human affairs we are usually concerned with a cluster of elements that stand at different distances from the observed effect. If a man kills himself sixteen days, five hours, and twenty-three minutes after receiving a piece of bad news, on what basis do we assign the cause of his suicide? We may say: "The idea of disgrace gradually became too much for him"; or if we know when he did the deed: "A man's vitality is lowest in the small hours," or "A man of

[38]Elizabeth Jordan, quoted in S. Nowell-Smith, *The Legend of the Master* (New York, 1948), 16.

John's character could not face bankruptcy." In other words we ascribe his death either to a slow and unfathomable psychological process, or to a physiological fact, or to a standard motive. We are not likely to ascribe it to the bullet and the gun, because that cause does not interest us: it interests only the Medical Examiner.

Generalizing from this example we conclude that a recital of what happened does not uncover *the* cause (several combined antecedents) of any event, but only a few of the *conditions* attending its emergence. Not only can we not isolate the cause, but we cannot properly define what it would be. When Pascal said that if Cleopatra's nose had been shorter this would have changed the face of the world (to say nothing of her own), he was pointing out that personality plays a role in History. He did not mean that Cleopatra's nose in all its beauty was *the* cause of her lover Mark Antony's defeat at Actium: it was one of the much earlier conditions. In giving an account of human events we fasten upon those points that seem to connect them with our present concerns and previous experience. If these connections are duly brought out we say we "understand."[39]

The thought occurs that we might come closer to pinning down *the* cause if we could only deal with well-defined kinds of events, say, automobile accidents. We classify these and learn that mechanical failure caused so many percent, speeding so many, and intoxication so many. Can this sort of statistical measurement be extended to History and make it a science? It is clear that although historical events are unique, some of them are enough alike to be called by the same name, and hence to suggest regularities. History does and does not repeat; and science deals, though in a different way, with the same paradoxical situation: no two laboratory "events" are alike, though designed to be so. Again, the events of history occur in the same

[39]For a subtle and authoritative account of causation as it is conceived in physical science and as it must be conceived in the "historical" realm, which includes all that is not science, see Henry Margenau, *Open Vistas* (New Haven, 1961), esp. 191–214.

universe and follow the same material "laws" as the objects of science. Living beings are subject to gravitation and decay, statesmen in transit are no different from other moving bodies, and what is most important, human minds work upon historical data with the same perceptions and logical rules as they do in science.

But a difference remains. One cannot pare down events and reproduce them at will under the controlled conditions that we call experiment. Nor, as we saw above, can the historian sort out his materials into independent units that will enable him to measure and relate them as constants and variables.[40] Even when we count automobile accidents we pursue our practical interest at the expense of strict causal analysis. The immediate mistake that caused the drunken driver's accident interests us no more than the remote cause that led him to drink—and the nearest "cause" of death may have been a thin skull.[41]

On Cause and Measurement

Every attempt to formalize causal description by assigning one "paramount" cause and several "contributory" causes ends in a deceptive kind of exactitude. For if, as Edward Lucas White once contended,[42] it took malaria-bearing mosquitoes and the spread of Christianity to undo the Roman Empire, the mosquitoes

---

[40]We can of course achieve this relation intuitively through historical *judgment*, as Garrett Mattingly, the astute historian of early modern times, pointed out: "Conscious that every human situation contains certain elements of uniformity and certain elements of uniqueness, we scrutinize each new one and compare it with everything we can find out about similar situations in the past, seeking to assign values to constants and to isolate the variables, to decide which factors are significant, what choices are actually present, and what the probable consequences are of choosing course A and rejecting B."

[41]For a trenchant discussion of the logic of historical analysis, see an article under that title by Ernest Nagel in *Scientific Monthly* (74, March 1952, 162–69).

[42]*In Why Rome Fell* (New York, 1927).

were as necessary as the Christians and neither is paramount to the other.[43]

The reporter of events is thus led to adopt a practical distinction about causality that has also commended itself to philosophers and scientists alike. They draw attention to the difference between causation that occurs in a long chain of events of various kinds and causation within a closed system. An example of the first is the forming of a cloud, the darkening of the sun to earth dwellers, the lowering of temperature, people putting on coats, a thunderstorm bursting, a person taking refuge under a tree and being struck by lightning and killed. This chain of "causes" is miscellaneous and each event in it unpredictable, not because it is not determined, but because it occurs outside any controllable limits. As against this, in the physics laboratory, an elastic body of known stresses and strains goes through a series of evolving states; at any moment a single definite distribution of measured stresses and strains follows that of the previous moment, which may therefore be regarded as its complete "cause," as *the* cause."

The distinctive feature of the first kind of causality is that there is no restriction on the number of events that may be related. It is open to the observer's insight to select the conditions that belong to the chain and have the merit of interesting him and his audience. It is for them to judge whether the resulting narrative is intelligible, consonant with the experience of the race, and useful in orienting the mind amid the welter of facts. The "single cause" is always fallacious and even too few conditions can distort. As a noted theorist said many years ago:

Nothing could be more artificial than the scientific separation of man's religious, aesthetic, economic, political, intellectual and bellicose

---

[43]See a striking archaeological hypothesis of the same simplicity: "Downfall of Indus Civilization Is Traced to Mud" (*New York Times*, May 23, 1966). And, reverting to the Romans, some advocates of the single, hidden cause have suggested gout, "the bacchanalian appetites of ancient Rome," or lead pots and pipes, or all three (*New York Times*, March 18, 1983).

properties. These may be studied, each by itself, with advantage, but specialization would lead to the most absurd results if there were not someone to study the process as a whole; and that someone is the historian.[44]

Such is the view properly called pragmatic.[45] Its concern is not with causes but with variously relevant conditions. In this light, the objection that historians select their facts to suit themselves is seen to be no objection but a necessity. They must think and choose, and they are judged by the intelligence and honesty with which they do both. Again, the objection that history cannot be true because it has to be rewritten every thirty years appears as a sign of the usefulness of history. The successive revisions of the past do not cancel each other out, they are additive: we know more and more about the past, as we know more and more about nature, eliminating untenable views as we go. Finally, the need to choose among conditions in order to delineate events points to the truth that history, like all narrative, must present a pattern to the mind, must have form. An unsorted pile of names and events is unintelligible and useless. It is organization that makes the past valuable, just as it is the organization of phenomena in scientific formulas that makes the study of nature valuable.

The ultimate question for the historian therefore is: What pattern?

[44]James Harvey Robinson, *The New History* (New York, 1913), 66.

[45]"Pragmatic" is here used in its technical, Jamesian sense; it does not mean "convenient" or "practical," but "tested by consequences rather than antecedents"—the pragmatic test.

CHAPTER 7

PATTERN, BIAS, AND REVISIONISM

The Reason of Historical Periods and Labels

When six historians were invited by a leading monthly journal to select by way of bicentennial tribute the most formative events in U.S. history, they suggested a total of 356 events; they agreed unanimously on five.[1]

Few historians would be surprised by this fact, and most would gladly have explained to anyone who asked that although the answers were rational, the question was based on a misapprehension. For to try to determine for oneself or for others *the* formative moments in history, whether 15 or 100, is an intellectual impossibility. To understand why this is so calls for an understanding of the related subjects of Pattern, Period, Bias, and System.

Everybody can see why the writing of history requires a pattern. The human mind cannot fix its attention on anything that does not present or suggest form. Throw down a dozen paper clips on a table and look at them for a few seconds: they are scattered at random, yet you will find yourself "seeing" a triangle of three in one corner, a sort of cross in the middle, and a little rosette at the left. The constellations in the sky are the product of this inevitable penchant for grouping-in-order-to-grasp.

[1]*Life Special Report: 100 Events that Shaped America* (1975).

The need is the same in story and in history. We expect them to offer us incidents in clusters that follow "rationally" upon one another. We may keep reading straight ahead uncritically, but on looking back we like to feel that the whole somehow possesses dramatic form. This does not mean continuous emotional excitement; it means an acceptable progression from a clear beginning to an intelligible end. This is why Macaulay, proposing to give a vast panorama of the events that filled the "momentous years" from 1685 to 1701, was so concerned with his arrangement. When his *History* was done he kept scrutinizing the form and comparing it with that of his favorite, Thucydides: "I admire him more than ever. He is the great historian. The others one may hope to match: him never . . . [but] . . . his arrangement is bad. . . . How much better is my order than that of Thucydides."[2]

Some few historians have at times repudiated this interest in "order" and declared that for history to be scientifically true the facts should arrange themselves. This is a misconception of both history and science. In the study of nature the facts do not arrange themselves either. A formula, or little form, implies the selection of certain phenomena that observation, followed by experiment, have related, first to a scale of measurement and then to other facts in fixed or variable connections. The choice of facts and of relations is dictated by human interest as well as by nature. It is curiosity that moves the inquirer to ascertain the relation between the behavior of a gas and the phenomena of heat and pressure. The facts, moreover, are seen through ideas (for example, the idea of a molecule) that are not immediately visible and ready to be noted down. They are searched for with a purpose in mind. The facts and connections once ascertained, a mind has to frame a hypothesis to arrive at what is properly called *theory*: a total view of related events.

All reporters of events work under the same necessity of giving shape to what they have found and verified. Chronology does supply a natural order among facts. But, as we shall see,

<hr>

[2]G. O. Trevelyan, *Life and Letters of Lord Macaulay* (first published 1876), diary entries for November 25 and December 4, 1848.

chronology is long and its contents are a mixed bag. For both these reasons it, too, needs a pattern before it can be thought and felt.[3] This leads the historian to carve out manageable periods: reigns, centuries, eras. He also finds ready-made certain other patterns or "constellations" created by the laity, contemporary or not, out of *their* need to group things: these groupings go by names such as Gothic and Baroque, Renaissance and Romantic. These the historian must accept as having meaning, even if the meaning has to be explained at length, and even if it remains less clear-cut than that of the molecule. For the historical labels refer to the thoughts and acts of once living beings, who were precisely not molecules.

Groups and their names usually arise in the course of intellectual or artistic debate. Thus the name "Hudson River School," now used in scholarly writing to describe a notable group of American painters, was first used by a critic in scorn of certain artists and their subjects. It was not an exact label, as one might guess, for the men attacked did not invariably paint the Hudson River or live on its banks. But the name is now indispensable, in the first place because it is an historical datum; and in the second, because it links fact and idea in the true manner of history. The ideas consist of certain pictorial principles and poetic intentions; the facts make up the biography of certain men, their dates, works, careers.

The Conditions of Pattern-Making

Having accepted certain historic groupings as given, we go on to ask: What elements of thought and observation go into the making of any constellation that unites the loose particles of fact? Not all periods, patterns, and labels are equally apt and useful. The first element in any pattern is a comparison of some sort, natural or artificial. We decide that X is more like Y than like M. As in the example of the scattered paper clips, we can

---

[3]For the relation of the chronological and topical treatments, see Chapter 8, p. 173ff.

argue that some of them naturally are in the form of a cross, or again that we choose to see them as a cross. Never mind this philosophical question. The researcher will profit more from the distinction between random (or historic) grouping and (systematic, purposive) grouping.

The first kind is that exemplified in the name Hudson River School. The critic who made this pattern to impress the readers of the New York *Tribune* with his disapproval did not conduct a survey of contemporary American painters and verify their common features. He was simply hurling an epithet at random—and it stuck.[4] But when we use it now we have to qualify its meaning and modify its scope.

A systematic grouping, on the other hand, is usually the work of a researcher who stands further away from the living reality than the contemporary critic, and who wishes to study a genuine set or class of facts. Thus when the late Crane Brinton prepared his book *The Jacobins,* he did not take merely the first half dozen whose names he happened to know, or content himself with the membership of the Paris group; he systematically sampled the membership of that historic party by examining the records of Jacobin Clubs all over France. Such a study resembles what we know as sociology; its principle is fundamental to all descriptive disciplines: generalization depends on adequate enumeration. If you want to make an assertion about the views of a board of directors, you must look up in the minutes the votes and opinions of all the members. With very large groups a sampling is possible, but your classification must cover the

---

[4]Compare the various origins of "Quakers," "Muckrakers," "Sea Beggars," "Diggers," "Fauves," "Cubists," "Rosicrucians," "the Bloomsbury Group," "Girondists," "Jacobins," "Jacobites," "Whigs," "Tories," "Spartacists," "Huguenots," "Know-Nothings," "Suffragettes," "Irreconcilables," "Existentialists," "Beatniks," "Hawks and Doves," "Supply-siders," "New Leftists," "Neo-Conservatives," "Libertarians." A useful work on this age-old social and political practice is George E. Shankle, *American Nicknames and Their Significance* (2nd ed., 1955) and for more general uses: Carl Sefakis, *Dictionary of Historic Nicknames* (1984) and the Gale inventory already cited, *Pseudonyms and Nicknames Dictionary* (1980).

ground. Definition determines the limits of the class, even though you are still grouping together people who differ in appearance and opinion from one another.

The next condition of pattern-making grows out of this human diversity, which makes it either impossible or fruitless to report on human affairs in cut-and-dried fashion. It would not be enough to give a tabulation of the directors' votes on various issues. To report the temper of the company accurately, we must know the words, the personalities, the intrigues, the emotions represented. And since the historian cannot and should not "tell all," he must select. We thus arrive at our first rule of pattern-making: *To be successful and right, a selection must face two ways: it must fairly correspond to the mass of evidence, and it must offer a graspable design to the beholder.*

The researcher never sees the facts fully displayed before him like someone selecting jewelry laid out on a counter. He has begun with but little knowledge of the subject and has gradually acquired a mass of information beyond the holding capacity of both the mind's eye and the memory. When he selects, therefore, he is to be compared not to the customer with the synoptic view, but to the traveler exploring new country. The explorer forms his opinions as he progresses, and changes them with increasing knowledge. Yet they are always conditioned by two things: the observer's temperament, including his preconceptions, and the motive or purpose of his search.

The Sources of Bias and Its Correctives

The researcher, it is clear, looks for his facts even more actively than the traveler. He must piece together the "scenery" of the past from fragments that lie scattered in many places. He soon develops a guiding idea to propel him along his route, a hypothesis ahead of the facts, which steadily reminds him of what to look for. Says one critic:

The clearer we are about the theme of our research, the clearer we become about our own bias. And the clearer we are about our own bias, the more honest and efficient we are likely to be in our own research. Many of the rules laid down about the correct methods of historical research are in fact disguised declarations of the purposes of the research itself.[5]

To which might be added: in research as in life one is far more likely to find what one looks for than what one does not care about.

Since guiding ideas affect both search and selection, let us call the researcher's temperament (that is, the whole tendency of his mind) and his present intentions and hypotheses, his total *interest.* We may then say without implying any blame that his interest will determine his discoveries, his selection, his pattern-making, and his exposition. This is unavoidable in all products of the mind. Mathematicians themselves recognize in the work of their colleagues the individuality that produces solutions of certain kinds or arrives at them in certain ways. In research and writing there are of course many kinds of qualities or "interest," ranging from the downright dishonest to that which in Thucydides elicited Macaulay's breathless admiration. Apart from degrees of talent, the dividing line between the good and bad kinds of interest is usually drawn through the point where interest begins to spoil the product. It is then called Bias.

Bias is an uncontrolled form of interest.[6] It is easily detected, but its presence does not tell us all we need to know about a report. Gibbon, for example, was biased in favor of pagan Rome and against Christianity, so much so that he devoted two long

[5]Arnaldo Momigliano, "A Hundred Years After Ranke" (*Diogenes,* 6, Summer 1954, 57–58).

[6]That bias can be controlled, indeed suppressed, by a trained mind that is also self-aware is vividly shown by a remark in a contemporary history: "[Professor] Nock," says the late Morton Smith in his work of discovery and interpretation, *The Secret Gospel,* "was a tower of strength in this. His philological knowledge was vast, his judgment impeccable, and his objectivity such that, in spite of his prejudice against Clementine authorship, he often pointed out evidence that went to confirm it" (1973, 27).

chapters to an ironic castigation of the early Church. As a result, one does not go to Gibbon for a sympathetic understanding of primitive Christianity, although what he reports is true, not made up. And the remainder of his history—the larger portion— stands firm. That valuable portion could not have been produced apart from the rest. The work as a whole would probably not have been undertaken and carried through without Gibbon's animus, his bias.

Again, Macaulay is sometimes dismissed with the phrase "the Whig historian." The description is not wrong, but the implication usually is. Macaulay's sympathies were with the Whigs in the Revolution of 1688 and with their descendants, the Liberals of his day, so his *History*—what? It stands. What he wrote is neither a party pamphlet, nor a whitewashing, nor anything less than a great history. One of his later opponents in politics, Lord Acton, who was deeply repelled by Macaulay's views, nevertheless called him "one of the greatest of all writers and masters."[7]

Because "bias" is used pejoratively, it is assumed that some workers are biased, others not. This is to think in black and white. Gaetano Salvemini put the situation better when he told his students: "Impartiality is a dream and honesty a duty. We cannot be impartial, but we can be intellectually honest." The student, the reader, each responds to the need for pattern and wants a motive, the one to drive his research, the other to take it in. Without "interest," both efforts will be useless. In judging

[7]James W. Thompson, *A History of Historical Writing* (1942, 2:300). On one occasion Acton told the Trinity College Society at Cambridge: "'I was once with two eminent men, the late Bishop of Oxford [William Stubbs] and the present Bishop of London [Mandell Creighton]. On another occasion I was with two far more eminent men, the two most learned men in the world. I need hardly tell you their names—they were Mommsen and Harnack. On each occasion the question arose: who was the greatest historian the world had ever produced. On each occasion the name first mentioned and on each occasion the name finally agreed upon, was that of Macaulay.'"

the way in which the writer's interest has contributed to the form, the reader asks:

1. Was the writer fastidious or crude in selecting and marshaling his facts? That is, was he hard upon his own hypotheses, fair-minded to his opponents, committed to the truth first and foremost?

2. Was he self-aware enough to recognize—perhaps to acknowledge the assumptions arising from his interest?

3. Does the work as a whole exhibit the indispensable scholarly virtues, however noticeable the bias?

In answering these questions, the critic himself will try to be as fair as he can. For whoever judges another's interest is moved by one of his own—an interest that is often heightened by the knowledge that others share it unquestioningly. At any one time, politics all over the globe is powered by thoughts of the past mixed with plans or hopes for the future—and this is not just unconsciously, but overtly in the form of arguments, appeals, and recriminations. As an English newspaper said about the unending conflict in Northern Ireland: "What can we do? No peace until historic facts are faced." Riots and murders continue. The probability that a critical inquiry would show an equality of misdeeds on either side does not deter the combatants from re-enacting history; in Ulster, the religious wars of the sixteenth and seventeenth centuries are not yet over.

In these conditions the effort of self-awareness required to overcome bias is, for most people, superhuman. For the researcher as he writes, measuring self-awareness means being alive to the implications of his words; there is no law requiring him to say outright: "These are my assumptions, how do you like them?" He may rest content with statements of principle that he hopes you will accept as true, or at least as working hypotheses. Take as an example a remark of Macaulay's:

During more than a hundred years . . . every [English] man has felt entire confidence that the state would protect him in the possession of what had been earned by his diligence and hoarded by his self-denial.

Under the benignant influence of peace and liberty, science has flourished and has been applied to practical purposes on a scale never before known. The consequence is that a change to which the history of the old world furnishes no parallel has taken place in our country.[8]

We easily infer that the writer favors peace, liberty, property, applied science, and the Industrial Revolution. He is also a Little Englander, patriotic but not imperialistic, an advocate of laissez-faire and of the moral traits that go with that philosophy: self-reliance, rationalism, and a respect for worldly achievements.

The value of perceiving all this as one reads an account of the past is that it permits one to judge the writer's own judgments. The reader proceeds by a sort of triangulation: here I stand; there, to left or right, stands Macaulay; and beyond are the events that he reports. Knowing his position in relation to mine, I can work out a perspective upon events such as I could not if I saw them exclusively through his eyes—or mine.

Practicing this triangulation is not the same as dismissing an author after having "doped out" that he is a Whig, a Catholic, a Dutchman, a Muslim, an alcoholic, or a divorced person. Dismissal or systematic discounting of what is said or written because of nationality, religion, or personal history is only the crude and dull form of the delicate assessment here called for. One might as well spare oneself the effort of reading at all if one is going to make the text a mere peg for toplofty dissent. The aim should be rather to obtain a positive return in knowledge, some of it held under caution until two, three, or four other accounts have modified or strengthened its solid parts.

The View from Inside

Reader's stereotyping, then, is no answer to the question of writer's bias. On the contrary, sympathy is prerequisite to understanding, for history presents people once alive and their

---

[8]*History of England from the Accession of James Second* (1899, 1:261).

active emotions, which can be understood in no other way. Woodrow Wilson, an accomplished historian, went even further:

The historian needs something more than sympathy, for sympathy may be condescending, pitying, contemptuous. . . . Sympathy there must be . . . but it must be the sympathy of the man who stands in the midst and sees like one within, not like one without, like a native, not like an alien. He must not sit like a judge exercising extraterritorial jurisdiction.[9]

Here, surely, is our old resource Imagination under another name. The fact that it is a dangerous power does not mean that it can be dispensed with. Imagining what facts we want and where they may be found also tells us what they mean. An Australian historian, Sir Keith Hancock, has told how in writing his first book on the Risorgimento in Tuscany he identified himself with each party, one after the other: "I was zealous in turn for the House of Austria, the House of Savoy, the Papacy, the Mazzinian People, and half a dozen brands of liberalism or democracy."[10] An imaginative identification with all the participants sets up in the researcher's mind that internal debate which re-creates the actuality. Juxtaposing his successive enthusiasms, Sir Keith formed a total view that none of the actors themselves had, and his intellect apportioned to each element its due. In his own words, "Getting inside the situation is the one opening movement, getting outside it is the concluding one."[11]

The impossibility—indeed, the undesirability—of eliminating interest and the consequent effort to detect and allow for bias reconciles us to the lack of unanimity in historical writing. The reasons for all variations and contradictions is of course perspective. A large subject is like a mountain, which no beholder ever sees entire: if he climbs it he discovers only selected

[9]"The Variety and Unity of History" (*Congress of Arts and Science, Universal Exposition, St. Louis,* 1904, ed., Howard J. Rogers, 1906, 2:17).

[10]*Country and Calling* (London, 1954), 220.

[11]Ibid., 221.

aspects; if he stands off, he sees but an outline and from one side only; if he flies over it, he flattens it out.

What is more, every ten or twenty years, contemporary events cause a shift of interest in the public mind. War, revolution, depression, dictatorship give respectively to international relations, domestic unrest, quasi-military parties a special importance that often directs researchers to a fresh aspect of the past. Accordingly, the cliché that history must be rewritten every generation should run somewhat differently: the past cannot help being reconceived by every generation, but the earlier reports upon it are in the main as good and true as they ever were. Anyone who would know the full history of any period will do well to read its successive treatments, just as the ordinary researcher who would know the truth of a single incident seeks out all its witnesses. The rewriting of history, rightly considered, does not substitute; it subtracts a little and adds more.

A further advantage of trying to harmonize the views of different periods into a larger but still coherent pattern is that in so doing one learns a great deal about the mind of each period. Pierre Bayle, the seventeenth-century critical historian, put this with some exaggeration: "I almost never read historians with a view to learning what occurred, but only in order to know what is said in each nation about what occurred."[12] A modern researcher into Bayle's own century expressed the nub of this more exactly when she said:

> The major changes in historical interpretation do not, as the layman often imagines, arise from the discovery of new evidence—the chest full of unsuspected documents . . . what is most likely to happen is that the historian will find what he is looking for, namely, the documents which will explain and illustrate his own point of view. But what *is* he looking for? Surely he is looking for the truth—for what really happened. It is his job as a scholar to form as exact an idea of past events as he can from the surviving evidence. But the instrument with which he

---

[12]"Critique générale de *l'Histoire du Calvinisme* de M. Maimbourg" (*Oeuvres Diverses*, The Hague, 1727, 2:10).

looks at the past is modern. It was made, and shaped, and it operates, in the present. It is his own mind. And however much he bends his thoughts toward the past, his own way of thinking, his outlook, his opinions are the products of the time in which he lives. So that all written history . . . [is] a compound of past and present.[13]

Revisionism Good and Bad

These shifts of outlook, then, are a constant in human experience itself. But within the last half century, something like a fresh motive has been added to this normal restlessness. It is called Revisionism and it springs from the conviction that all earlier views of men and events are wrong, vitiated by prejudice or falsified by lack of modern methods. The prejudice is supposed to come from the very principles of Western civilization. The missing methods are supposed to be supplied by science, defined as depth psychology and quantitative sociology. The influence of Marxism, the disgust with the status quo, a sense of oppression have inspired the belief that nothing deemed true before can be true now. The change is thus not one of perspective or interest but, as it were, of reality itself. Some Revisionists aim at creating total contempt for the recorded past.

The movement, moreover, owes part of its animus to the temper of the modern arts, which have accustomed the public to the idea that any work deserving attention must destroy existing beliefs or turn them upside down. Only the offbeat, startling, provocative, and "revolutionary" has merit; the rest is deemed dull imitation. The model is doubtless science, which steadily overturns and defies common sense. In revisionist history and biography heroes and villains are apt to change places, while causes and results contradict, not just some detail or tendency, but the received and hitherto probable explanations. Thus scholars have tried to show that slaveholding in the South was not as harsh as abolitionists said it was, that the railroad had little

[13]C. V. Wedgwood, "The Present in the Past" (*Listener,* 53 February 10, 1955, 235).

or no influence in developing the continent, and that the country's power of assimilation—the "melting pot" that made Irish, Sicilians, Finns, Jews, Hungarians, Germans, Swedes, Greeks, and other Europeans into Americans—was a fiction.

The application of the new methods has given results ranging from the useful to the absurd. The useful results have not been histories but sociological studies of past times and situations. An historian could well make use of them in the course of his or her narrative, to depict conditions of life and states of fact or of mind. But it remains to be seen which of those innumerable studies by historians not trained in sociology or statistical method are reliable enough for the social historian with a keen sense of evidence.

Another unexpected direction that Revisionism has taken is the contention that denies or casts doubt on the possibility of writing history itself. By comparing the multitude of detail in life—especially life in high civilizations—with the amount of sources available, one can arrive at an arithmetical conviction of inadequacy. This nihilism is nothing new; it cropped up in ancient times and it recurred in the eighteenth century. But it is easily countered by a few reflections. The first is that history does not profess "to tell all." Nor is "all" necessary for an understanding of human situations. This is particularly true of the history of one continuous civilization, the latest portion of which is familiar, being the historian's and his reader's. Further, individual memory shows that one's own history is unquestionably real and it can be verified by letters, diaries, and official documents. If points of doubt remain as to motive or other matters of quality and degree, the narrative is still satisfying. One may therefore say that history is imperfect, like other human achievements, but it is not impossible.

The Philosophy and "Laws" of History

Yet one more type of interest that continues to impel certain historians is that of discovering "the laws" of history. The search for them goes by various names—it purports to give the "philosophy of history," or it establishes an historical "system," or it lays down "the law of historical evolution" as in Marx's "materialistic conception of history."

The latest of these systems, Arnold Toynbee's *Study of History,*[14] is the most inductive, at least in the beginning, but it too winds up with a recurrent pattern, in which regularity is disclosed amid the "apparent" disorder of events. One might say that just as Bias is the excess of Interest, so System is the excess of Pattern.

What validates any pattern, as we saw, is that it permits *a* meaning to be attached to a group or chain of otherwise disconnected facts. What prompts the systematic historian is the desire to find *the* meaning of *all* the facts—the meaning of History and thus of man's destiny on earth. He starts from the assumption that nothing in the chaos of known human events for the last 6,000 years can be pointless. His faith is strong that somewhere and at some time the good and evil, the successes and failures, the pluses and minuses must produce a kind of total that, when read off, will have universal significance. History to him is not a vast network of incomplete stories, upon which patterns slightly clearer than life's confusion are imposed for convenience; rather it is *one* story, with a beginning, a middle, and an end.

In such an absolute system, the believer must show that despite surface differences, there is uniformity underneath. He is then bound to explain how the governing agency "underneath" produces the welter above, and he is thus brought to the view that some one powerful force, acting by necessity, has woven the great web of History. Systematic historians, in short, are committed to the doctrine of the Single Cause.

Whoever enjoys reading history will want to satisfy curiosity by taking up one or another of these systematists. From Augustine to Toynbee, the offering is rich and rewarding. For one thing, in the course of demonstration notable passages of

[14]Twelve volumes (London, 1934–1961). An abridgment in two volumes was made by D. C. Somervell (1947, 1957).

FIGURE **12**   *PHILOSOPHIES OF HISTORY: LINEAR PROGRESSION*

The BIBLE (c. 8th century B.C. 2nd century of our era)
1. Partial destruction but hope of messiah
2. End of the world and day of judgment

VIRGIL (c. 20 B.C.)
Golden age not in past but in future

ST. AUGUSTINE (A.D. 413–426)
Human history a part of eternal destiny of man; hence greatness and fall of Rome intelligible as moral and religious lesson

BOSSUET (1681)
The progress of revelation from the Jews to the Romans and to Western Europe demonstrates the action of God in history

CONDORCET (1793)
The progress already made by reason through eight stages opens the prospect of a world that will be ruled entirely by knowledge, reason, and brotherly love

SAINT-SIMON (1825)
Three stages of intellectual development usher in harmony and a Christian technocracy

COMTE (1830–1842)
Three stages of intellectual development usher in positivist thought, with the triumph of science and a rationalist religion of humanity

HEGEL (1820–1830)
A dialectical interplay moves all history, whose three stages of freedom usher in the freedom of all in a strong but just state

SPENCER (1850)
Natural forces move all things from the simple and alike to the complex and unlike, which in human affairs means moral and mechanical progress

BUCKLE (1857)
Intellect working under freedom achieves increasing order and power

MARX (1848–1867)
The dialectical movement is rooted in matter taking the form of economic production. Successive class struggles usher in freedom and justice in a state without need of government

DARWIN (1871)
Natural struggle and sexual selection produce higher societies that increasingly recognize civil and moral law

---

narrative history occur. For another, many of the works in this genre have been political and cultural forces in themselves. Augustine, Vico, Hegel, Comte, Marx—to name only a few— have influenced thought and action. As shown in Figures 12 and 13, the best-known philosophies of history fall into two categories, the linear and the cyclical. The former implies indefinite progress; the latter implies development and decay along a curve that brings civilizations back to their humble beginnings.

But apart from the fine fragments and the brilliant display of ingenuity, have the systematizers a use for the researcher working today? An indirect one, no doubt, yet important: their work shows how a scheme leads to a thorough review of large periods

FIGURE 13 *PHILOSOPHIES OF HISTORY: CYCLICAL PROGRESSION*

PLATO (388–368 B.C.)
1. Egyptian (?) fable of periodic destruction by fire
2. Tale of the lost Atlantis

LUCRETIUS (c. 55 B.C.)
Atoms form worlds and revert to atoms

VICO (A.D. 1725)
Progress of nations through divine, heroic, human stages and return to primitive

VOLTAIRE (1750)
Irregular recurrence and decay of high civilizations: four ages in 2,000 years

MALTHUS (1798)
The perpetual action of want, war, and disease keeps mankind from ever "perfecting" itself as hoped for by the *philosophes*

GOBINEAU (1853–1855)
Race mixture brings about and then destroys civilization

NIETZSCHE (1855–1889)
Necessity working through all things without interference from (nonexistent) spirit brings about the return of all events in exact sequence forever

FLINDERS PETRIE (1911)
Civilizations rise and die from the effects of size and complexity

SPENGLER (1918–1922)
Forms (morphology) determine cultural growth and breed decay, causing the death of the societies based upon them

TOYNBEE (1934–1955)
The organic response of civilizations to inner or outer challenges propels them until the spirit (psychological and religious) abandons them

---

Among the "cyclical historians" one can distinguish those who posit a periodic destruction followed by rebuilding; those who believe in an "organic" law of rise and fall; and those who infer "eternal recurrence" from laws of material necessity. As to this recurrence, Shakespeare wrote a striking quatrain in Sonnet 59:

> If there be nothing new, but that which is
> Hath been before, how are our brains beguiled
> Which, laboring for invention, bear amiss
> The second burden of a former child.

and brings about the breaking up and recasting of old patterns of understanding. In so doing, the philosophers of history have drawn attention to the importance of neglected classes of fact. Vico's revision of ancient history influenced legal and linguistic studies and in the nineteenth century helped establish the idea of social evolution. Hegel's dialectic of history reinforced the vision that regimes and nations are small things when compared with the sweep of civilization, and that the unfathomable agitation of human beings conceals the potency of new ideas and great movements. Marx led historians to study economic conditions in as much detail as political and military. Gobineau dwelt on the significance of culture and custom and the anthropological method. Petrie showed what phenomena were common to advanced civilizations—feminism, for example, and the urban life of the "mass man"—and helped destroy the faith in unending progress. Spengler gave sharper contour to the meaning of certain historical terms, such as "classic" and "Faustian," and drew seductive projections of certain ages, such as that of Louis XIV.[15] And Toynbee, besides strengthening the notion of a civilization as an historical unit, showed that the breakdown of civilizations comes not alone from external attacks but also from inner failures of nerve and brain.[16]

No philosopher has demonstrated "the laws" of history, and every one—Toynbee as much as Spengler, though differently—has violated the elementary canon of historiography by neglecting contrary evidence. They have forced facts into arbitrary classifications; given credence to the single cause; called into play the reductive fallacy—"this is nothing but—"; lost, in short, the imagination of the real, because of an overmastering desire for a principle that will explain the career of mankind. Systems, the researcher will conclude, are of incidental use; not what they assert but only what they suggest can be converted to the legitimate uses of reporting the past.

[15]*The Decline of the West,* New York, 1926 (authorized English translation of *Der Untergang des Abendlandes*), 1:174.

[16]In a closely argued thesis on the same vast subjects, William H. McNeill takes issue with the Spengler-Toynbee view that cultures "fall" as the result of internal defects or failures. He offers the counterproposition that the cultures of mankind have always been interrelated and that changes in their relative strengths are owing to periodic cultural "explosions" or "disturbances" that upset the established cultural balance in the world *The Rise of the West: A History of the Human Community* (1963, new ed. 1991).

Part II

WRITING, SPEAKING, AND PUBLISHING

CHAPTER 8

ORGANIZING: PARAGRAPH, CHAPTER, AND PART

The Function of Form and of Forms

Everything so far said in this book about researching and reporting has urged or implied the importance of Form. Without Form in every sense, the facts of the past, like the jumbled visions of a sleeper in a dream, elude us. The attentive researcher soon discovers another truth: facts and ideas in disorder cannot be conveyed to another's mind without loss and are hardly likely to remain very long in his own. The mind demands some degree of order and symmetry. A shop window in which the objects for sale had been thrown helter-skelter would not only give no pleasure to the passerby, but would make it hard for anybody to notice anything in particular.

As we said earlier, even a haphazard grouping has form of some kind, but when we speak of Form with approval we mean attractive and suitable form. Its role is continuous, for in the act of *im*pressing something on the mind, Form also *ex*presses. For example, in the sentence you have just read, the contrast of the ideas "impress" and express" is driven in, as well as brought out, by the echo between the two words and by a formal device: italicizing the first syllables of a pair of words partly alike. The same thing could be said without the device—but would it convey the meaning as well? True, one often distinguishes "contents" from "form," but this separation is abstract. We know the contents only through the form, though we may guess at what the contents would be if the form were more clear-cut. It is the duty of the researcher to make sure that the contents he is delivering are precisely those he intended. Form and intention should fit like skin on flesh.

In written matter, the most frequent failure of form is that which comes from wrong emphasis. A writer must distribute emphasis in the right places. Because the reader cannot give equal attention to every part, his mind needs guidance to those parts—of a sentence or a book—that must be attended to for a correct understanding. On the printed page, a "little form" such as italics is a signpost telling the reader what is stressed. A footnote is likewise a form, whose makeup and uses will be described later on. The larger forms—sentence, paragraph— have less definable ways of producing emphasis than italics or footnotes, but length, beginnings, interruptions, and internal arrangements are pointers too.

Right now, we shall look at the largest forms: part, chapter, and paragraph, which are the masses that impress the reader while expressing the truth. All direct the attention, and so does the shape of any passage taken at random, even though its form goes by no special name. Consider the difficulty of following and retaining the disjointed ideas in this extract from what is a most scholarly and valuable work:

The most important document for seventeenth-century balladry is the Percy MS. Of this, and of the editing which its contents appear to have undergone, something has already been said. It contains no less than forty-six ballads, often unfortunately left in fragments by Humphrey Pitt's housemaids, and of these no less than nineteen are not found elsewhere. Several types are represented. There is a second text of *Adam Bell*. There are eight ballads of Robin Hood, but of these only one is unique, the tale of *Guy of Gisborne*, which has already been traced as existing in some form as far back as 1475. That of *Friar Tuck* may also be of early origin. There are six ballads including four unique ones, the themes of which are taken from medieval romance. There are fourteen, five of them unique, which can only be described as imaginative. But a main interest of the collector appears to have been in historical ballads, of which there are no less than seventeen, eight unique ones and nine others. Perhaps some of these would be better described as pseudo-historical, or at the most quasi-historical. Of *Sir Aldingar* enough has perhaps been said. The personages of *Hugh Spencer* and *Sir John Butler* existed, but the incidents described in the ballads lack verification. Of the strictly historical ballads *Durham Field, Chevy Chase, Musselburgh Field,* and *Sir Andrew Barton* describe battles on land and sea between English and Scottish, and are written from an English standpoint. *The Rose of England*, which celebrates the coming of Henry VII and the battle of Bosworth, is on a purely English theme. So is *Thomas Cromwell*. And although the themes of *Earl Bothwell* and *King James* and *Brown* are Scottish, the tone is still English. The Scots are 'false' and 'cruel', and 'false Scotland' is contrasted with 'merry England'.[1]

The trouble with this passage, plainly, is that the facts have not been organized. The separate bits of information are all there, but the full meaning is not, because grouping, subordination, and logical links are missing. Ordinarily, the reader has not the time, and most often has not the knowledge, to put everything in its place and restore the intended meaning for himself. What the learned author has served up is his notes raw. If the word "form" by itself has become a term of praise, it is partly because the world recognizes what labor goes into achieving it. It takes effort to put everything where it belongs, to make one thing follow upon another, to leave nothing essential out. Form is always the result of a struggle.

A book reviewer's complaint adds to this maxim a piece of useful advice: "Within the various chapters, he tends to leave out those vital little phrases and sentences that relate the parts to the whole, that remind us what his point is, where he's going and where he's been." And since it is inspiring to see a

---

[1]Edmund K. Chambers, *English Literature at the Close of the Middle Ages* (Oxford, 1945), 162–163. Near the beginning it sounds as if *nineteen house-maids* are not found elsewhere.

workman at grips with his material, the student should read in the letters and diaries of Macaulay what an amount of thinking and worrying, of doing and undoing, went into composing the *History of England*.[2] When the first part was out Macaulay reread his work and then the eighth book of Thycydides,

which, I am sorry to say, I found much better than mine. . . . On the whole he is the first of historians. What is good in him is better than anything that can be found elsewhere. But his dry parts are dreadfully dry; and his arrangement is bad. Mere chronological order is not the order for a complicated narrative.[3]

A year later, still fretting about arrangement, Macaulay notes:

To make the narrative flow along as it ought, every part naturally springing from that which precedes; to carry the reader backward and forward across St. George's Channel without distracting his attention, is not easy. Yet it may be done. I believe that this art of transitions is as important, or nearly so, to history, as the art of narration.[4]

Nearly four years after this, when one might have assumed that long practice had brought facility, Macaulay is still fighting against the same odds as any other writer:

Chapter XIV will require a good deal of work. I toiled on it some hours, and now and then felt dispirited. But we must be resolute and work doggedly, as Johnson said. . . . Arrangement and transition are arts which I value much, but which I do not flatter myself that I have attained.[5]

And to conclude, a month later: "I worked hard at altering the arrangement of the first three chapters of the third volume. What

---

[2]In any edition of G. O. Tevelyan's *Life and Letters of Macaulay* the principal passages will be found under these dates: December 18, 1838; November 5, 1841, through July 1843; December 19, 1845; and July 17, 1848 ff.

[3]Trevelyan, op. cit., Diary, November 29–December 4, 1848.

[4]Ibid. (April 15, 1850).

[5]Ibid. (Diary, January 1, 1854).

labour it is to make a tolerable book, and how little readers know how much trouble the ordering of the parts has cost the writer!"[6]

"The ordering of the parts"—that is the first problem, once the writer has acquired a body of material and must design the book. Chronology, Macaulay tells us, is not the answer; its order will only produce chronicles, which are notoriously unreadable.

If not chronological, what other kind of order is there? The *topical*. This is the order dictated by subject instead of time. And subjects, as we saw in Chapter 2, are characterized by unity. They are units suitable for description. The reporter of events who wants to be read will adopt the topical order. Yes, but not without modification. The pure topical order, exhausting one topic and jumping to the next, will deprive a story of continuity and coherence. A history is a recital of events that took place in Time; this must never be forgotten. You kill interest as surely by leaving out the time sequence as by breaking up the natural clusters of ideas. Nothing replaces the strong effect of beholding one mass of facts *after* another, as we can verify by recalling those films of which we happened to see the second half first.

The two fundamental forms of organization may be contrasted by imagining a biography built on the one and then on the other plan:

CHRONOLOGICAL ORDER

X is born, goes to school, breaks his leg, learns to smoke, is expelled from college, studies law, meets and courts Jane Smith, finds a five-dollar bill, is called a liar, gets into towering rage, marries Susan Black, is elected mayor, goes fishing, is thought a radical, plays the stock market, suffers from asthma, sues paper for libel, reads in bed, loses senatorial race, employs bodyguard, is accused of treason, goes to Mayo Clinic, dies. Will probated, widow remarries, memoirs published.

The fault of a strict chronological order is that it mixes events great and small without due subordination and that it combines

[6]Ibid. (February 6, 1854).

incidents that occur only once with permanent truths about habits and tastes, character and belief: it is a parody of life. The mind asks for something better than this jumble and says: "One thing at a time," meaning that it wants one subject, one idea gone into thoroughly, even if the parts of it were separated by many years. Yet the purely topical treatment will not do either:

TOPICAL ORDER

1. Character: in boyhood, youth, maturity, old age
2. Hobbies: in boyhood, youth, maturity, old age
3. Health: in boyhood, youth, maturity, old age
4. Income: in boyhood, youth, maturity, old age
5. Friends: in boyhood, youth, maturity, old age

Such a run up and down a man's life span would be tedious in the extreme, and while entailing an enormous amount of repetition, would not leave a clear portrait. The only way therefore is *to combine, in all but the briefest narratives, the topical and the chronological arrangements.* "Combining" defines the task and suggests the difficulty.

The Steps in Organizing

In the combined form, the chronology moves forward while embracing each topic and giving an occasional backward or forward glance as needed. Each small section of the work deals with a topic or one of its natural subdivisions at some length, and *completely as far as that subject goes.*

The full bearing of this last sentence is important to grasp. Suppose, to continue our biographical example, that X's character is referred to in twenty places but is extensively discussed in three, these places corresponding to youth, maturity, and old age. In each place, enough must be said to engage the reader's interest and to settle whatever question X's character raises. Nothing is more annoying than to find a few facts in one spot, a judgment in another, then more details about the earlier events because a fresh incident brings them up, and elsewhere again a dispute with another writer about the previous judgment. Such scattering leaves a confused and often contradictory impression, coupled with the surmise that the writer himself has not cleared his own mind.

A biographer who was also a poet has given a vivid analogy for what has just been discussed. He described a famous stage performer named the Great Wieland, whose act

> consisted in spinning plates on a long trestle table. Starting with three or four, he would soon have a dozen spinning, and be obliged to run from one end of the table to the other, in order to give a reviving twist of the fingers to one that was on the point of collapse . . . the number of plates grew and grew, and the audience would cry out with excitement. . . . I saw him several times, and he never let a single plate wobble to a stop.
>
> Everyone who attempts to write an account of a complex period or undertaking sooner or later finds himself in the Great Wieland's position, though not always equipped with the same skill. A story has many aspects, all of which have to be kept alive in the reader's mind; concentrate on one and the others will fall; keep to a strict chronological sequence, and you will fail to trace the growth of individual elements; attend to every element, and you will have to dodge about in time, running like Wieland from one century back into the one before to keep interest alive.[7]

As Macaulay pointed out, the combining of Topic and Time calls for the art of Transition. The means of transition — words, sentences, paragraphs, sections — take the reader by the elbow, so to speak, and make him face in the right direction for the next topic. Transitions are devices of emphasis. They belong to Form and to forms, whether they are small words like "hence," "but," "accordingly," "nevertheless," or long passages that sum up and forecast in one pivoting movement of thought.

[7] L. A. G. Strong, *The Rolling Road* (London, 1956), 82.

The problem to solve can now be seen in its fullness: to be effective, a mass of words must have *its* proper Form, which must satisfy the conflicting demands of Unity (one thing at a time) and Chronology (a series of things one after the other). And it must also simultaneously hold the reader's interest through Coherence (smooth passage from one thing to another). To find this arrangement there is no formula.

Now go back to the stage where the researcher confronts the mass of notes he has taken. Its form, we hope, is not that of complete but of modified chaos. Thanks to system the cards or slips or notebook entries are indexed so as to produce (we will suppose) six broad categories.[8] To vary the example, instead of a biography imagine a piece of business history:

1. The founding of the company
2. First success and next twenty years
3. The big lawsuit
4. Reorganization fails
5. Takeover and expansion
6. Research and charitable enterprises
7. Present prospects

Apply a test: Are these matters equal in importance? If so, their treatment should be of approximately equal length. How long should the longest of these parts be? The stack of classified notes gives some idea. Supposing numbers 4 and 5 run to about fifty pages each, we see at once that the two largest of our six divisions must be thought of as parts and not chapters. (A fifty-page chapter, though not impossible, is ordinarily too long.) But our concern is now with chapters: we want to settle on some headings to cover subdivisions of equal and moderate length—say twenty-five to thirty double-spaced typewritten pages—7,500 to 9,000 words. Hence numbers 4 and 5, which are parts, amount together to four or five chapters.

[8]See p. 23.

The Chapter: Role, Size, and Title

A chapter is not a set form like the fourteen-line sonnet, but it has some of the properties of a set form: it has unity and completeness, and it may be assumed to have about the length just stated. The function of a chapter is to dispose of one good-sized topic comfortably and give the reader as much as he can take in at one sitting. It is also the right length for an essay. Moreover, if this approximate wordage is adopted for one chapter, it will generally be possible to make the others roughly equal. Making chapters fifteen or forty pages long would probably cause difficulties; one could not keep them relatively even. Of course, one can—sometimes must—vary the length from chapter to chapter, but there is a marked advantage to having similar units to juggle with in the search for the right sequence. Note that the longer the chapters, the fewer the breaking-off points in the work, and hence the fewer rearrangements that are possible. If the chapters are too brief, too many breaks occur and coherence gives way to choppiness.

With the goal of equal and rounded-off units in mind, the researcher turns back to his notes and finds, on matching them with his six divisions, that whereas numbers 1 and 2 (the founding of the company and first success and next twenty years) each propose a single topic falling neatly into a pair of chapters, the next two (the big lawsuit and reorganization fails) are badly entangled. The company's reorganization was proposed before the lawsuit, and this in fact brought on the case. Besides, the unsuccessful reorganization was the start of the next set of events (takeover and expansion). In short, the middle portion is one big snarl.

The solution is to start with one distinct subject that could be separated from the rest and see what this leaves. If it destroys all possibility of making a realignment that will fit chronology and topical unity, it is probably too large a piece. So, take a scrap of paper and jot down each successive chunk of material, until the pieces form "natural" clusters. These emerge whenever things hang together more than they do with neighboring matters. Going over one's notes slowly and watching for key words will help, but remember there is no substitute for imagination—"How would it be if—?" To make the trial and error progress, one makes successive tables of contents, that is, chapter headings that will have the same weight and one switches them till the series sounds convincing. One may wind up with something like this—the wording to be improved later:

1. Founding the company
2. Success and first twenty years
3. Cracking at the seams
4. The big lawsuit
5. Reorganization: new management inadequate
6. The year of the takeover
7. The conglomerate empire
8. Research and charitable enterprises
9. Present doldrums and prospects for the future

With nine units, the writer's previous estimate of c. 250 pages divides into chapters of plus or minus 25, as desired, allowing extras for notes and index.

Next, take a look at the foreseeable character of each chapter from the point of view of narrative: 1 and 2 have forward motion from the inevitable "background" through the early struggles to the end of twenty years full of persons and incidents. Then comes a more static chapter, cracking at the seams, which is largely descriptive and which resolves itself into a new drama, the big lawsuit.

After this there is description again, to make clear the reorganization; then the account moves ahead once more through the scrimmage of the takeover and the details of the subsidiaries added one by one to make up the conglomerate. Next comes a picture of the firm at its high point; then perhaps a backtracking to the very beginning: "Old Mr. Bradley had always wanted to add a research unit but not until . . . , and so on." The same for the outlays to education and the like. The story of these two side-enterprises keeps the reader moving back and forth from beginning to end and affords the reader a subtle review of the ground he has covered since page 1. To leave him there would be inconclusive. Hence, a chapter to tie all the loose ends together and close on the idea of prospects. To test the scheme, the writer must make sure that the several chapters add up to the story as a whole, with nothing left out and no overlapping of subjects, though with as many cross references as are necessary for internal clarity.

Composing: By Instinct or by Outline?

Having reached this point you are not at the end of your struggle, but you have something like a structure. It remains to allot your notes to each chapter, after which you begin with one chapter and try to construct *it*. The same considerations of chronology, topical unity, coherence, and transition apply throughout: the part, the chapter, and the paragraph should have equally sound Form. But there is a difference: for the paragraph, you cannot plan a structure. A series of paragraphs each built to one pattern like the pieces of a prefabricated house would be intolerable. The same holds for a chapter. These cautions raise the question of outlines.

Writers divide fairly evenly into those who find outlines useful or indispensable, and those to whom they are a nuisance. By all means use them if they do not cost you too much in time, work, and spontaneity. But do not force yourself if making them up does not come easily, or if once drawn up the outline drags you back. Certainly the best order for the parts of a paper is the order that comes out of one's sense of the subject and seems dictated by it. To a writer who develops that sense from the growth of the data under his hand, the outline is bound to feel stiff and suspiciously logical. When the time comes to fill it out, the material runs away and the outline loses control over the enterprise. Conscience then inspires vain efforts to patch up the outline while groping for new transitions where the writing got off the prearranged track.

For such a writer the better procedure is to use the outline not as a guide beforehand but as a verifier afterward. We may picture the sequence of events something like this: you have set aside all but one batch of organized notes. A run through them (yes, once again) suggests that they fall quite evidently into three subgroups—perhaps four or five, but three is normal because every subject and subsubject has a beginning (exposition), a middle (complication), and an end (resolution or conclusion).

You now have a small number of smaller piles and notes.[9] You take the first pile in order, shuffle its contents until a rough sequence is established not so much in the cards as in your mind. You put them to one side and start writing. Some people need to look at their notes while composing; others prefer to gaze on the subject with the inner eye of memory and imagination. In either case the mind must take part in the work. Composing does not consist in merely blowing up each note to full grammatical size and tacking it on to the next; it consists—at least if you want to be read with any pleasure—in *thinking* your subject from A to Z just as you want your reader to grasp it.

Your ideas pull one another out of the wordless dark into the articulate light—you are writing ahead. Your facts and ideas dovetail naturally, with only occasional effort, even when the words halt and have to be changed. Incomplete or rough, the sequence of expressions corresponds to the understanding you have gained by reflection on top of research. The frequent rereading of the notes has made you feel that you know the story by heart; you can recount it. The *story* flows despite your pen's stuttering. Suddenly, you run into a snag. It may be one of two kinds: the course you are on obviously leads to the spot you see ahead, but at your feet there yawns a gap. How to get across?

---

[9]If the notes are not on cards or detached slips, the sorting is done by a further, more exact marginal indexing. This suits people who prefer not to handle or look at their notes while writing, but who arrange them mentally and simply refresh their memory now and again by consulting the notebook.

FIGURE **14** *The Use of Card Notes in Organizing*

18

E 807. W328 1989
Chicago Pub. Lib.

Ward, Geoffrey C.
A First-class Temperament:
The Emergence of Franklin Roosevelt
New York, Harper & Row, 1989
XVI, 889 p.
(good on relations with
mother. Also excellent index)

18

FDR at Wh. Hse 5/15/18 waiting with Pet
al for first airmail from My Al
Smith's name came up as NY gov.
possibility. FDR said Smith being
Catholic would have trouble upstate
H. demurred — improper concern when
youths of all faiths suffering war
casualties.
pp. 381-2

As recommended before, the systematic researcher uses two cards, a book card and a note card for the extracts. The book card contains the book citation and records the call number and the library where the book was found, plus any time-saving comments as to its features and value. The researcher gives each book card a serial number, which saves the trouble of repeating the citation on each note card. The book cards are kept in numerical order until rearranged for making up the bibliography. The note card is keyed to the book card by a number in the upper left-hand corner.

FIGURE 15   *INCORPORATING THE NOTE INTO THE OUTLINE*

---

18   III B 2 a

FDR at 2th Hse 5/15/18 waiting with Pet
al for first airmail from NY. Al
Smith's name came up as NY gov
possibility. FDR said Smith being
Catholic would have trouble upstate
H. demurred — improper concern when
youths of all faiths suffering war
casualties.

                                     pp. 381-2

The researcher who uses an outline has assigned numbers and letters in the usual way to each head and subhead of the outline. When ready to write any one portion of his work, he goes through the cards, sorting and marking them with the letters and numbers that show where they belong. In this case, the note has been assigned to section III B2a as shown in the upper right-hand corner.

The answer lies in another question: Is it a fact that is wanting to connect the parts? If so it must be obtained—later. Or is it an idea, a transition? If so, mark the spot by some conventional sign in the margin, an *X* or a wavy line, pick up the thread wherever you can, and keep going.

The lack of certain facts is important to discover at this stage, and the way of composing here recommended offers the advantage that by going mentally from next to next you discover the flaws as you would if you were a reader. If you merely sew your notes together as they occur in the bundles of your first classification, you will probably conceal the gaps and the reader will discover them. If what you lack is a deft transition, do not rack your brains. When you come to revise your first draft the right words may pop into your head, or else you will quickly see what small rearrangements will bring the gaping edges together.

Troubleshooting after Lapses

The lack of proper order and connection, of *composition* in the strict sense, is most glaring in the narration of physical events, where our daily experience supplies an immediate test. Here is an example:

> There was an office facing them, at the rear of the hall, and a man and woman were regarding them from a box window which opened above a ledge on which lay a register book. They were middle-aged folk: [a] man [and a] woman, . . . who examined the newcomers with enquiring gaze. [10]

In reading fast, one may not notice the double flaw in this description. But just visualize what happens (as any reader of a report is entitled to do): in line 1 a man and a woman are looking at the newcomers as they enter. Immediately before and after, the newcomers survey the box window, ledge, register— all quite uninteresting compared with the two gazing at them; the reader has to shift from one set of observers to another. And at the end, after a long description here omitted, the pair are still "examining the newcomers with an enquiring gaze" as they were doing four lines above.

The second kind of snag in writing is the discovery that you have steered around in a circle. The natural linking of ideas, instead of moving you ahead, has brought you back to a point earlier in your story. In this predicament a scratch outline, made on the spot, can serve as straightener. Cast your eye back to your beginning, jotting down as you go the main and secondary

[10]J. S. Fletcher, *The Middle Temple Murder* (1919), 36.

ideas, using the same key word for each idea that belongs to one subject, being sure to reduce each sentence to its simplest thought in order to classify it; otherwise you will not clear up the mess. You find where you got off the track by seeing where, let us say, ideas E, F, G, and H were followed by F again. This may have led you to avoid a second G and H. You leaped ahead to K, then felt disquieted by the chasm and stopped to take stock.

The solution is scissors and paste.[11] Cut out the intruding ideas but keep any good passage that you have written (K), though it is out of place, and set it aside. Go back to the good original section (E F G H), see if there is anything valuable in the second reference to F, inserting it near the first if desirable, and throw away the rest. Sew together any wounds created by this surgery and keep looking ahead until the place for K comes in sight. Remember that for these remedial purposes all subjects have not one but a dozen handles to grasp them by. Depending on which you seize and which you present to be seized, you produce logical flow or jerkiness.

Here are figures to make the procedure clear. S is a subject with branches radiating from it—relevant circumstances that you want to mention in order to build up the unity of S. But along each branch is a point where you can get so far from the round core that you cannot get back. The dotted line marks how far you can go without getting stranded. Bear in mind that S, when completed, must present a link to another topic, T. If you go beyond the end of S_5, you will never come within reach of T_1. A little foresight tells you that by keeping in sight the core of S and making the last of your journey S_5 you can easily seize hold of T_1.

This way of working will help you to link chapters as well as subsections. There is always some topic that can come at the end of the chapter to relate it to the next, and that supplies a

---

[11]Or the equivalent operation on your computer, see pp. 281, 293f.

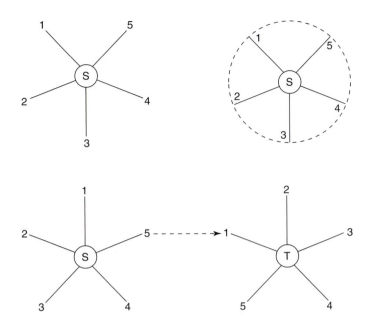

good beginning for the chapter following. Interlocking ideas makes for a tight book, yet it is not invariably necessary to fashion this kind of chain. Sometimes a new chapter will hark back to a much earlier topic in order to throw light on the forthcoming facts, and this backward jump often provides variety in what would otherwise be a forced march at a relentless pace.

No matter what is to be done at a given spot, it is indispensable to give the reader a clue. He will follow with docility for many paragraphs if the road is straight or gently winding. But if you want him to turn a corner you must firmly guide him: "We now see why in those years when . . ."; or "From that day when he met his future wife"; or "Casting our minds ahead of the point we have reached"; or "Before we can understand the issue at stake, we must recall (or examine or describe)"; and so on. It is amazing what a reader will gladly absorb if he is occasionally told why and given a hint of where the facts will take him.

These exceptions to the rule of always going forward are inherent in topical treatment. Look again at the table of contents made up for the company history. In Chapter 8 the reader is brought back to the beginning twice. When this is necessary, the trip forward should be speeded up in such a way that any needed repetition is made to seem new; otherwise the reader has the feeling of being on a merry-go-round.

The most frequent cause of interference with forward motion and straight chronology occurs oddly enough at the start of a book or article. The reason is that a subject can begin in one of two ways: the natural one, which research has discovered, and the conventional one, which is whatever the reader is assumed to know. This pair must be reduced to one by compromise between the two or postponement of the less enticing. A writer whose work calls for sustained attention through many pages wants to grip the readers from the outset and engage them so completely that they will be compelled to turn the pages. The first chapter of any book, the first page of any report, the first paragraph of any review are tests of the art of composition. Where they break into the subject, what goes into them, how they insert themselves into the reader's stream of thought and stock of knowledge, and what they promise of future interest, are so many delicate questions asking for answers.

Films use the flashback as one kind of answer, one that is as old as Homer's *Iliad*. In scholarship, the device, well handled, justifies itself. Take Lionel Trilling's *Matthew Arnold*. The logical beginning is Chapter 2, entitled "His Father and His England." But the effective beginning is the first chapter, mysteriously entitled "A," which opens with this beguiling sentence: "The secretary of old Lord Lansdowne, the liberal peer, was a singularly handsome young man, whose manners were Olympian and whose waistcoats were remarkable." After this one certainly wants to know more, which is not a feeling that always occurs at the sight of every block of print.

Altering the normal order can also be used to take care of conditions to be gone into before the subject proper. A smooth transition to the main topic is then called for. Thus Macaulay's *History* begins with a statement of his purpose, which is to write the story of England from the accession of James II to recent times. But for this he must give "the background," and we hear about Celtic Britain, the Norman Conquest, the Papacy, and a quantity of other familiar landmarks, followed by some of the main themes of the work, presented in their earliest historical forms, the whole moving forward in seven-league boots.

His Chapter 2 is chronologically more unified and static: it surveys the political and religious history of the seventeenth century and ends with mention of the death of Charles II. Chapter 3, famous as "Macaulay's Third Chapter," is panoramic. It is a bird's-eye view of social and cultural England in 1685. We are by then on the spot and almost at the time of the true opening. Chapter 4 catches up the end left dangling in 2 by *describing* the death of Charles II, and with the words "That morning . . ." we are finally at the "natural" starting point announced some 200 pages back.[12]

A good beginning is good not only for the reader but also for the writer. It is like a running start, or rather, like propulsion from a rifled barrel: it keeps one going in a straight line. Yet it often happens that the perfect beginning cannot be found by

---

[12]Macaulay worried about a proper beginning for a long time. "The great difficulty of a work of this kind," he wrote ten years before its publication, "is the beginning. How is it to be joined on to the preceding events? Where am I to commence it? I cannot plunge, slap dash, into the middle of events and characters. I cannot, on the other hand, write a history of the whole reign of James the Second as a preface to the history of William the Third. If I did, a history of Charles the Second would still be necessary as a preface to that of the reign of James the Second. I sympathise with the poor man who began the war of Troy *'gemino ab ovo'* [starting with the egg from which Helen—the cause of the war—was born]. But, after much consideration, I think I can manage, by the help of an introductory chapter or two, to glide imperceptibly into the full current of my narrative" (Diary in Trevelyan, op. cit., December 18, 1838).

mere thought. You choose what you think good and start writing, but the thought wanders, the facts do not fall in naturally. In this situation, keep on for a time until a direction becomes clear. When you have finished six or eight pages, reread, and you will generally find that somewhere on page 2 or 3 is the true place to start. What went before was akin to a dog's walking round and round to beat down the grass before settling down.

The Book Review and the Paragraph

We have been talking about books. You may believe that you are not ready to compose on the large scale. Is it possible to shrink all this advice to the dimensions of a short piece and—equally useful—to the dimensions of a paragraph? The answer is Yes as regards the short piece. The more practiced you become in the composition of papers ranging from the three-page book review to the thirty-page report, the better you will be able to handle the chapter and the planning of the book.

The longish report (forty to fifty pages) should be considered as a miniature book rather than an enlarged essay. It has "chapters" and possibly "parts" of its own, though the so-called chapters may be as short as five pages. For these subdivisions it is helpful to have headings, though they are not indispensable. What is essential is that the sections be separated, by numerals or by blank spaces. An unbroken stretch of many pages is hard to read, even in a novel, and very hard to compose. The writer needs mileposts, just as the reader needs breathing space.

For writers of the shorter forms, here is a set of suggestions about the book review. We will assume that it is written for a periodical, where the space allotted will usually not exceed 1,500 words. The beginning, we know, is important. The first of your ten paragraphs or so should present an idea of interest to the readers who will leaf through the journal. If your first words are "This book . . ." they will not be able to distinguish your review from perhaps six others, and they will be entitled to conclude that you have not expended much thought on enlisting their attention. The opening statement takes the readers from where they presumably stand in point of knowledge and brings them to the book under review. The briefest possible description of its aim, scope, and place in the world therefore follows the baited opening sentence and completes the first paragraph.

The second classifies the book: what thesis, tendency, bias does it uphold, suggest, evince? Paragraphs 3 to 5 go into the author's main contentions and discuss them. Do not repeat anything you said in the classificatory paragraph, but rather give detailed evidence of the grounds for your classification.

Paragraphs 6 and 7 may deal with additional or contrary points to be found in other authors or in your own research; but so far, these only amend or qualify what is acceptable in the new book. In 8 and 9 you deliver your chief objections and summarize shortcomings. If you have found errors, mention only the important ones—do not waste space on typographical or minor slips. From errors you modulate into the broad field: how is our conception of it changed by the book? What further work is needed to clear up doubtful points? Where have gaps been left that must be filled? You have now one more paragraph in which to strike a balance of merits and faults, ending with some words about the author—*not* yourself or the subject.

For with book reviewing goes a moral obligation: you hold the author's fate in your hands as far as one group of readers is concerned. Author and work should, through you, be given the floor. What you say in the review will, rightly or wrongly, be taken seriously. You are in honor bound to be scrupulously fair. Never use the author's admissions against him, saying, "Mr. X entirely neglects the foreign implications," when it was he who warned you of this in the preface. Do not expect him to have written the book *you* have in mind. Recognize the amount of work that has gone into the product and be magnanimous: you may be severe on serious faults of interpretation and inference; but unless minor ones are continual, forget them while you concentrate on avoiding yours.

More than in the long work, article, or report, it is in the paragraph that the writer's yearning for freedom can be indulged—up to a point. There is no formula for beginning or ending paragraphs that will not produce a dull, mechanical sound. The topic sentence, as its name indicates, comes early and announces the topic. But especially in reporting events, the topic sentence does not always live up to its promise of unifying the paragraph. It is often used by good writers from habit, but composing such sentences one after the other is a mistake. Ask yourself, rather, what intertwined subjects the dozen lines of print will contain; what is the little core *S* and what are the branches it sends out as you employ your facts and use your ideas to join them. In the paragraph as elsewhere this is a matter of linkage. The fault in the paragraph quoted at the beginning of this chapter is not the lack of a topic sentence: it has one; the fault is that the ensuing facts and ideas are not firmly tied together by kinds but loosely associated.

Linking can be systematically practiced until it becomes habitual. In general—but only in general—the good writer makes the last thought in sentence A suggest the first thought in sentence B. At its most rigid this would give us the pattern: "Henry Adams has written a book. The book is a history of the Jefferson and Madison administrations. Those administrations cover the years 1801–1817. Those years were notable for . . . ," and so on. Perfect coherence but grisly reading. The coherence to aim at is that of a normally constituted mind, which likes variety in continuity. If in revising your first draft your mind as reader is not satisfied with your mind as writer, make a mental note of the sort of jumpiness that ails you in composing. No writer attains adequate coherence throughout a first draft. Everyone *must* revise, which means cut, add missing links, catch and kill repetitions—in short, we tinker to improve and polish.

These operations will in time become second nature, but at first the tendency when reading over one's copy is to find it perfectly lucid and forceful, not to say sublime. This is because the mind that has framed it keeps on supplying its deficiencies through the memory of what was meant. One must therefore lay aside one's manuscript for several days and return to it as if it were written by someone else. And since this may not provoke sufficient self-criticism, one must scan each statement for its accuracy of form as well as relevance of contents, the two virtues required of our work before it is sent on its journey to printer and public.

CHAPTER 9

PLAIN WORDS: THE WAR ON JARGON AND CLICHÉS

Keep Aware of Words

To the general public "revise" is a noble word and "tinker" is a trivial one, but to the writer the difference between them is only the difference between the details of the hard work and the effect it achieves. The successful revision of a book in typescript or on screen is made up of an appalling number of small, local alterations. Short of the total recasting of a passage, revision is nothing but steady tinkering.

Apprenticeship under a vigilant critic will gradually teach a novice writer how to find or change all the wrong or clumsy words that bespangle every first draft. The image of tailoring that the word "alterations" connotes is a good one to bear in mind. A first draft is blundering and stiff—you must shorten something here, lengthen it there, move a stop or a link forward or back, smooth out a wrinkle, make the garment fit. The words are not only the garment of the thought, they are its body as well; so that the pulling and adjusting has to go on until the thought you hoped to present and the thought on paper coincide and displace the wrong thought or no-thought that got written down at first.

This operation suggests what we must do to start our custom-tailoring: learn to see what does not fit. Whoever wants to write

193

and be read must develop a new habit of attending to words—
not just the important words on occasions of formal writing,
but to all words at all times. A student of painting does not
think it outside his duty to attend at all times to shape and
color, or a musician to sounds and rhythms. The good writer
has developed for words the eye of a jewel expert who knows
the worth of his gems at a glance. The word expert is able to
juggle each term's multiple meanings with ease. When words
form sentences, he must be as alive as a lover or a diplomat to
the shades they convey through their overtones; he is aware
of his audience and thus of the proper tone for the particular
message. In short, the writer is fully conscious, and whatever
he is writing has a peculiar purpose. Out of these two necessities
comes the doctrine of the *mot juste,* or "inevitable word" for a
given spot, proper words in proper places. Unfortunately, the
inevitable here is something most of us are able to avoid with
the greatest of ease. Take an example:

> Although this book differs from Harrisse's on Columbus, it is also
> important.

At least three words in this sentence are improper and darken
understanding: "although," "differs," and "also." How does one
come to see this? "Although" and "also" taken together imply
that a book which "differs" from a certain other book is not
important. And "differs" by itself is absurd, since every work
differs from every other. The writer probably meant something
like this: "Although this book disputes Harrisse's views on
many points, it is not negligible," or "its interpretation is valuable." But more likely still, he had no such formulated idea.
What he wanted to say was: "Here is a book; it opposes
Harrisse's view on Columbus; I think it important."

There is of course nothing criminal in writing a first draft
full of such non-sense, or to begin with jerky, simpleminded
remarks. The important thing is that in the next draft the writer
should have moved away from both these faults and produced
a mature and tenable statement. You discover what you really

think by hacking away at your first spontaneous utterance. How to give your idea its definitive form is the subject of the next chapter. In this one we are concerned with the first step, which is to discover where your words make your idea *un*tenable. The sole method is: an unremitting scrutiny of words.

The State of the Language

The modern assumption that all words in current use are good enough to carry the meaning intended by the user is hardly borne out in practice. One continually hears of "failure of communication" as the cause of some mishap, trivial or serious. In part this is because the language has undergone influences that have much increased the degree of confusion that is normal at most times and that careful writers disentangle as they work.

The researcher who has taken pains to verify his findings and wants them received by others as precisely as possible, must overcome many and insidious obstacles. For one thing, his early schooling has probably failed to impart the techniques of plain writing; for another, everybody is exposed through print and broadcast to a stream of vague or misleading expressions that come to mind first in one's own speech. Take the common "let me address the issue very briefly." Does *address* mean *describe, discuss, make clear, deal with, settle?* And is the *issue* a *difficulty, question, objection, puzzle,* or *predicament?* The listener gets a drift and not a meaning. Equally bad is the effort to counter the recurrent *address* by sounding "fancy" through deliberate misuse, as in: "I wanted to *engage* the Big Bang theory with new objections." It is no less vague and it spoils a good word.

Corruptions of grammar affect the choice of tenses: "If she knew about his early days she may not have married him." This mixes "If she knows, she may not marry" with "If she had known, she might not have." Worse, because ambiguous, is the neglect of the subjunctive: "The court insists that the procedure is followed." Is the court defending its performance? The *is* says so.

Or is the court demanding of others that the procedure *be* (= should be) followed?—quite a difference.[1]

The writer eager to improve will make his task easier if he labels the types of malpractice to which the modern vernacular invites. It will help to spot them and to keep weeding them out of first drafts. The main types are: (1) Jargon, (2) Vogue Words, (3) Neologisms, (4) Misused and Misplaced Technicalities, (5) Failure to Follow Distinctions, (6) Malaprops, (7) Twisted Idioms, (8) Wrong Prepositions, (9) Misdirected Verbs, (10) Faulty Constructions, (11) Figurative Phrasing, and (12) Euphemisms. For a sampling of each kind, see Figure 18, p. 209.

Jargon: Origin and Sources

Critics of current prose often refer to all the offenses just listed as Jargon. In its original form jargon is legitimate; it is the special tongue of a trade or art—what we now call technical terms—of music or carpentry or sailing. These terms are indispensable; they usually have no synonyms and must be accepted regardless of form or logic. When you discover that to a sailor the "main-sheet" is not a sail but a rope, there is nothing you can do about

---

[1]In view of this cluster of dangers to prose, the dictionary becomes the needed guide to root meanings and the thesaurus (Roget's is fuller than that found on your computer program) a treasury of replacements for words worn threadbare. For questions of grammar and usage, a good many manuals are available, their growing number in recent years testifying to the increasing muddle and the desire to avoid its contagion. Here are recommendations. The two pioneer works, Fowler's *Modern English Usage* and Gowers' *Plain Words* can still instruct about principles. (This cannot be said of the two revisions of Fowler.) Consult Wilson Follett's *Modern American Usage* (2nd ed., 1999), which imparts correctness without compromise. Bryan A. Garner's *Dictionary of American Usage* (2000) is more latitudinarian and adds some instruction in grammar at large. For advice on diction, syntax, and composition, the well-known and justly popular *Elements of Style* by Strunk and White supplies the basics, and *Simple & Direct* by Jacques Barzun (4th ed., 2001) covers the subject in detail and on the main topics gives groups of sentences for practice in correcting.

it; and all professionals keep it clear by using it correctly. Do the same for the common tongue.

Like jargon, most vogue words are good in their original sense. It is when *agenda* is continually used for *hidden purpose* or *secret plan* that it becomes false and tedious. Mindless repetition for a wrong purpose is what makes vogue words vague. So every variety of faddish wordage should rightly be called pseudo-jargon. Its source is the wide world of affairs. Advertising pelts us with slogans to make ordinary objects alluring; bureaucrats think they enliven their routine by changing its vocabulary; statesmen and journalists try to hold our attention with catch-words and metaphors.[2] All this is an indirect tribute to poetry, but the residue left in the mind is "jargon."

A final caution: do not be tempted to make things easier for your reader by creating acronyms and sets of initials. There are enough in circulation to tax the most retentive memory,[3] and many mean four or five different things. If your subject calls for discussing the General Research Division of the Tutankhamen Intercontinental Foundation, squelch the impulse to juggle with GRDTI and its BOT and SFD—the Board of Trustees and the Special Field Director. Readers will follow your thought if you refer simply to the division, the board, the director, and other suitable variants: the foundation, the organization, the section, the trustees, the head; each is chosen as it suits best the topic at hand. With the ugly rash off the page, your text will be a pleasure to read.

In view of these dangers, the dictionary becomes the chief reference work on the researcher's shelf—or rather on his desk—to be used more often than is necessary, so as to make sure that

[2]William Safire in his *New York Times* Sunday column studies the products of this factory, traces their origin, records their passing, and discusses their approximate meaning.

[3]To uncover the meaning of a term that is hiding under a set of initials, consult *Acronyms, Initialisms, & Abbreviations Dictionary,* 3 vols., 1991. It contains more than half a million entries and it is kept up to date by supplements. Jennifer Mossman, its compiler, has also provided a *Dictionary of Medical and Health Acronyms* (1991).

the words he knows "perfectly well" are not in fact words that he knows *im*perfectly.[4] The chances are good, for example, that more than one reader of this book did not appreciate the distinction on p. 69n between *genuine* and *authentic*. And in some contexts at least, they probably use with false or blurred meanings such words as *connive, drastic, disinterested, deprecate, minimize, suppositious, evince,* and *decimate*. They probably neglect the useful difference between such pairs as *specific* and *particular, nomenclature* and *terminology, growth* and *development, component* and *constituent, mixture* and *compound, autonomy* and *independence, constant* and *continual*—in short, they find synonyms on every hand, whereas an amusing tradition has it that English can show but one pair of exact synonyms, namely, "gorse" and "furze."

Be Strict about Signposts

Unfortunately, some of the most important words you cannot, in a sense, look up. The small guiding and linking words that recur on every page are plain without definition. But do you sufficiently query their fitness in your prose? An "although," an "also," a "but," a "because" can overthrow your meaning while your attention flags. It might be supposed that anyone who writes English at all would know how to use "a" and "the" and avoid confusing them. But scanning one's language to make sure of small distinctions is so out of favor nowadays that the misuse of the definite and indefinite articles is continual. Look at this sentence: "She then married the relative of the theater manager." One might make a guessing game out of such statements: "How many relatives did the theater manager have?" Again, one reads reports of "an ailing so-and-so." Surely it is *the* ailing public figure, not one of an assortment bearing the same name.

---

[4]For writers, regardless of specialization, the desk dictionary recommended here is *Webster's New World College Dictionary* (4th ed., 2001), though some may prefer *The American Heritage Dictionary of the English Language* (4th ed., 2000), which is more permissive.

FIGURE **16** *Brevity Not Always the Soul of Wit*

"Hopkins, YR. ABRV. ENG. STMTS. LV. MCH. 2 B DSRD."

Even an occasional use of abbreviations, unless they are the most common and universal, is discourteous to the reader. This maxim does not relate to technical discourse. For computer language see p. 295 and n.

Other writers misuse "but," making it an elegant variation of "and," or as a universal joint with no distinct meaning: "The company overextended its operations in hopes of stimulating its liquid position, but the disastrous end product was not hard to foresee." "But" marks an opposition, and in this sequence of ideas there is none. The word serves here merely to connect the last idea with each of the two that precede. The first idea, which ends with "operations," requires "and" to tie it to the third, since there is no opposition between overextension and bad consequences; there *is* opposition between the high hopes and the bad results that followed. Hence the misleading "but." The sentence is a bad mix and must be recast. (Avoid also the frequent doubling of the sense in "but nor was there any reason for alarm." *Nor* is sufficient to mark the opposition contained in *but*.)

The same caution applies to the myriad "howevers" that dot the printed page, usually at the head of the sentence. With some writers this mannerism says no more than that they are taking breath: ". . . escalation of the war . . . Aahh—however, . . . bitter criticism is being expressed everywhere . . . Aahh—however, . . . the enemy is not surrendering. Aahh—however, . . ."

The severe scrutiny recommended for *a, the, and, but, however* is to be applied to all other linking words. They are signals that guide the thought along its proper path and they must be kept accurate. On this ground the doublings—*and/or, as to whether, if and when, unless and until*—are not only clumsy, but also needless, which is enough to condemn them. If you understand the meaning of *or*, you see that it includes *and*; if you know how to use *whether*, you spare your readers the redundance of *as to whether*; if you grasp the force of *if*, you perceive that it provides for *when*.

Picture All Verbal Images

When we pass from link words to nouns and verbs, the test is concreteness and lucidity. You ask your words: Can this be touched or seen? If you write long strings of abstract nouns and use "have" or "are" and the passive voice instead of strong active verbs, your thought will be akin to a faded photograph. Try reading this at a normal speed and then try to recall what it says.

Our organization has by common consent now achieved its objective of amplifying our groundbreaking position on the cutting edge of policy determination facilitation for the areas and fields contemplated by the innovation delineated in our mission statement, the first in the field more than a decade ago, and the result of the passage of time has only proved the consolidation of our basic thrust of ascertaining and packaging policy ammunition modules in graded calibration to the end of immediate adaptable utilization by decision makers without further modification for the specific use intended by lawmakers and all responsible agents of management alike.

The sentence is too long, lacks concrete nouns and active verbs, and defies the rhythm of speech. The result is a general haze.

The tendency of our culture, steeped as it is in technicalities, is to seek them out for common use or make-up fakes that sound technical. Take *venue*. Its technical sense is legal, the geographical place of a trial. So in other contexts the right word lies somewhere in a long list of words denoting *place: site, locale, district, ground, yard, zone, lawn, environment, surroundings,* and so on up to *heaven* and *hell,* together with *house, hall, theater, school, dwelling, home, castle, jail, cellar, bunker* and so on down to the grave.

These replacements for *venue* make clear the merits of concrete terms. What we here call "cover words" are made up to dwell in abstractions. A *facility* covers buildings, parking lot, wire fence, and speed zone, which usually need neither mention nor cover. Building is enough. Writers who justly fear overabstraction, try to avoid it by figurative language and bright, "efficient" words that happen to be in vogue. These too are objectionable: they recur too often, grow stale quickly, and even while fresh sound unpleasantly smart.

To the alert mind, all words convey an image—the representation more or less vivid of an act or a situation. When we say "do you grasp my meaning?" the listener half pictures a hand seizing something. When the answer is "No, I don't get you," the image is less vivid, yet it is clearly in the same plane: both remarks depict taking hold. In hasty speaking or writing one easily passes from image to image, saying perhaps: "It is difficult to grasp a meaning that is couched in florid language." The three images of "seizing," "lying on a bed," and "adorned as with flowers" do not develop a single coherent image, and though the result is intelligible enough it is neither sharp nor strong. Most of us think in such loosely connected images; conscious writers make an effort to trim and adjust them. The fear of "mixed metaphor" has become a bugbear because it can be ludicrous, but incoherent imagery often passes unnoticed by both writer and reader. What is the harm? The harm is that it conceals all or part of the meaning.

Consider the passage examined on p. 201; it is general and indefinite: what did the company do when they "overextended operations"? How did they think this was going to help them? What *was* the disastrous result? Let us suppose some facts: the company opened ten new branch stores, hoping that the money would roll in and add to the cash balance. But half the stores failed and the firm sank deeper into debt. If this is what happened, why not say so? We then *see* something and pass judgment upon it. The images raised go together; they put us in the very presence of the overextension, the hope, the stimulus, the "liquid position" (here a technical term), and the "end product."

The merit of this rewording is practical. Given a chance to *see,* a vigilant stockholder could have *foreseen* and said, "It can't be done. The installation of the new stores will eat up our profits for six months and the company needs cash in less than three. I move a vote of No Confidence in the Board of Directors." Imagery, if familiar enough and put together plausibly, will lull the half-attentive into accepting any amount of nonsense.

Analyze the following sentences taken at random from the inexhaustible supply in one's daily reading matter:

On the offensive side, the Air Force foresees a lethally vital future for its intercontinental strategic missiles.

But it was another [court] case that plummeted Carpenter to the pinnacle of the Wisconsin bar.

While on the money side of our business a point worth noting is the trend which continues to develop in commercial banking with respect to deposit growth.

And from student work:

The workers were pressed into back-to-back houses like sardines in a rabbit-warren.

Such were the innovative solutions which could foreground a shifting of boundaries between the problems.

The habitual maker of such visual monsters may from time to time catch himself at it and remove them. But most of the time he or she will continue to frame sentences made up of expressions like "integrate the major material," "a context that lends perspective," "a background that ushers in the realization of," or "drafted with a loophole which is now in the hands of the secretary." The authors of these improbabilities were in a state of waking sleep, like the reporter who in describing the setting of an outdoor game wrote: "The birds filled the tree-tops with their morning song, making the air moist, cool, and pleasant."[5]

Decide Which Images Are Alive

The test of the images that tempt us to put them on paper is twofold: are they alive and are they compatible? Since most words have the power to raise images, it would be impossible to write if some of these images were not neutralized by their remoteness or deadness. For example, when a supermarket chain is said to "open a branch" the image is dead—as in supermarket *chain*—and therefore acceptable. If our literal vision were aroused, the phrase would be absurd. "To stimulate conversation" is also a dead image; the two ideas of a push given and a man speaking produce no clash of images. But as we saw

[5]Quoted by William James in *Principles of Psychology* (1890, 1:263).

above, "stimulate" (or "rebuilding") and "liquid position" do clash. On coming together the two expressions spring into life again and draw attention away from meaning by their incongruity. They arise suddenly in some advertising, political, or academic circle, and they catch on, for no apparent reason but novelty and modishness.

In the sentence containing "liquid position" occurs the term "end product." Jargon lovers prefer this phrase to the simple "product." Now it is conceivable that in some industries it may avoid confusion to distinguish between by-products and end products. But in ordinary speech no such need exists. "End product," "end result" are tiresome tautologies. The first was particularly uncalled for above, where the meaning is actually "consequence," and not "product." But perhaps we should be grateful that we do not as yet hear of the "end consequence," "end outcome," and "end upshot."

In the light of these objections the conscientious writer will train himself to resist the laziness implicit in all tricks of speech, all ready-made expressions that sound clever-new (or once did), all hackneyed tags and quotations, all seeming shortcuts—for example, the tacking on of "-wise" to some other word as a quick way to get nothing said: "The two nations got together tradewise." (Started to trade? increased their trade? signed a trade agreement?) He will avoid the same trick with "-conscious" and "-minded"—for example, "community-conscious" and "air-minded"—and will not pile up nouns without connectives as in "child sex education" and "population theory evidence." The lesson here is: to be heard and heeded you must do more than lay your ideas side by side; you must *articulate* them.

Finally, do not substitute semi-synonyms for the words that say something outright; avoid, for example, the widely prevalent use of "feel" for "think"—"Whitehead feels that Nature is a continuum." He does no such thing: he thinks, believes, argues, maintains, assumes, supposes, posits, postulates, imagines, demonstrates, proves—which is it? The same flabbiness occurs in "Karl Marx had the benefit of Engels's thinking" (i.e., Engels's thought, views, opinions, knowledge, advice, etc.).

FIGURE **17** *THERE IS NO FORMULA FOR STYLE*

"'It was the best of times, it was the worst of times . . .'
For goodness sake, Mr. Dickens, make up your mind!"

The truculent editor is quoting the famous opening words of Dickens's novel about the French Revolution, *A Tale of Two Cities*. The remainder of the paragraph keeps on with strong contrasts, to create the atmosphere of approaching conflict. The editor's challenge to the author is ridiculous, because it makes a good rule into an absolute. In another novel, *Bleak House*, Dickens begins with a sentence fragment: "London." It is followed by another, longer one. Then: "Implacable November weather." And yet another—successive "faults" of syntax. The effect is magical; there are no absolutes in good writing. Fitness is all.

There is no such thing as a man's "thinking" apart from the indefinite activity. This flabby usage is not a parallel to "I enjoyed the violinist's *playing*," which is a sensible remark, but rather to "I am going to write the story of Napoleon's living." To sum up, jargon, clichés, and tricks of speech are not merely hand-me-downs and faults of writing, but forms of escape. They denote an emotional weakness, a shuffling refusal to be pinned down to a declaration.

Give Up Omnibus Words and Dressing Gowns

It would be a mistake to think that because they prevail, jargon and cliché are the only enemies of good prose. Other types of words are equally harmful to the twin virtues of vocabulary, felicity and force. They are perfectly good words, which can be well used; they do damage only by being in the wrong place. Writers of histories and reports tend to be fond of such words as *trend, factor, forces, situation, movement, condition, elements, circumstances*. Loosely used, they are blank cartridges—they merely make a noise. The way to restore their force is to use them for distinct purposes and invariably where they belong. A *trend* denotes a clear or measurable collective tendency. It expresses motion, increase. There is a trend toward early marriage or building smaller houses, but it is not true that "These new digital refrigerators are a regular trend." Similarly, a factor is something that makes. Hence it is not true that "The gap was a factor he could not bridge."

Whenever possible, use the name of the thing or person—not "the maritime elements were disaffected," but "the sailors were rebellious" or "the seaboard population." As recommended earlier, keep your eye on what your reader could go out and see or touch, and write accordingly.

In the same class as "omnibus" words are certain adjectives that writers of textbooks have made depressingly habitual. These books contain nothing but *bitter* attacks, *crushing* defeats, *shrewd* diplomats, and *ruthless* ambition. Such standard epithets deserve a rest. Attacks can be angry, vehement, violent, reckless, impetuous, sinister, unforgivable, and perhaps a dozen other things. Let us have each a little different. They were so in reality and they would be more easily remembered when free of the label that makes them all alike.

The parroting habit also leads writers to clutter up their prose with what Gowers happily named "adverbial dressing gowns." He meant such pairs as *seriously* consider, *fully* recognize, *wholly* unjustifiable, *thoroughly* mistaken. He calls them dressing gowns because the writer is shying away from the naked word they wrap around. Strip the main word and see how it gains strength. To say "His act was unjustifiable" is far stronger than "His act was wholly unjustifiable." The adverb strains to prove; with it you are frothing at the mouth; without it you have judged and there is nothing to add.

A third group of encumbrances is long words and circumlocutions. No rule can be given about the length of words it is best to use. The length of the same word varies with the context. In the first sentence of this paragraph, "circumlocution" is the shortest way to say what is meant; elsewhere, it may not be as in "Refrain from circumlocution," where the idea is: "Don't beat around the bush." Once you have mastered "translation" in this sense you should be able to adapt your diction to the occasion. In the classic musical *Guys and Dolls,* the dialogue is an artful mixture of slang, jargon, and highbrow bookishness. The effect is comic, yet one meets people who miss the virtuosity of the script and who complain that the dialogue sounds "uneven."

Observe Idiom and Implications

The researcher taking notes must be able to summon up half a dozen words or phrases in place of the text he is reading and choose among them for his brief rewording. And if this quick version is to be the core of his later description, it must be correct idiomatically and in every other way. Idiom is generally "cast-iron," to use one of Fowler's terms. You *must* say "hard put to it" not simply "hard put." Again, it is "acquiesce *in* the proposal," not *to.* If you slip here, it is probably because of "he agreed to," but note at the same time that "agree to" has a different meaning from "agree with," like "compare to" and "compare with." Idiom follows neither logic nor illogic; it simply is and has to be learned. Submitting to the fixity of idiom, good writers seldom tamper with common phrases that, superficially considered, seem to allow change. Write "past his prime," not "past his distinguished prime." Leave to the advertiser the privilege of saying "at its tastiest best"; and if you must qualify, do it outside the phrase, e.g., not "he put a reluctant stop to . . . ," but "he reluctantly put a stop"—which also has the advantage of better logic.

Connotations or overtones are still harder to learn, though many are second nature to practiced readers. Just as everybody knows that one *rides* a horse and *drives* a car, so all know that one *celebrates* a wedding and *conducts* a funeral; one *reciprocates* a favor and *retaliates* an injury. Such usages may be regarded as halfway between idiom and right diction. A writer should not confuse "hard work" with "hard labor," "avoid" with "prevent," "fortuitous" with "fortunate." Some words have acquired subtle implications often disregarded. "Drastic," for instance, which has become so popular, suggests an act that affects both the doer and the victim, though perhaps unequally. The shopkeeper who announces "Drastic cut in prices" is correct—the drastic act hurts him while wreaking havoc among the price tags. To use "drastic" as a mere synonym for "violent" or "thoroughgoing" is to waste a choice overtone, which after a while will cease resounding and be lost for good. People will then ask, "How do you express the idea of injuring yourself so as to injure your enemy more?"

For practice in self-criticism let us look at a pair of sentences from essays by advanced students and apply the principles laid down in this chapter. The first defines the German Customs Union that preceded the Empire:

1. "A basically geographical concept permeated with political overtones dependent on arbitrary historical and political boundaries of the included states."

FIGURE **18**   *WORDS THAT BLUR MEANING*

1. *Jargon:* dimension / traumatic / parameter (for limit) / exercise facility (for gym) / paradigm (for model) / metaphor (for emblem or example) / major thrust (for main point) / general resource center (for library) / interface (for link) / infrastructure (for lower ranks—or streets and bridges) / dysfunctional (for "doesn't work") / dichotomy (for difference) / pre-empt (for prevent) / pre-owned (for secondhand) / point in time (for moment) / bottom line (for clincher) / icon (for hero) / problematic (for doubtful—or for puzzling) / testament (for testimony, evidence).

2. *Vogue Words:* avid / sensitive / volatile / abrasive / gap (credibility, gender, etc.) / empathy / cusp / creative / strategy / hopefully / scenario / agenda / module / innovative / polarize / synergy.

3. *Neologisms:* acerb(ic) / acid(ic) / gift (as verb) / wellness / parenting / mentoring / morph / infotainment / all words compounded with -thon, -tron, -matic, -mation, multi- and other scraps of pseudo Greek or Latin.

4. *Misused or Misplaced Technicalities:* quantum (jump, leap) / catalyst / venue / -itis (for addiction or obsession) / and all needless verbs in -ize (prioritize, finalize, folderize, laymanize).

5. *Failure to Make Distinctions:* fiscal and financial / assure and ensure / euphuism and euphemism / flout and flaunt / perspicacious and perspicuous / comity and community / sensuous and sensual / comprise and compose / desire and desiderate / podium and lectern / conventional and traditional.

6. *Malaprops:* cohort (for companion) / peer (for fellow-) / meld (for combine) / torturous (for tortuous) / critical (for ill) / personal (for private) / gender (for sex) / embattled (for besieged or beset) / legendary (for famous or excellent).

7. *Twisted Idioms:* hard put (lacking to *it*) / suffice to say (lacking *it*) / by the boards, down the tubes, (omit *s*) / one on one (for one to one, in conferring, etc.) / and nor, but nor (omit *and, but*) / as of now, as of yet (omit *as of*) / have no bones (make no bones) / by a hare's breath (hair's breadth).

8. *Wrong Prepositions:* a writer with distinction (of) / acquiesce to (in) / worthy for (of) / identical to (with) / compliance in (with) / this dates to (dates back to; or is dated, without *to;* or dates from).

9. *Misdirected Verbs:* this door is alarmed / the company must divest (lacks *itself of*) / boggle the mind (the mind boggles, i.e., halts, resists) / it rankled him (omit *him*) / this translates to ten dollars (is equivalent to) / she was convinced to buy (persuaded to buy) / commit (without myself, etc.).

10. *Faulty Constructions:* based on fresh information, they . . . (basing themselves) / if I knew, I wouldn't have (if I had known) / it is not true, as the report says (ambiguous: does report say it is true or not true?) / with better luck they may have survived (might) / I didn't see him yet (haven't) / the officer insisted that she remained (remain) / it's got to be a risk (must be) / and all German-style constructions, e.g., "to-the-floor-draped stools."

11. *Figurative Phrases:* cutting edge / Catch 22 / send a message / pushing the envelope / window of opportunity / get off the dime / dead-cat bounce / forward leaning.

12. *Euphemisms:* senior citizen / significant other / visually challenged / maintenance engineer (for janitor / unauthorized premature disclosure (for leak).

A critical reader's comments would run: *basically* is both jargon and an adverbial dressing gown. *Concept* is jargon for *idea* or *conception*. "Permeated *with*" is wrong; the idiom requires *by*. Moreover, the image is absurd: overtones cannot permeate a concept, and a geographical one at that. The rest is inoffensive but clumsy and vague.

> 2. "Memoirs must be studied for falsifications and for the author's own point of view, as well as sources, whether documentary or in the nature of narrative without official certification."

Comments: Memoirs are not *studied* for falsification; they are examined or scanned. "Falsifications" is the wrong word, anyway—try "errors" or "falsehoods." The sentence limps badly, but that fault belongs to our next chapter. "Sources . . . in the nature of narrative" are nothing but narratives. "Official certification" is jargon here for *official* by itself, which should go before "documents" in the rewritten: "as well as sources in the form of official documents or plain narratives."

The concluding thought about putting ideas into words is this: the ease with which even trained eyes can overlook error, confusion, and nonsense should make every writer at once endlessly cautious and forever modest. At least half a dozen competent readers—colleagues, editors, and the author himself—must have gone over the preface of a valuable work on economics, which closes with these words: "Obviously, none of the people named above has the least responsibility for whatever may be found in this book. I alone am to blame."

As the words stand, the author "blames himself" for whatever may be found, that is, the entire contents of his book. The mistake is more amusing than grievous, and certainly not hard to forgive. Perhaps it should be remembered as stating the rule by which every writer must write and revise: "I alone am to blame."

CHAPTER 10

CLEAR SENTENCES: EMPHASIS, TONE, AND RHYTHM

Live Sentences for Lively Thoughts

As needs hardly be said, meaning does not come from single words, but from words put together in groups—phrases, clauses, sentences. A mysterious bond links each of these groups of words with our ideas, and this relation leads in turn to the miracle by which ideas pass from one mind to another. The reason for weighing words with care is to make sure that these units of speech correspond truly to the parts of one's inner vision; the reason for building sentences with care is to make sure that the parts hang together correctly for truth and conveniently for understanding.

Everyone's mind, however eager it may be for information, offers a certain resistance to the reception of somebody else's ideas. Before one can take them in, the shape, connection, and tendency of one's own ideas have to yield to those same features in the other person's. Accordingly, the writer must somehow induce in that other the willingness to receive the foreign matter. He does so with the aid of devices which, when regularly used, are called the qualities of his speech or writing.

These qualities go by such names as: Clarity, Order, Logic, Ease, Unity, Coherence, Rhythm, Force, Simplicity, Naturalness, Grace, Wit, and Motion. But these are not distinct things; they overlap and can reinforce or obscure one another, being but aspects of the single power called Style. Neither style nor any of its qualities can be aimed at altogether by itself. Nor are the pleasing characteristics of a writer's style laid on some pre-existing surface the way sheathing and plaster are laid on the rough boards of a half-finished house. Rather, they are the by-product of an intense effort to make words work. By "making them work" we mean here reaching the mind of another and affecting it in such a way as to reproduce there our state of mind. This is done by removing the hurdles to understanding, while preserving as much as you can of your spontaneous utterance. All attempts at imitating a recognized style, whether biblical, Lincolnesque, or "stark" for modernity, defeat them-selves. You cannot be someone other than yourself.

The qualities we have listed should therefore be regarded not as goals but as additional points in self-questioning. You do not say: "Now I am going to be clear, logical, coherent." You go over a sentence and ask: "Can someone else follow?" Perhaps not. Then what is the matter? "I see: this does not match that. And here—is this ambiguous, repetitious?" Clarity is there when oth-ers can follow; coherence when thoughts hang together; logic when their combination is valid. You may wonder: "Is there no way to write so as to avoid at least some at this patching after the fact?" There is—and learning how is the subject of this chapter. But note at the outset that any helpful hints will only reduce the amount of rewriting to be done, never remove its necessity.

It is an interesting proof of what has just been said that no satisfactory definition of a sentence has ever been given: there is no formula to build one with. Yet every educated person knows a sentence when he sees one. But any models or formulas for sentence making will be useless, and even paralyzing, unless they are taken with imagination. A sentence is not some-thing rigid, static, and absolute; a sentence is above all func-tional, dynamic, and relative. A perfectly good sentence may be all wrong when it follows or precedes another. For the thought has to keep moving from sentence to sentence and the joints must be firm. If you need a structural image of

The Sentence, think of it as an organism possessing a skeleton, muscles, and skin.

Like a skeleton, a sentence is a piece of construction. Traditional grammar in fact speaks of related words as forming "a construction," and calls it awkward or harmonious, allowable or contrary to usage. But do not let construction suggest a table or a house; true, a sentence has to stand on its feet, but we liken it to a skeleton because a sentence has to move like the thought it carries. Motion is perhaps the fundamental quality of good writing. A reader who knows nothing about the principles of writing may be incapable of describing what is wrong as he makes heavy weather through a book. But he feels very keenly whether his mind advances or sticks, goes straight or in circles, marches steadily forward or jerks two steps ahead and three back.

In order to move, the parts of the sentence skeleton must be properly jointed; the muscles and connective tissue must be strong and inserted at the right places; the burden of ideas must not be too great for the structure. And to cover all this machinery and make it pleasing, the surface must be smooth and reasonably varied in appearance. Translating this into writers' terms, we say: clauses and phrases must fall into the right pattern (syntax) and the words must be chosen so that the tone and rhythm of the whole are appropriate. A telegraphic message may be exact and well knit, but it lacks grace and sounds unnatural. It moves but does not flow. One cannot imagine reading three hundred pages in telegraphic style. The words omitted in that style and that are restored in ordinary prose are no decoration or added charm; they are simply the rounded contour of the thought, reduced in the telegram to the bare bones.

The return of this likeness to bones shows that we have come full circle in our attempt to describe what a sentence is and what it does. But you may think—and rightly—that what you need even more than a description is direct advice, and for this we must look at examples—and you must study them with our analogies in mind.

Mismatching of Parts

Let us begin with the schoolbook example: "The wind blew across the desert where the corpse lay and whistled." The sentence moves indeed, and the information it contains is plain enough; but before we quite grasp it we laugh. And this alters the meaning, which was not intended to be jocular in the last three words. How to fix it? Our first impulse is to insert a comma after "lay." But the result gives an odd impression, as if "and whistled" was a dangling afterthought. Try it aloud and you will hear that a comma pause after "lay" makes "and whistled" sound puzzling. The only way the sentence sounds rhythmically satisfying is without the pause.

The trouble is that the meaning and the construction are at odds; bad rhythm gives the flaw away, the limb "and whistled" is attached to the wrong part of the body. The joke comes from the bad linking of parts. We draw from this error our first rule of sentence-making: *bring as close together as possible the parts that occur together in the world or go together in your mind.*

Now apply the rule: "The wind blew across the desert and whistled where the corpse lay." No longer comic, but wrong again, because the new close-linking suggests that the whistling took place only near the corpse. Try again: "The wind blew and whistled across the desert where the corpse lay." At last we have the limbs correctly distributed—the arm is not attached to the hip. Our sentence passes the test as far as avoiding absurdity and false suggestion.

But say it aloud once more and you will notice that it still sounds odd. It leaves the voice up in the air, and with the voice, the meaning. Why? The emphases are off beat. In an ordinary declarative sentence, the two spots of emphasis are the beginning and the end. Hence the two most important elements in the thought must occupy those spots. In our example the main elements obviously are: the whistling wind and the corpse. Whether the corpse lay or stood or leaned is a detail. The last idea sounding in our mind's ear must be "the corpse." Can this be managed? "The wind blew and whistled across the desert where lay the corpse." A trifle better, but far from perfect, because modern English shies away from inversions and to defy usage is to lose force. To sound natural we must stick to "where the corpse lay."

By this time we are sick and tired of wrestling with these twelve words and we conclude that they cannot be juggled into a proper shape. We are ready to scrap the sentence and go at the idea by a different route, when a fresh form occurs to us. "The corpse lay in the desert, across which the wind blew and whistled." This is the best yet. The form is right and if the whole subject were less dramatic we could let it stand. But there is a stiffness about "across which" that suits a description of scenery rather than that of lonely death. This impression means that we have been made aware of Tone while trying to secure Right Emphasis, Right Linking, and Right Rhythm. These features of the sentence, we know, are not separable and we become aware that a sentence is a compromise among various demands.

If the Tone of "across which" is unsuitable, what *can* we do with that wretched corpse? Try once more: "The corpse lay in the desert, and over it the wind blew and whistled."[1] Still disappointing: a compound sentence is too weak for this gruesome vision; it separates what eye and ear grasp together. We have dismembered and reconstructed without success.

The true solution lies in the so-called periodic sentence, whose form heightens suspense and generally favors rhythm: "Across the desert where the corpse lay, the wind blew and whistled." A peculiarity of the periodic sentence is that its suspensive opening phrase does not monopolize the emphasis we associate with beginnings; the stress falls on the end of the clause in the effort to complete the meaning. From our experience with a single bad sentence, we can now confirm our first rule of

[1]The inveterate verifier is curious about the fact and asks, *Does* the wind whistle when it blows across an unobstructed waste?

thumb and add three others for framing and straightening out sentences:

1. Right linking is the prime requisite. Begin by seeing to it that things related are not divided, and that things remote are not falsely joined.

2. Right emphasis comes next. It is what gives momentum to the thought, what makes the sentence move. It starts from a point of superior interest, travels through a valley of detail, and reaches a second point of high interest, which ends the journey by completing or advancing our understanding of the first.

3. When our emphases are right, the rhythm is likely to be right also, for our speaking habits naturally follow our habits of wording and of thought.[2]

4. At any point in the structure, the phrasing must be in keeping with the tenor of the whole. This is a matter partly of diction and partly of construction. The two together produce Tone.

To these four propositions there is an important "Don't" corollary: Although a comma that is missing from a sound sentence should be put in, a defective sentence cannot be cured by a comma. When you are tempted to waste time in this effort, just remember "and whistled."

Five-Legged Sheep and Other Monsters

With these truths in mind, we can refine a little on the art of construction, though with no hope of exhausting the subject of sentence-building. Return to the difficult art of linking. The desire to bring kindred things together often tempts the unwary

---

[2]This does not mean that in speaking we usually place our words right for emphasis but that we sound them right, and hence the rhythm is natural. One says: "They *are* good—in *my* opinion." To convey the same meaning in print, one must write: "They are, in my opinion, good." Still, judging the written word, explain the rather different meanings of: "In my opinion, they are good" and "They are, in my opinion, good."

to use phrases that can be read in two ways. When that happens, the reader is sent on the wrong track; he must back up and make a fresh start, or perhaps remain in doubt about the right fusion of ideas. Suppose one reads:

> If there is lost motion in the rods and boxes in a boiler of steam generating capacity and a valve distributing power properly when the lever is hooked down, it develops into a pound that is annoying and detrimental to the machinery.

The reader's trouble begins at "steam generating capacity." Should this be "steam-generating," an adjective modifying "capacity"? Or should it be "a boiler of steam, generating [power at] capacity"? Below, a similar hesitation arises at "valve distributing power." Doubt is settled by our knowledge that valves distribute power and not the other way round—"valve-distributing power" is nonsense—but we have had to stop and figure this out. Because this second phrase parallels the first, our retentive ear entices us to give their parallel forms a parallel meaning. Next we are stopped again at whatever "it" is that "develops into a pound." After talk of steam power, the word "pound" is ambiguous. We soon see that it is not a pound of pressure that is meant but a pound*ing*. We have been halted a third time. Finally, another parallel between the two adjectives toward the end tells us that this pounding is "annoying . . . to the machinery."

On the whole, this sentence written to teach engineers can tell us more about writing than about machinery. It tells us that parallelism is so important a device that its use must be kept pure. Do not give parallel forms to disparate ideas and always carry out the parallels you start with. And never suppose that variation is more elegant. Note the accumulation of horrors in the paragraph that follows:

> When it came right down to it, he was no more able to spell out a conceptual pattern than, in the last analysis, he felt he could muster up the imagination to face such explosive problems of ethics as his sadly unhappy life had left him no room to size up with detachment.

With the words "he was no more able to," the writer made a contract with the reader. Those words forecast a "than," to be followed by a second action parallel to the first. The contract here is broken. The "than" duly comes, but its proper adjunct is forgotten while the writer pursues his wandering thought down winding channels. Jargon and rank images ("spell out a pattern," "explosive problems," "room to size up") are mixed with clichés ("in the last analysis") and tautologies ("sadly unhappy"). And the redundancies spoil the parallel: "he [felt he] could," and the words following "imagination." The cure is to give up the "no more than" construction and make two sentences, one about the conceptual patterns—whatever they may be—and one about the ethical problems of a sadly unhappy life without room.

The remark made in passing about *it* when we examined the sentence from the engineer's manual furnishes yet another rule of good construction: *the antecedents of pronouns must always be unmistakable.* In the welter of rods, boxes, and valves no one can tell what "it" is that "develops into a pound." It cannot be the engine, which is not even mentioned. The motion, no doubt, develops into (causes, generates?) a pounding, but the only motion mentioned is four lines above and it is *lost* motion. Technically, it is a kind of motion, but in syntax it does not exist. The grammatical crime is that six nouns in the singular precede "it," and two would be enough to create confusion. By rights, the last in order should be the true antecedent, but that happens to be "lever," which makes nonsense. The "it" is an orphaned relative with no references to show when questioned.

Modern Prose: Its Virtues and Vices

After so much wallowing in uncertainty we are eager for a good sentence. Here is one embodying a double parallel and making of it a dramatic image: "Too blind to avert danger, too cowardly to withstand it, the most ancient government of Europe made not an instant's resistance: the peasants of Unterwald died upon their mountains, the holders of Venice clung to their lives."

The modern reader who appreciates this sentence may say that in spite of its clarity, richness, and rhythmic excellence, it is alien to our mode of thought and hence beyond our power to imitate. We no longer enjoy these complex and balanced forms; they seem to us artificial. We prefer to write simply, as we speak—or so we like to believe. If the engineer's sentence above, and the biographer's right after are fair samples of simpler prose, we must say that complexity is still with us, but unorganized. We are not so straightforward as we pretend; the truth is that we could not "write as we speak" even if we wanted to.

What prevents the written word from reproducing speech is that, in speaking, the voice, stress, facial expression, and gesture contribute a quantity of meaning that fills out the insufficiency of colloquial phrasing. Read the transcript of court testimony and you will see how difficult it is to understand. You have to guess how every remark was spoken, inflected, made clear by something other than words. In good writing the writer supplies these elements which complete utterance. Hence the use of transitional and qualifying words that are almost entirely absent from conversation.

This necessity, of course, also leads to the other extreme. The writer may try to fill out his spontaneous sentence with many words—to stop the gaps, to bottle up the meaning that always threatens to fizz away. Up to a point the effort succeeds. But superfluous words destroy explicitness. The fault of beginners and inattentive writers is that their sentences say the thing twice. Here is a government office memorandum: "I believe we all function best in a positive, supportive work environment where we are each able to develop mutual respect for co-workers and work at a job that gives us a sense of self-fulfillment in the 'work' category of our human activities."

The sentence has not been stripped down to its fairly simple meaning: "positive and supportive environment" is jargon and remains vague until we make out that the *where* clause is what the writer means by positive and supportive. Then the idea of mutual respect is attached to *each*, as if one person could develop anything *mutual*. Finally, the definition of the desirable environment suffers from the afterthought concerning our feelings about the job itself. Next, this is topped by a tautology: where does self-fulfillment from a job belong except in the "work category"? Every phrase shows up a writer who did not sort out his ideas. He wrote down his thoughts just as they tumbled into his consciousness. The excess is not simply dropped by the reader; it stops his mind long enough to make him wonder whether he is missing some special nuance. Since he is not, his effort has been wasted.

From this type of fault we draw the generality that, all else being equal, *the ease with which thought can be gathered from words is in inverse ratio to their total length.* We do not say "to their number," for the length of the individual words may be part of the impediment; it is a fact that each syllable the eye and the mind take in causes a kind of friction, as in physical work. But we cautioned: "all else being equal," means that occasions are frequent in which long words and long sentences are called for. The moral is, any sentence that goes on and on in a string of words ending in "-ity" or "-tion," hooked together with of's, to's, and which's must be whittled down to size with a hatchet.

Consider this statement, which professes to make clearer one of Shakespeare's plays:

> The creation of character, indeed, is not to be regarded as the unique or even principal, end of Shakespeare's dramatic creations, in which plot and motive, themselves handled with greater flexibility and insight, tend increasingly to find their proper context in a more ample artistic unity which embraces and illuminates them; but in the delineation of personality beyond the limits of convention his language first attained some sense of its full possibilities.

No mind, including the author's, can take in at one scoop the message here delivered. There is no excuse for offering to the public a dozen chapters in this vein. Sprawling is not this writer's only sin against sense. He gives us an anthology of faults: (1) Awkward repetition: "creation" in line 1, "creations" in line 2.

(2) Tautology: "themselves" in line 3, and the clause from "find their proper context . . ." down to "embraces" ("context," "unity," and "embraces" say the same thing three times). (3) Illogic: what are we told by the comparison "greater" and "more ample"? than what? "Increasingly" suggests "as time went on," but we must guess this. (4) Pronouns adrift: "their" in line 4 and "them" in line 5 have two possible antecedents—"dramatic creations" on the one hand, and "plot and motive" on the other. (5) Vagueness from abstraction: what does it *mean* "to handle plot and motive with greater flexibility and insight"? "to find a proper context"? "to be embraced and illuminated by a more ample artistic unity"? "to delineate personality beyond the limits of convention"? And how can a writer's language "attain some sense of *its* full possibilities?

The worst faults of "serious writing" are here conveniently grouped, the "noun plague" dominating them all. Not one plausible agent performs a recognizable act denoted by a strong verb. All is passive and diffuse and jargon-ridden. As an antidote, let us turn to another writer on Shakespeare:

> Structurally, Tate has made a few serious alterations. The most important is Bolingbroke's winning of the rabble. This is amusingly done and probably acted well enough. More serious is the "elevation" of Richard's character, a feat on which Tate plumes himself in the Preface. As a matter of fact, it spoils the play.[3]

Despite its choppiness, which might become tedious and lacking in charm, and would preclude subtle thoughts, this passage at least answers the reader's wish for lucid prose. What makes it such is: plausible agents, recognizable actions, strong verbs. Of these, there are still too few. A more searching writer would have preferred: "Tate has altered but few structural parts. . . ." The logic, then, could be stricter: if "the most important" alteration is the one about Bolingbroke, how can the one about Richard be "more serious"? And to a good ear, the sentence

---

[3]Hazelton Spencer, *Shakespeare Improved* (Cambridge, MA, 1927), 262.

"This is amusingly done and probably acted well enough" sounds disjointed. The shift in voice calls for a second subject: "and *it* probably acted . . ."; the passive "is done" will not go in harness with the active verb "acted."

Punctuating for Smooth Reading

On an earlier page we laid down the rule that a badly made sentence can never be cured by inserting a comma. The debatable subject of punctuation deserves a few words here. A full discussion would be out of place—and inconclusive. If you want more, consult the compact handbook *American Punctuation* by George Summey (1949) or R. E. Allen, *Get Ahead in Punctuation* (2002).

The modern tendency is to punctuate as little as possible; readers are expected to see without guide-marks the groups of words that in an earlier day were organized by punctuation. This very change yields a sort of principle: be sure to mark off what will otherwise cause a stumble. Example: "America could outbid Europe in every market for goods in this country had not yet been depleted and were exportable." Without a comma after *market*, the reader inevitably sees "market for goods" as a unit and has to backtrack. The same mischief can occur with a single qualifying word: "Throughout the text is illegible." But when the meaning of such an introductory word (or a short clause) runs toward its complement with no danger of false linking, the sentence can do without a separating comma. In brief, at the first level, the comma, punctuate by meaning.

This precept leads logically to further guidelines. When the sentence calls for two or more commas, the next division requires the mark next higher, the semicolon. The eye can then make out the right division of parts. For an example, turn to Figure 7, p. 60, and read the next-to-last block of print. Without the semicolons it would be a chaos of phrases and clauses.

No reader of this book needs to be told the next convention: the end of a sentence needs a period, unless it puts a question or utters an exclamation. But watch for indirect questions, which must stand without question marks: "They wondered what was to happen next" is an affirmative statement, not a question, despite the "what was."

Bad punctuation occurs perhaps more often in the use of dashes and hyphens than elsewhere. Dashes in pairs act like parentheses to set off an idea that is in effect an aside. It may explain, as in: "A computer batch file—one that contains several commands—is a great convenience." A single dash has a different effect when put at the end of the main idea; it also signals an aside, an example, a reason closely related to what precedes: "By thus combining keys one commands forty or more functions— a great convenience."

So much is clear. Trouble comes in sentences that have somehow acquired three dashes. How can the reader know which to pair? If all three are intended as singles, the doubt is worse yet. Make sure that you dash your work in the light of reason, just as you would if you used parentheses; of these it would not occur to you to sprinkle three.

How to hyphenate a word split at the end of a line arouses fiery passions among copy editors and authors of manuals. No system has been found consistently applicable, but that failure should cause no weeping. So long as the reader is not brought up short by a split that creates an ambiguous or ludicrous pseudo word, he will accept any system; indeed he will not even notice the hyphens.

There remains the question of words with internal hyphens: *make-believe, self-distrust, face-lift,* and the like. Some editors (and some writers) would write all the above without hyphens, merely spaced apart; others fuse them together. John Dos Passos wrote *picturegallery* and other hybrids of the sort. Others find in the accentuation of double words a principle to follow, but accent varies: English ice-*cream* is American *ice* cream and in this country also pronunciation varies by regions. Agreement about hyphens will never be reached on any list of terms, and it really does not matter, so long as one's practice is not outré. The eye accepts *babysitter* as readily as *baby-sitter,* but it balks at *antiintellectual* and other mergers that violate familiar arrangements of letters or sounds. Only pedants make war on all hyphens, as if the mark somehow fouled the text.

What does matter—and neglect here shows the unprofessional—is to hyphen at every compounding of words that are to serve as adjectives. When the normally unlinked *eighteenth century* is to modify a noun the hyphen must be inserted: "eighteenth-century furniture." Disregard of this convention makes even a short paper irritating to read.

Another piece of slovenliness with hyphens is found in the form "the war lasted from 1914–1918." The hyphen represents the word *to* only when the dates are taken by themselves: "The first World War (1914–1918)," and it never stands for *and* as in "He held office between 1984–88." Good usage in linking has lately been perverted even more by the substitution of the slash or virgule (/) for the hyphen: "the East/West lack of understanding." What is objectionable is the doubt it creates. In the lawyer's *and/or,* which probably started the fad, the slash stands for *or.* In the bed/breakfast rate, it stands for *and,* though in "the price quoted gives you the lunch/dinner option," it is again *or*— you have a choice of one of the two main meals. But in the East/West phrase it means neither *or* nor *and*; it means *between.* These are enough ambiguities to reject the slash, except in lists or tables, where it simply separates items more clearly than would a comma or semicolon.

Now what about the exclamation mark? Seldom use it!

Carpentry or Cabinetmaking?

The recommendations detailed in the present chapter are but an extension of our original proposition that good writing is an intense effort to make words work. The critiques of the quoted passages boil down to the demand that each word—noun, verb, adverb, or any other kind—should contribute something to the sense, and this with economy. If one word can do the work of two, use one. If you absolutely need a phrase, make it short.

If the thought is complex and the sentence has to contain several clauses, see to it that each clause expends its energy where none will be wasted, that is, close to the idea it enlarges or qualifies.

A good rule to follow in order to achieve coherence with the least trouble is to stick to the subject, voice, or construction. Do not start with one idea or form and change it in mid-career. The writer on p. 221 switched from passive verb to active and lost momentum. Another will write: "The topic one selects should be clear and precise and when one comes to look for the materials on it, it will be found that the subject itself serves as a guide to their selection." This is no doubt a faithful transcript of the way the thought arose in one mind, but its form is ill adapted to its penetrating another. Cling to the grammatical subject and see where it leads: "The topic one selects should be clear and precise—so that IT will guide the researcher—when HE comes to look for *his* materials" (twenty-four words in place of thirty-five, and continuous motion instead of three hitches—from "the topic" to "when one comes" to an indefinite "it" and back to "the subject" again).

Remain faithful to subject and construction and you will be surprised at the ease, speed, and clarity you attain. The thick connective tissue, the clanking chains "as regards," "as far as . . . is concerned," "in relation to," and the like, will fall away; associated ideas will be next to next; and your thought will be quickly caught by the reader who, by definition, is always on the run.

For models of this kind of writing, study the advertising cards in any public vehicle. The ideas conveyed may be stupid, commonplace, or untrue; the words themselves may be flossy or jargonlike, but the construction is usually impeccable. One reason is that advertisers know they have only thirty seconds to make an impression. Another and clinching reason is that they employ first-rate writing talents. When these are used to publicize government programs or, occasionally, political appeals, they produce classic utterances. What could be better than: "Eighteen million Californians need a fighting Senator with experience, ideas, and a heart."

Note how the attention is arrested, without fuss, by the opening phrase, which addresses every voter in the state, and how adroitly the emphases are managed: having started with our interesting selves we wind up with an appeal to the feelings. But "ideas" are not wholly forgotten, though "experience," as the chief political virtue, comes first in the series. Notice also the function of the single adjective "fighting." It is a strong word, but here it is more than that. Without it, the sentence might be a bare statement of need, suggesting no candidate to fill it. But with the epithet, it is clear that the declaration aims at someone, and behold, his picture is underneath it.

You may say that the ease, lucidity, and force of this bid for votes comes from the inherent simplicity of the idea. Not so. It is always easy to write a muddy sentence, and it would be surprising if the one we have been admiring had been struck off impromptu. The normal tendency is to join chunks of wordage together as they come and then tap them here and there with a hammer till they more or less resemble a structure.

Here are two examples of composition—if indeed the first fragment can claim the name. The first writer is a high-school teacher of English whose summer-school examination paper suggests how illiterate those who teach others can be:

Hemingway works is the beginning of all modern American Literature. He doesn't write too much conversation in his books. Just enough to make the idea go across and his descriptions are brief with many adverbs.

Compare a hammered-down affair that is brisker and more literate but not much more satisfactory:

"Thousands of years ago men first learned the secret of conducting water through crude pipes." ["Crude" is out of place here, since the secret sought was how to conduct water through pipes—which turned out to be crude.] "Long before the birth of Christ, the Chinese transported water through bamboo." [Christ is brought in for vividness, but the effect fails by making one wonder what His birth contributed to plumbing.] ". . . and there is much evidence of the fine water supply systems of the Romans." [By this point, the writer has lost grip on vividness, relevance, and rhythm.]

The unpalatable truth is that since a really well-made sentence is not born, like the live body we compared it to, it can only be the result of much planing and fitting, of close measuring for balance, and of hidden jointing for solidity and smoothness—it is cabinetmaker's work, plus the living force that gives movement and stirs the inert frame into an animated whole. The joiner's task calls for words that will bind the ideas together from end to end. Yet, in a second draft it may be desirable to omit some of the cross references. Where the reader's mind will take the jump alone, it is a waste to prod him. For example,

What course of procedure does this suggest? In spite of all the study on the broad topic of productivity, the sum total of knowledge useful to management is small. Government and economic research agencies should be encouraged to expand studies of productivity.

This passage is clear and rapid because in the first sentence "this" refers adequately to the preceding paragraph and because in the second sentence the subject (productivity) is named again in a passing manner that allows our attention to dwell on the aspect of it that matters, namely, the *study* of productivity. The writer then omits a further reference after "the sum total of knowledge"—we know very well it is not knowledge at large, but knowledge about productivity. At the last gasp, however, the writer slipped up: he repeated "studies of productivity" at an emphatic place, almost as if this were a new topic he was introducing. He might have said instead: "Government, etc., should be encouraged to enlarge this sum by extending [not 'expanding'] such studies."

There is one place in any article or book where to fail in directness is fatal. That is the beginning. To catch your reader, the hook must be baited with a palatable morsel. A writer will therefore toil over his opening sentence. Let his ideal be the one that opens Jane Austen's *Pride and Prejudice*: "It is a truth universally acknowledged that a single man in possession of a good

FIGURE **19**   *LINCOLN AS STYLIST*

"Mr. President, don't you think it might be better to say
something simple, like, 'eighty-seven years ago'?"

Because of the popular myth about the Gettysburg Address, this scene is at
once recognized as Lincoln on his way to the battlefield in 1863; he is presumably improvising the text on any old sheet of paper. Actually, he made
two or more drafts before leaving the Executive Mansion (not then officially
called the White House). As for breaking the rule of simplicity, he knew that
an opening must be sonorous and arresting to command instant attention.

fortune must be in want of a wife." This far from truthful proposition is a perfect opening, because it foretells in the smallest
compass what we are about to be concerned with—marriage
and money—and that we are to be concerned with them in the
spirit of irony.

Conclusions, too, are important, being the last words ringing in the reader's ear. They may be as difficult to compose as the beginning was, if you have said a great deal and want to recall it in one, final, pregnant sentence. But it can be done. Here is the conclusion to an account of England's defeat of the Great Armada: "This triumph of sea power insured the survival of the Reformation in England and to a lesser extent in Germany, and helped maintain Holland's independence from Spain."

The Sound of the Sense

The two examples given of opening and closing are models because they combine a number of the qualities every reader longs for in what he reads—clarity, balance, movement, force, and ease. Jane Austen's has grace and wit besides. But the models further resemble each other in having a tone: we hear a voice and it is pleasing. Tone cannot be defined except negatively, when it is bad. Anyone can tell when a writer is talking down— that is the condescending tone. There are also the pompous, the chattering, the precious, the chummy, the toplofty, the cynical and sneering, the vulgar out of the corner of the mouth—the varieties of bad tone are many; they correspond to all the possible mixtures of human attitudes.

The curious thing is that a good writer will occasionally fall into a tone that he himself would reprove, yet will never notice the lapse. Either he is seduced by "language," for example when he is precious or pedantic, or else betrayed by his feelings about the subject, when he is cynical or arrogant. These are reasons, not excuses. The reader is quick to notice and resent what rings false. A writer may therefore have to be on guard against some congenial affectation. Until spoiled by sophistication, children who write are free of such things. Daisy Ashford, the nine-year-old author of *The Young Visiters* has perfect tone. Pick up the book anywhere and no matter how difficult the subject, the tone suits:

The Abbey was indeed thronged next day when Ethel and Bernard cantered up in a very fine carriage drawn by two prancing steeds who foamed a good deal. In the porch stood several clean altar boys who conducted the lucky pair up the aile while the organ pealed a merry blast. The mighty edifice was packed and seated in the front row was the Earl of Clincham looking very brisk as he was going to give Ethel away at the correct moment. Beside him sat Mr. Salteena all in black and looking bitterly sad and he ground his teeth as Ethel came marching up.[4]

What admirable control of rhythm and tone! The difficulty of exercising control has inspired a rule of thumb: If you are especially fond of a passage, strike it out; but the injunction goes too far, since "fondness" can express a sound judgment about a sentence well worked over. The only clue to bad tone is reading one's writing after an interval and responding to the text like an unprepared reader. Phrases will then begin to sound hollow; they will be judged severely as falsehoods or padding or irrelevance.

Most writers aim at a virtue beyond propriety of tone, and it is in this effort that some overreach themselves and produce what is ironically stigmatized as "fine writing." This sarcastic term does not mean that writing cannot or should not be fine. Masterpieces of prose are there to prove that the quality is both desirable and achievable. The objection is to the striving after a fineness that is put on, i.e., not apt; borrowed or, echoing another's genuine feeling.

True fineness is at once the result of work and of a born writer's personality. A decisive example is the ending of Lincoln's First Inaugural, for which his Secretary of State, William H. Seward, had proposed a first draft as follows:

I close. We are not, we must not be, aliens or enemies, but fellow-countrymen and brethren. Although passion has strained our bonds of affection too hardly, they must not, I am sure they will not, be broken. The mystic chords which proceeding from so many battlefields and so many patriot graves, pass through all the hearts and hearths in this broad continent of ours, will yet again harmonize in their ancient music when breathed upon by the guardian angel of the nation.

[4]1919, 99.

FIGURE **20** *QUESTIONS TO ASK ONESELF IN WRITING*
         AND REVISING

I. a. Has my paper (chapter) a single informing theme, with its proper developments, or is it merely a series of loosely connected ideas and images?

   b. Does my beginning begin and does my conclusion conclude? (A beginning should not go back to the Flood, and a conclusion is not the same thing as a summing up.)

   c. Is each of my paragraphs a division with a purpose; that is, does it organize a number of sentences into a treatment of one idea and its modifications?

   d. Is each sentence built to stand on its own feet or is it thrown off balance by the load of qualifiers or the drag of afterthoughts?

   e. Have I made proper use of transitional words and phrases to keep all connections clear? For example, *nevertheless, moreover, even, still, of course* (in its use of minimizing the idea before), *to be sure, admittedly.* (The transitional word or phrase is usually better in the course of the sentence than at the beginning.)

II. a. What is the tone of my piece? Is it too stiff and too formal, trying for the effect of authority? Is it perhaps too relaxed, too familiar, too facetious? Or is it, as it should be, simple, direct?

   b. Are there any passages that I especially prize? If so, am I sure that, in my creative enthusiasm, I am not delighted with something "fancy"?

   c. Have I been aware of the reader and have I consulted his convenience? Or have I, on the contrary, been easy only on myself and used a private language?

   d. Could I, if called upon to do so, explain the exact meaning and function of every word I have used? For example, *subjective, objective, realistic, impact, value, metaphor.*

   e. Are my images aids to the reader or merely ways for me to escape the difficulty of explicit thought?

III. a. Is it perfectly clear to which noun or noun-clause my pronouns refer? (The *slightest* ambiguity is fatal.)

   b. Have I tried to give an air of judicious reserve by repeating the words *somewhat, rather, perhaps,* and have I used for this purpose the illiterate "to an extent"? Or, conversely, have I overdone the emphatic with *very, invariably, tremendous, extraordinary,* and the like?

   c. Have I arbitrarily broken or altered the idiomatic links between certain words, particularly between verbs and their allied prepositions, committing such solecisms as: *disagree . . . to, equally . . . as, prefer . . . than?*

   d. Have I imported from science or other disciplines in which I am interested a vocabulary out of place in public writing? What jargon and vogue words have slipped out by force of habit? For example: interface, area, parameter, frame of reference, methodology, in terms of, synergy, approach.

   e. Have I preferred the familiar word to the far-fetched? the concrete to the abstract? the single to the circumlocution? the short to the long?

Lincoln worked it over four times and produced the well-known words:

I am loath to close. We are not enemies, but friends. We must not be enemies. Though passion may have strained, it must not break our bonds of affection. The mystic chords of memory, stretching from every battlefield, and patriot grave, to every living heart and hearthstone, all over this broad land, will yet swell the chorus of the Union, when again touched, as surely they will be, by the better angels of our nature.

Lincoln did not, in one sense, change a single idea of Seward's. But in another sense he changed them all. By a greater simplicity of vision, a truer feeling for the logic of the suggested words, and a superior sensitivity to rhythm, he produced his own incomparable music. Seward had merely lined up some appropriate propositions. Seward is (as we say) adequate, but he lacks the complete felicity that thinks of everything needful and sets it in its proper place. Just compare Seward's "guardian angel," who is a cliché of the political platform and not a force, with Lincoln's "better angels of our nature," who stand here for conscience and generous impulse in each *living heart.* There was still a chance of averting bloodshed by appealing to "our nature," whereas Seward's plea was a dead letter before the ink was dry.

To sum up, the search for "complete felicity" is, first and last, the only general rule for good writing. Find out what you mean—what you would go to the stake for—and put it down without frills or apologetic gestures. Exhaust the means of literary expression, and you will produce sentences that parse and move and carry the ring of your voice. Keep your eye constantly on your subject—that portion occupying your field of vision at the moment—and you will achieve, in addition to ease and lucidity, force. Contrary to common belief, this trinity of virtues does not mean that sentences must bark, or be cast in the same mold, or remain drearily declarative. Nor does keeping the subject ever in view mean that the writer's own personality vanishes. It mingles, rather, with every phrase he sets down, yet without interposing a thick mist of ego between the reader and the page.

Examine, by way of conclusion and summary of our suggestions, the following paragraph, taken from an English scholar's introduction to a volume of letters. Notice how much information is amassed and conveyed without being thrust at the reader; and respond also to the quiet working of a style in which no word is wasted and through which the native impulses of an urbane mind are revealed:

Saint Evremond admits that the company of his friends and their conversation were more important to him than his writings, which occupied his time only when there was nothing better to do. Like his contemporaries at the courts of Louis XIV and Charles II, he regarded literature as one of the necessary accomplishments of a person of quality, not as a means of earning money or reputation. And though posterity remembers him as a man of letters, he himself claimed to be remembered as a soldier first and afterwards as a courtier. For the fate of his compositions after they had left his pen he cared as little as tradition says he cared about his personal appearance in his old age. He wrote, as it has been said of another, for his own and for his friends' delight, and for the delight also, though he could not have foreseen it, of the pirate printers. They, of course, turned his carelessness to good account, and flourished on the proceeds of innumerable and horribly garbled impressions of his essays, exposed for sale on the bookstalls of London, Paris, and Amsterdam. Hitherto he has given no delight to the bibliographer, and I confess that I have profited little from an examination of a very large number of those unauthorized publications. At the same time my acquaintance with them, and with the one authentic edition of his collected works, has not altered my belief that a selection of his writings, even in translation, is worth reading, and therefore worth reprinting.[5]

---

[5]John Hayward, ed., *The Letters of Saint Evremond* (London, 1930), xiii.

CHAPTER 11

THE ARTS OF QUOTING AND TRANSLATING

Three Recurrent Tasks

Whether a researcher writes well or badly, he finds himself repeatedly quoting and citing. This is true regardless of his subject. And unless that subject is purely local, he also finds himself using sources in a foreign language, which require translation.

Quoting other writers and citing the places where their words are to be found are by now such a common practice that it is easy to look upon the habit as natural, not to say instinctive. It is of course nothing of the kind, but a very sophisticated act, peculiar to a civilization that uses printed books, believes in evidence, and makes a point of assigning credit or blame in a detailed, verifiable way.[1]

Accordingly, the conventions of quoting and citing should be mastered by anyone whose work makes him a steady user of these devices. Citing is in fact so stylized and yet so adaptable to varying needs that we shall devote to it most of the next chapter. The present one will deal with the two forms of quoting—in the original and in translation. They are capable of

---

[1]The vagaries of quoters and misquoters are studied and illustrated by Paul F. Boller, Jr., in his books *Quotemanship: The Use and Abuse of Quotations for Polemical and Other Purposes* (1967) and *They Never Said It: A Book of Fake Quotes, Misquotes, and Misleading Attributions,* written with John George (1989).

more flexible handling than is sometimes suspected, and a study of the technique will contribute to simplicity and efficiency if not to art.

The Philosophy of Quoting

Formerly, the practice was limited to scholars, and was taken as a sign of the unoriginal, timid, pedantic mind. Emerson, by no means an unscholarly man, expressed a common feeling when he said: "I hate quotations. Tell me what you know." And another scholarly New Englander, John Jay Chapman, pointed out that what the great quoters seize upon, they alter as they repeat it.[2]

What was said in Chapter 2 about taking notes by rewording texts for assimilation holds good on the larger scale of the finished work. If you have not made other people's knowledge your own by mixing it with your thoughts and your labor of recomposition, you are not a writer but a compiler; you have not written a report but done a scissors-and-paste job. And the chief defect of such an evasion of responsibility is that the piece will probably be tedious to read and lacking in strength and light. In many a Ph.D. one reads page after page in this vein: "on this point he said: . . ." and "in reply, he stated: . . ." These are varied with: "Six months later, Thomson declared: . . ." and "Jennings thereupon differed as follows: . . ."

Unless your words and your thoughts predominate in your work, you cannot give form to *"your* story." The writers you quote had different purposes from yours, and you cannot make a forward-moving whole out of their unmolded fragments. This truth leads to the first principle of the art of quoting: *Quotations are illustrations, not proofs*. The proof of what you say is the whole body of facts and ideas that you present. From time to time you give a *sample* of this evidence to clinch your argument or to avail yourself of a characteristic or felicitous utterance. But it is not

---

[2]*Lucian, Plato, and Greek Morals* (Boston, 1931), 3–4.

the length, depth, or weight of quotation that convinces your reader.[3]

From this principle, two rules of thumb: (1) Quotations must be kept short, and (2) they must be merged into the text. The form of quoting that we have just used to state two rules— stopping dead, a colon, and a new sentence—is convenient in books of instruction; it is awkward in writing that describes, argues, or narrates. The better form is that which we use in the next line; it makes part of your sentence "the portion of the author's original words that [you] could not have put more concisely" without losing accuracy. Longer quotations cannot, of course, be inserted entire into your own sentence, but your words can lead to the brink of the other author's remarks so that, *with or without an ushering verb, the two speakers join to produce one effect,* like singers in a duet. Here is a passage from the biography of an English trial lawyer, where the author wants to make use of an important letter:

He was bitterly disappointed when his old friend Clavell Salter was given the first vacancy. "I am told that S. is to be recommended," he wrote to Lord Edmund Talbot, "Well, he is a splendid chap and a great friend of mine of thirty years standing. I think he will tell you he owes much to me in the early days. . . ." The letter is that of a bitterly disappointed man, and ends with a prophecy about his future, which came almost exactly true. "Well, I am fifty-nine; if my health lasts, I suppose I can enjoy another ten years hard work at the Bar." Within a few months of ten years after the date of the letter he died, almost in harness. Shortly after this disappointment he was approached as to the writing of his memoirs and he discussed the project and even wrote a few pages. "What will you call the book?" he was asked. "Better call it *The Story of a Failure,*" he said sadly, and laid aside his pen.[4]

---

[3]An apparent exception to this rule occurs when you try to prove a point by reproducing documents. The exception is only apparent, because documents that are longer than half a page or so should be made an appendix and briefly "called out" in the text.

[4]Edward Marjoribanks, *The Life of Sir Edward Marshall Hall* (London, 1929), 377.

If instead of this running narrative and commentary, the biographer had used the lazy way of heralding each quoted remark with "he said" or one of its variants, we should have halted and started four times. Notice that the method of Merged Quotation has the advantage of preventing the kind of repetition that *Punch* once picked up from the London *Times*:

Land at Freshwater, Isle of Wight, is being prepared as a rocket-motor testing site, the Ministry of Supply said yesterday. "This land is being prepared for the ground testing of rocket motors," a Ministry official explained.

"Clear now?" asked *Punch*.

Whole books have been composed on this system: (1) announcing what the quotation says or implies, (2) giving the quotation, and (3) rehashing what has just been said. To the reader this is death in triplicate, and for the publisher a waste of paper and print. Besides, in the merged quotation the original lead-in and lead-out are dropped; only the body of the statement plays a part in your presentation.

Some final caveats: a researcher must quote only what he has himself read (or heard), and he must weigh carefully his choice of source when variant texts present themselves. It is a shortcut but rarely an advantage to use another writer's quotation as one's own; the risks are not worth the time saved. Editors of learned journals estimate that as many as 15 percent of all footnotes contain errors of one kind or another, even in the work of careful scholars; their quotations are probably no more accurate.

Researchers should also remember that quoted passages in books—and still more often in the contents of Web sites—have sometimes been sanitized, not necessarily for wicked reasons, but to make them shorter, neater, or more usable. Again, the words in a public speech may be misspoken[5], as when a

[5]See Rachel Smolkin, "What Did He Say?" (*American Journalism Review*, Vol. 24, No. 7, September, 2002, pp. 36–39).

president urged his fellow Americans to volunteer for "4,000 years" of service. He meant "4,000 hours," and in the same speech he misnamed a well-known official. Should the transcript for the permanent record of his presidency correct these mistakes? Should it include an audience's response with cheers or jeers, to say nothing of the usual halting and backtracking of extempore remarks?

Some purists argue that the record must be literal, like a tape. This is patently an absurd standard. Stenographers will miss or mishear words, and tape recordings often have blurs and gaps that cannot be left so. Audiences are used to the usual slips of tongue and mind and expect the final version of an important statement to represent the speaker's intention. In a researcher's article or book the quotation should reproduce this model.

The Mechanics of Quotation

Certain forms must, as we said, always be observed in quoting. Modern quotatiousness, which has made us aware of whose words are which, and that has inspired the announcer's ". . . and I quote . . . " (or the careless speaker's "quote . . . unquote")[6] has made us all obey a common reporting system; Its mechanics have both a practical and moral meaning; the system became universal because people saw exactitude as respect for a man's opinion; it acknowledges the influence of context upon meaning; and it protects the author's rights in literary property. The most important conventions that rule the quoting of words in print have been exemplified throughout this book. Set down in a row, they come to over half a dozen:

1. A quotation is introduced and closed by double quotation marks. A quotation within a quotation carries single quotation

---

[6]There is no need for either of these verbal devices; they are affectation based on the formality of the written word. Moreover, "unquote" is nonsense born of confusion with "end quote."

marks, and a third internal quotation, if required, brings double ones again.

2. The omission of a word, phrase, or sentence is shown by three dots. If that omission comes at the end of a sentence, the fourth dot that you will see stands for the period at the end of the original sentence.

3. If intelligibility requires the addition of a word or short phrase—seldom more—the added words should be enclosed in square brackets.[7] These words will generally be possessive adjectives—for example, [her], [your]—or the definite article [the], or a pair of words expanding a pronoun, such as an "it" that would be ambiguous. One replaces this "it" with: [the document], or some such unmistakable substitute. One may also supply a word where ambiguity might result from the lack of a context: see the word [court] in the quotation on p. 203.

4. The spelling, capitalization, and punctuation of the quoted passage must be faithfully reproduced unless (a) you modernize these features when quoting older texts, in which case you mention your practice at some convenient point; or (b) you correct a typographical or other obvious error, in which case a footnote is required to notify the reader only if meaning is involved. If you wish to draw attention to an error without correcting it, put [*sic*] after it in square brackets.

5. The foregoing rule also dictates the familiar tag at the end of a quotation: [My italics]; it is perhaps a shade less obtrusive to use the phrase "Italics added." In any case, a writer should avoid sprinkling italics over other people's prose. If you choose your quotation with forethought and set it with care, it will generally not need any italicizing to make its point. If on rereading you think the force of the quotation somehow does not make itself felt, try cutting down the quoted words to those that actually contain the point.

---

[7]In legal scholarship, brackets are put around any capital letter that is supplied by the quoter when he changes the grammatical role of a word. This is rarely necessary in historical or report writing.

6. The quoting of titles is more properly called "citing." It gives rise to the second invariable rule of modern scholarship:[8] all book titles are printed in italics (words underlined in typescript); all essay titles are in roman type and enclosed within double quotation marks.[9] The two forms are thus distinguishable at a glance.

But a question divides opinion as to the wording of a title when cited. Some readers feel awkwardness when they see: "This he achieved in his *The Call of the Wild.*" It is ungrammatical to use two definers: "Then he picked up his the hat." The remedy is simple: omit "his," which adds nothing to the meaning. Hence many writers cut off the *A* and *The* of a title when they cite in running text: "Motley's *Rise of the Dutch Republic.*" This practice is long established. When you follow it, take care to note the possible significance of *A* in a title. The author may have wanted to sound tentative as in: AN *Economic Interpretation of the Constitution* by Charles A. Beard. In such a case, insert a cushion word before the *An* (or *A* or *The*): in his next work, her first novel, etc.

But watch again: we fall into gibberish if having properly elided a redundant article, we begin to use the decapitated title as if it were complete: "He then published *Rise of the Dutch Republic.*" The use of *a* and *the* in all contexts is a measure of a writer's awareness of his obligations.

7. There should be firmer rules about the *right* to quote; legal doctrine is on this point indefinite. The principle of "fair use" sets no clear limits to the kind or amount that may be quoted without special permission. This is true for prose but not for quoting poetry or the lyrics of a song, even a few lines. Most publishers routinely request that the author ask permission of the copyright holder for every quotation. But do you ask for six words?

---

[8]For the first, see Chapter 2, p. 26.

[9]Some periodicals devoted to book reviewing dislike the appearance of frequent italics in their pages and require book titles to be named within quotation marks. This practice does not lessen the importance of the rule or the unanimity with which it is observed in the world of research.

Obviously not. Some publishers allow quoting 250 to 500 words without permission being sought.

All American university presses allow one another's authors a thousand words. For the rest, you must write to the quoted author's publisher, giving the length, opening and closing words, and page references of the passage, and also the name of your own publisher. Do so well ahead of your publication date, for you may have to write again, to the author or to a third party—the holder of the copyright.[10] Most British authors will express surprise at your wanting a written permission for what they do every day without formalities.

"Credit" should naturally be given for all that you borrow, including original ideas that you restate in your own words. But there is no need to be overcome by gratitude: you are keeping an author's thought and fame alive when you quote and name him or her, and for this either is in your debt. Some publishers will specify for your acknowledgment a formula of their own, occasionally quite long and in a style reminiscent of funerary inscriptions. But open a current book and you will see that thanks are given in a list of all copyright owners on an Acknowledgment page, or that each is named briefly at the point where the material is used.

Quoting from unpublished manuscripts—letters, diaries, journals, and unfinished literary pieces—once regarded as not usable by researchers without permission—has now become moot. There is a strong demand for their free use, but they are now deemed copyrighted by the very act of their creation and cannot be used even if they are open to the public in libraries and declared unrestricted by the depositor. Many authors and journalists believe that restricting the use violates a putative "right to know." They argue that the prohibition protects public

---

[10]These restrictions do not apply to government documents, from which you may quote ad lib unless the quoted portions themselves contain copyrighted material, as indicated in the document itself. On copyright issues respecting electronic sources, consult Raymond T. Nimmer, *Information Law* (2 vols., 2002).

figures from a close scrutiny of their lives and careers. Whatever the merits of the argument, if in doubt, request your editor to consult the firm's copyright lawyer.[11]

In permissible quoting, must you always name the author? Many obvious quotations need no author's name. For instance, if you are so unadventurous that you find yourself quoting "To be or not to be," leave the author in decent obscurity. If you quote for a purely decorative purpose an anecdote that is going the rounds and that you found in your local newspaper, or a trifling news item from the same source, no reference is needed to the place and date (see the extract from *Punch* above, p. 238). Remember, in other words, that quoting is for illustration and that citing is for possible verification. What is illustrative but unimportant (and in any case not likely to have been garbled or forged) does not need to be verified, and it would therefore be pedantry to refer the reader to its source. Like Emerson, he wants you to tell him what you know.

Difficulties and Dangers of Translation

When what you want to tell your reader is the statement of a foreign authority, the wish to quote carries with it the duty to translate. We willingly assume that you can read the language you intend to quote from, but this is the least of the prerequisites, even though the opinion is widespread that anyone who knows two languages pretty well can translate from the one into the other. Nothing could be further from the truth.[12]

---

[11]On copyright protection for your own work, see p. 291ff.

[12]An extreme yet frequent example is that of the person who, because he reads and understands a foreign language, thinks he can write it. Some years ago, an Italian publisher of scholarly books sent to his American patrons a magnificently printed and illustrated folder announcing a new edition of a medieval text. The description in "English" was in this style: "Indispensable and basic to those who deal Dante's problems of Midiaeval Mysticism, *The Book of the Figures,* consisting in two volumes cloth bound and with superior cut gilt, reproduces the Reggian Codex and the other one, analogous, of Oxford, with very rich colour tables, which offer to the studious Enquirers a limpid Historical Document. . . . This new Edition will gain new consensus, especially out of Italy."

The result of the misconception is that readers and critics keep complaining of the unreadable matter palmed off on them as translations. The principles of the art of translating are apparently unsuspected or ignored by those most in need of them—authors, publishers, journalists, researchers, and students generally.

In a world whose inhabitants are more and more involved with one another across the frontiers of politics and language, it is obvious that translation is a daily necessity. Yet good translators being scarce, the world's work is hampered or spoiled by mistranslation. This leads on occasion to grave misunderstanding and does nothing to allay any preexisting friction. The problem at its simplest often occurs between the two branches of what we still think of as one language, namely English and American. Churchill once mentioned that the word "table," in "tabling a motion," plunged an important war council into a "long and even acrimonious discussion," because the Americans took "table" to mean indefinite postponement, whereas the English understood it to mean "put down for subsequent discussion."[13] Again, the familiar words of science and technology, many of which are international, sometimes mislead through unexpected overlappings or false similarities, as when the French *éther* is made to stand for both "ether" and "ester."

Such misunderstandings define the first duty of the translator: he must thoroughly understand the meaning and connotation of the words in his original—not their general purport, but their precise uses. In short, the researcher who translates must once again be a critical scanner of words, a haggler over shades of meaning. The briefer the passage to translate the more important is hairline preciseness, for the occasional errors in a long work tend to be corrected by the context, whereas a fragment eight lines long affords no such corrective.

---

[13]See G. V. Carey, *American into English: A Handbook for Translators* (London, 1953), 1 and 87; and Norman W. Schur, *British English, A to Zed* (2001).

Even supposing that the scholar, reporter, or technician has learned in one or more foreign tongues all the words in his special vocabulary; he is still far from fully equipped. For "what the original means" is not the same thing as "knowing the meaning of every word." It is words together that give a statement its peculiar force and clear implications. Take a phrase that recurs in political declarations coming from France. A quite simple statement by a minister in office will begin with: "*Je sais bien que. . . .*" Throughout the English and American press this will be translated as either "I know well that . . ." or "I well know that. . . ." Neither sounds quite right, for English or American speakers never use this expression. What they do say that looks faintly connected with the original French is the somewhat accusing: "You know very well that [you leaked the story]." Or in the first person singular, the quite different: "I know very well [what I did]"; which implies: "And it isn't what you think." But neither use of this *well* has any relation to the French phrase. What is the force of *bien,* and how do we translate it? Forget "well" altogether; *bien* here must be translated: "Of course." What the politician said is our concessive remark "Of course, I know [that this has already been tried, *but* . . .]."

Dictionaries and "False Friends"

The second rule of translation is that to find the full meaning of words as required by the first rule, we must go beyond the immediate dictionary meaning to the significance of its role in the particular sentence. About *bien,* the author of a handbook for translators asserts: "It is only exceptionally that it should be translated 'well,' "[14] and he gives half a column of examples and

[14]J. G. Anderson, *Le Mot Juste: An Anglo-French Lexicon* (London, 1932), 44. A revised edition was brought out by L. C. Harmer in 1938. See in addition *Mistakable French* by Philip Thody and Howard Evans (1985), which lists under ten categories from Law to Literature words easily confused.

equivalents. What is true of all these troublesome little words in every language—*doch* in German, *più* in Italian, *más* in Spanish—is true in a different way of the abstract and substantive words. You cannot be sure that when you have the denotation firmly in mind you also have the right connotation.

Worse, you will find that words coming from the same root have had different histories in two or more languages and have diverged. A dais in English is a platform; in French it is a canopy. A person described as *constipado* in Spanish merely has a cold. A *Friseur* in Germany will not curl or frizz your hair but will cut it. A vexatious example of the same slippage of sense in diplomacy came to light at the League of Nations after the First World War. The French *contrôle* was frequently translated "control" until it appeared that in French the word means "supervise, pass upon, make sure of compliance," while in English it means "govern completely." Thus a French conductor who punches your ticket is a *contrôleur;* this is etymologically correct, since the root of the word is *contre-rôle,* a counter-roll or, as we now say, a checklist.[15]

Sticking to French, one may cite a few of the commonest words that have become traps in translating, most frequently in newspaper reports: *admettre* does not always mean "admit," as in *"Le gouvernement ne peut pas admettre que. . . ."* The meaning is a softened "allow": "The government will not grant that. . . ." Again, goods described as *en provenance des Etats-Unis* do not necessarily "originate" in the United States; they are merely being shipped from there. Once an Anglo-French committee was stumped by the description of a proposed course of action as *fastidieux.* Plainly "fastidious" made no sense. It turns out to mean "wearisome," "dull and fatiguing." Finally, there are tricky words such as *demander* and *ressentir,* which mean "ask"

---

[15]The French meaning occurs in English in the single phrase "control experiment," which is a check upon other work, with no idea of "control" in the ordinary sense.

and not "demand," "feel" or "experience" and not "resent." But hold on. The derived noun *ressentiment* does carry the notion of anger or rancor, even more strongly than does "resentment." Such are the pitfalls of language.

The consequences of missing such nuances or supplying gratuitous ones in translation are patent. But the problem rarely comes to public attention as it did when the United States, through the late Ambassador Edwin O. Reischauer, formally persuaded the Japanese government to change its official translation of the word "containment," the term for America's Cold War policy. The Japanese had long been using the word *fujikome,* which Reischauer, learned in Japanese, saw as having a connotation of aggressiveness, suggestive of a bulldozer at work. The Japanese Ministry of Foreign Affairs finally changed the translation to *sekitome,* a milder word meaning simply "to check" or "to dam."

It follows that every translator needs all the help he or she can get from (1) dictionaries, (2) special lexicons and manuals for translators that can protect you from "false friends," as they are called, (3) extensive reading in the many languages required by his work, (4) a studious pursuit of etymology and word connections in *both* of the languages involved, and (5) the advice of educated native speakers of the foreign language.

Except for traveling light, a pocket dictionary is worthless. You need the best foreign-English dictionary *and* a reliable all-foreign dictionary in that language. The best bilingual dictionaries of the modern tongues are those that (1) list more than one equivalent, (2) supplement these with examples of use, and (3) have been revised by scholars within the previous quarter-century.

Literalism and Paraphrase

The reader of foreign languages will also be interested in everything he encounters that bears on translation. There is, for example, a lively little book by the late Monsignor Ronald

Knox that deals with the difficulties and controversies he ran into when translating the Bible.[16] Now the Bible may be all Greek and Hebrew to you, but in these essays by Knox you come upon illuminating remarks that are applicable to translating to or from any language. For example:

> Among the many good things . . . [Hilaire] Belloc has done . . . is a little brochure . . . on Translation. The great principle he there lays down is that the business of a translator is not to ask "How shall I make this foreigner talk English?" But "What would an Englishman have said to express this?" For instance, he says, if you are faced with the French sentence, *"Il y avait dans cet homme je ne sais quoi de suffisance,"* you do not want to write "There was in this man I know not what of self-sufficiency"; you want to write, "there was a touch of complacency about him. . . ."
>
> Anybody who has really tackled the business of translation, at least where the classical languages are concerned, will tell you that the bother is not finding the equivalent for this or that word, it is finding how to turn the sentence. . . . The translator, let me suggest in passing, must never be frightened of the word "paraphrase"; it is a bogey of the half-educated. As I have already tried to point out, it is almost impossible to translate a *sentence* without paraphrasing; it is a paraphrase when you translate "Comment vous portez-vous?" by "How are you?"[17]

This last caution is worth expanding a little in order to banish once and for all the fear many writers and researchers have of being wrong when they depart from the word-by-word contents of their original. The term "paraphrase" frightens them because they know that a paraphrase from English verse to English prose entails a loss of meaning; you cannot paraphrase the soliloquies in *Hamlet* and say: "This is Shakespeare's meaning." It can only be a rough approximation. But in translating from a foreign language, what is loosely called paraphrasing is

---

[16]*On Englishing the Bible* (London, 1949). See also Adam Nicolson, *God's Secretaries: The Making of the King James Bible* (2003).
[17]Ibid., 4 and 12.

the only wording that deserves to be called a translation, no other being possible. To reinforce the Belloc example, take the French expression: *"C'est une autre paire de manches."* The *only* possible translation of those words is: "That's a horse of another color." Plainly, none of the significant French words has received its normal equivalent. The French says nothing about horses or their color; it talks of a pair of sleeves. But the horse is no "paraphrase" of sleeves; it is their correct equivalent. To put into English each word separately would be to write nonsense. For an enjoyable lesson on this point, and the humor to be drawn from willfully forgetting it, read in Mark Twain's "Private History of the 'Jumping Frog' Story" the portion that gives in English his impression of the French version of the tale. Take it as an absolute rule that translation occurs not between words but between meanings. Father Knox gives the example of *en effet,* which he finds everybody translating "in effect" when the meaning is not in the least "in effect" but "sure enough"—no paraphrase, but an exact rendering of the meaning of the two French words.

To Translate Is to "Carry Over"

What all the warning examples boil down to is this: *Accurate translating requires, in addition to a transfer of the full contents, a transfer of their full intention.* This is plain enough at any point where a rhetorical device occurs in the original, such as irony, which conveys the opposite of what is said. When Thomas Nugent in the eighteenth century translated Montesquieu's *Esprit des Lois,* he completely missed the irony of a famous passage about slavery so completely, that he felt called upon to add a footnote of apology for the author whom he took to be defending the institution. The apology should have been addressed to the author thus misrepresented. Such blunders inspired the Italian proverb *"Traduttore, traditore"*—"A translator is a traitor."

The researcher wants to be the very reverse of a traitor. His motto is Fidelity. But because of lack of good advice, poor teaching in school, and no sound tradition, fidelity is easily misconstrued into Literalism. The translator defends the word-for-word by pointing to the original with a "that's what it says!" There is no "it." There is a foreigner's thought, and you must think, too, if you are to discharge your duty of reproducing it. And to do this you must have mastered your own language. Unless you can summon up the right turn of phrase in your native tongue, you will betray its counterpart in the original text. The foreignness of it will show through; you will be giving not a translation but a transliteration. At times, to add yet one more shade, you may want to quote your author's own wording; you give it in italics in parentheses. But your text gives the *thought.*

One way to define faithful translation would be to say that a certain paragraph in a foreign work contains, over and above its cargo of information, eleven additional features—an alliteration, a play on words, a rhythmical halt, an allusion to a famous poem, a colloquial turn, a long learned word where a short common one was expected, and so on. The translator, noting these points, will try to reproduce somewhere in his version each element or effect. Not until he has exhausted his resources will he consider the original sentence to have been fully "carried over."

Some examples of successive attempts at this perfection of rendering will make the task and its method clear. Our first example is again from the French, the language that translators agree is the most unlike English in the movement of its thought and the most deceptively like English in its vocabulary. It thus combines in the highest degree the two difficulties that must be met in every piece of translation. The following passage comes from a work which has been twice translated in our time, and which would benefit from a third effort that would retain the happy turns of the previous two. Here is the original:

Un des plus grands personnages de ce temps-là, un des hommes les plus marquants dans l'Église et dans l'État, nous a conté, ce soir (janvier 1822), chez Mme de M . . . . , les dangers fort réels qu'il avait courus du temps de la Terreur.

"J'avais eu le malheur d'être au nombre des membres les plus marquants de l'Assemblée constituante: je me tins à Paris, cherchant à me cacher tant bien que mal, tant qu'il y eut quelque espoir de succès pour la bonne cause. Enfin, les dangers augmentant et les étrangers ne faisant rien d'énergique pour nous, je me déterminai à partir, mais il fallait partir sans passeport."[18]

In 1915 this was translated as follows:

One of the most important persons of our age, one of the most prominent men in the Church and in the State, related to us this evening (January, 1822), at Madame de M -'s, the very real dangers he had gone through under the Terror.

"I had the misfortune to be one of the most prominent members of the Constituent Assembly. I stayed in Paris, trying to hide myself as best I could, so long as there was any hope of success for the good cause. At last, as the danger grew greater and greater, while the foreigner made no energetic move in our favour, I decided to leave—only I had to leave without a passport."[19]

A dozen years later an anonymous version, said to have been done under the supervision of the well-known translator, C. K. Scott-Moncrieff, appeared in New York and has since been reprinted in a popular series. It is on the whole less accurate than the first. Our passage comes out in this form:

One of the most illustrious persons of his time, and one of the foremost men in both Church and State affairs, told us this evening (January 1822), at Madam M's house, some of the very real dangers he had run at the time of the Terror.

"I had had the misfortune to be one of the most important members of the constituent Assembly: I remained in Paris, trying to hide myself as best I might, so long as there was any hope of success for the good cause. At last, as the dangers were increasing and other countries were making no effort to help us, I decided to leave, but I had no passport."[20]

---

[18]Stendhal [Henri Beyle], *De l'Amour*, "Fragments Divers" (1822), 166.
[19]Translation by Philip and Cecil N. Sidney Woolf (London, 1915), 329.
[20]Translation by H. B. V. (New York, 1927); Black and Gold Edition (New York, 1947), 341.

The meaning of the original is simple and the text presents no grammatical difficulty; the reader of the English "understands" it, as he thinks, through and through. Nevertheless some points are in doubt, since at those points the meaning has struck two pairs of translators rather differently. Quite apart from the resulting hesitation, the reader may feel that he would like to know what the "good cause" is, which both translate literally. Could closer attention to nuance achieve greater fidelity? Let us try, adding explanatory comments and signposts as we go:

One of the greatest figures [*not* "persons" and *not* "illustrious"] of that age ["his age" would conflict with what follows], *who was* [needed for the sentence to sound English] among the foremost men *in Church and State* [English idiom], told us at Madame de M's this evening (January 1822) [the natural English order for Place and Time is to put the shorter modifier first] *about* the very real dangers to which he had been exposed [one *runs* a risk but not a danger] during the Terror.

"I had [the pluperfect is literal but throws us off] the misfortune of being *among the foremost* [phrase repeated from above, as in the original] members of the *National Assembly* [the more familiar name in English, little used in French]. I *hung on* in Paris [= the true force of the original], trying to hide [*not* 'hide myself,' which suggests children playing] *in one way or another* [*not* 'as best I could,' which goes without saying], so long as there was any hope of success for *our cause* [that is, the 'good cause' was naturally his own, but it is also that of the people he is addressing]. At last, the danger increasing [singular, since he is not counting but gauging] while the foreign powers [not 'countries,' which is weak, nor 'the foreigner,' which is vague] *were taking no strong action* in our behalf, I *made up my mind* ['decided' gives no sense of a gradual resolution] to leave—only, [comma essential; otherwise the sentence means 'no one but I'] I had to leave without a passport." [Here as elsewhere the second translator omits a whole idea.]

Now if a few quite simple lines are capable of improvement by the application of a little critical thought, it is easy to imagine how much attention long and complex passages require. Our shelves are full of works in "famous" translations that yet contain page after page of gibberish—the gibberish that comes of a "careful" literalism. For examples of this fatal fault, one has only to leaf through the two volumes of Henry Reeve's well-known translation of Tocqueville's *Democracy in America*. Here is the beginning of Chapter 2:

> A man has come into the world; his early years are spent without notice in the pleasures and activities of childhood. As he grows up, the world receives him when his manhood begins, and he enters into contact with his fellows. He is then studied for the first time, and it is imagined that the germ of the vices and the virtues of his maturer years is then formed.[21]

This nonsense should be enough to dispel the idea that because of look-alikes the French and English vocabularies make translation easy. All translation is hard. Practice and challenge make the task congenial to the person who is a lucid writer. To translate is, after all, to set down your own thoughts. True, you are borrowing them; you have, so to speak, overheard a secret uttered by a foreign agent, and your knowledge of the foreign tongue enables you to understand its full bearing. To repeat it depends on your knowledge of your own tongue.

An example from the German, again comparing two translations, will show how important is this last capacity. Goethe tells in his autobiography how as an eight-year-old he and his family were much excited by the outbreak of the Seven Years' War and the ensuing partisanship for or against Frederick the Great:

> *Und so war ich denn auch preussisch oder, um richtiger zu reden, Fritzisch gesinnt: denn was ging uns Preussen an? Es war die Persoenlichkeit des grossen Koenigs, die auf alle Gemueter wirkte. Ich freute mich mit dem Vater unserer Siege, schrieb sehr gern die Siegslieder ab, und fast noch lieber die Spottlieder auf die Gegenpartei, so platt die Reime auch sein möchten.*[22]

---

[21]Alexis de Tocqueville, *Democracy in America*, the Henry Reeve translation, as revised by Francis Bowen, further corrected and edited by Phillips Bradley (1945), 1:26.

[22]Goethe, *Dichtung und Wahrheit*, Book 2, paragraph 4.

The standard translation, originally by John Oxenford, and then revised anonymously, reads as follows:

So it was that my sympathies were on the side of Prussia, or more accurately, of Fritz; what, after all, was Prussia to us? It was the personality of the great King that impressed everyone. I rejoiced with my father in our conquests, willingly copied the songs of victory, and perhaps yet more willingly the lampoons directed against the other side, poor as the rhymes might be.[23]

The people who had a hand in that version did not satisfy one reader of a later generation, who re-translated the whole:

And so my views were Prussian, or, to speak more correctly, those of Frederick, for what did we care about Prussia? It was the personality of the great King which moved all hearts; I rejoiced with my father over our victories, most readily copied out the songs of triumph and almost more readily the lampoons against the other party, however poor the rhymes might be.[24]

In this pair of renderings almost the only part that seems assured is: "It was the personality of the great King." As for the rest, in either version, the least that can be said is that it does not come up to the jauntiness of the original. Here we have the old poet looking back on the first enthusiasm of his childhood, recalling a distant hero worship, half-political, half-poetical; how shall we express it when he has done it so well in the simplest, clearest German? We can only try—and very likely fail:

And so here I was, a regular Prussian, or to put it more exactly a Fritz man: for what did Prussia mean to us? It was the personality of the great King that captured the imagination. With my father I gloried in our victories. I eagerly made copies of the victory songs, and perhaps even more eagerly of the songs that made fun of the other side, no matter how lame their lyrics.

---

[23]*Poetry and Truth*, revised translation based on that of John Oxenford and A. S. W. Morrison, revised by Minna Steele Smith (London, 1913), 1:35.

[24]R. O. Moon, *Goethe's Autobiography* (Washington, DC, 1949), 34.

So much for the goals of fullness and felicity. A peculiar danger the researcher must guard against when he has been plunged for some time in foreign sources is the inability to distinguish between the idiom he understands "like a native" and his own. This failing overcomes even the best translators of scholarly and other books. For example, a writer on French political parties will speak of "the militants" who attended a meeting, meaning "the rank and file"; or again, a student of Italian culture will write "The Illuminism" instead of "The Enlightenment"; just as a reporter on contemporary German life may slip into the habit of piling up adjectives in front of his nouns ("an easy-to-suspect assertion") without noticing that in coining such expressions he is Germanizing at variance with the genius of the English language.

The safeguard against this excessive adaptability of the mind is to translate in three steps: (1) a rough draft, quickly made with the original at hand; (2) a second draft, some days later based on the first, with the original out of sight. You will find odd combinations of words, a twisted idiom, a verb in the same tense as the original that are not English usage. You correct and improve; (3) a third and possibly final draft, for which you consult the original, phrase by phrase, to make sure that *all the ideas and implications have found a place somewhere in your version.* Then, perhaps, you have a piece of prose that may pass for a translation.[25]

---

[25]The mechanical problems of translating coinage and weights and measures, and of transliterating Russian, Chinese, and other proper names, are so special and varied that they cannot be taken up in a book dealing with fundamentals. Current practice, moreover, is chaotic. Whereas the Chinese some years ago adopted *pinyin*, a sensible system of equivalent letters that show how to pronounce, say, Mao Zedong, our authors do not apply it to established former spellings, e.g., Chiang Kai-shek, which is sounded Jyang Kyshek. Lately, too, the familiar Koran has begun to appear as Qur'an and Mohammed as Muḥammad, with a meaningless dot under the ḥ. Names transliterated from Russian, Polish, Hungarian, and Turkish continue to defy reason, in deference to an imaginary accuracy which is nothing better than pedantry.

CHAPTER 12

THE RULES OF CITING: FOOTNOTES AND BIBLIOGRAPHY

Types and Functions of Footnotes

An important double biography of Benedict Arnold and Major André was originally issued with an announcement to the purchaser: "Source references available on request from the publishers, in a pamphlet designed to be affixed to the book."[1] By mailing a postcard to the publishers, one received a booklet of twenty-five pages, a package of footnotes. Passing over the question of where the library reader of the book would seek its documentation when the booklet was mislaid or out of print, we must raise the larger question: What are footnotes for? Are they a standard accessory of every good work other than fiction, or are they optional for both the writer and the reader? Publishers generally believe that scholarly works are more likely to attract readers if shorn of footnotes. Still, in the absence of footnotes many readers feel deprived of things they want to know.[2]

Footnotes are of two kinds. The first explains an assertion in the body of the work and is therefore reading matter. This kind of footnote is used when the elucidation or elaboration of a

---

[1]James T. Flexner, *The Traitor and the Spy* (1953).

[2]See Gertrude Himmelfarb's front-page article, "Where Have All the Footnotes Gone?" (*New York Times Book Review,* June 16, 1991) and letters in response, ibid. (July 14, 1991).

remark in the text would break the thread of the story or otherwise distract from continuity. Such comments and sidelights are sometimes so numerous and so full that they take up more space than the words they supplement. This abuse is to be avoided, for as one facetious objector pointed out, "it is quite a chore to keep focussing up and down the page, especially if you have old eyes or a touch of astigmatism."[3] Yet it would be wrong to outlaw this form of running commentary. When skillfully used it serves to fill out the narrative with details that would clog the mainstream but that greatly enrich the understanding.[4] There is no warrant for the maxim "if it's important, put it in the text; if it's not, leave it out." The caution against excess footnoting can be summed up as: don't write another book or article running parallel to the first.

The form of the explanatory footnote consists of declarative sentences, usually in a more conversational tone than the rest of the book, like a stage aside. For example, in the main text of *The Age of the Great Depression,* Dixon Wecter wrote that a new magazine named *Ballyhoo* "rocketed to a two-million circulation largely by debunking the specious salesmanship of the Twenties."[5] To this neutral report of fact he added the footnote: "Its creator was a disillusioned Manhattan editor and artist, Norman Anthony, but the name which *Ballyhoo* made famous was that of a fictional high-powered advertising man, one Elmer Zilch. In a chapter called 'Jackpot!' Anthony gave the history of this magazine in *How to Grow Old Disgracefully* (New York, 1946)." This lively information was too detailed for a place in a survey of the years 1929–1931. The author is in effect saying that he knows more than what he relates on the scale of his main narrative, but if you will step outside, he will extend his remarks.

In textbooks, footnotes may be unwanted, but they cannot be ruled out even there. They may serve to give equivalents for

[3]Frank Sullivan, "A Garland of Ibids for Van Wyck Brooks" (*New Yorker,* 17, April 19, 1941, 15).

[4]See, for example, Lawrence A. Cremin, *The Transformation of the School* (1961).

[5]Vol. 13 of *The History of American Life* (New York, 1927–1948), 15.

foreign coinage or land measures, or supply the original words of foreign quotations, or identify a little-known character mentioned in passing. A footnote that is important but too long is matter for an appendix. James G. Randall in *Lincoln the President* took this means of conveying the information on Lincoln's relationship with Ann Rutledge.[6]

The second kind of footnote refers to a source; it records the origin of, or the authority for, a statement in the text. Footnotes of this type are used for both direct and indirect quotations. They form the main part of the "apparatus" that distinguishes a work of scholarship from a popular work. They create confidence in a book by enabling anyone to verify the assertion made. In addition, they permit the author to acknowledge his debts.

Using the proper form for this kind of footnote demands careful attention. Even though no one method has been universally adopted, it is a shorthand easy to learn and decipher. The researcher will choose between two systems: that codified by the Modern Language Association;[7] or that described in the Chicago Manual.[8] Other learned groups use other systems to suit their special needs (see Figure 21).

Whatever the style—and the variations from one publisher to the next are slight—the principle underlying all the forms is the same; it is implicit in the purpose of the reference footnote: give the essential details in short compass. The note must be so framed that the reader can immediately tell the type of source cited—a manuscript or a printed article, a newspaper or a book, a letter or a conversation. These distinctions are important, for in estimating evidence its sources are weighed, not counted. Each kind impresses the reader in a different way. For example, a magazine article is generally written with more care than a

[6] 1946–1952, 4 vols., 2:321–342.

[7] *MLA Handbook for Writers of Research Papers* (revised by Joseph Gibaldi, 6th ed., 2003).

[8] *The Chicago Manual of Style* (15th ed., 2003). A paperbound digest of the Chicago rules by Kate L. Turabian has been popular: *A Manual for Writers of Term Papers, Theses, and Dissertations.* It has been revised most recently by John Grossman and Alice Bennett (8th ed., 1996).

FIGURE 21   *THREE WAYS OF CITING*

Modern Language Association:
Koch, Kathy. "Truck Safety." *CQ Researcher* 12 March 1999. CQ Electronic Library. Richland Coll. Lib., Dallas. 25 Jan. 2002 [and on the Internet:] http://library. cqpress.com
American Psychological Association:
Koch, K. (1999). *Truck Safety. CQ Researcher, 9*, 209–32.
Chicago Manual of Style:
Koch, Kathy. "Truck Safety." *CQ Researcher* 9. (March 12, 1999): 209–232.

Variations on these sample ways are permissible, provided the information needed to track down the article or book is there and clearly set out. The punctuation is likewise at one's discretion so long as it is clear and consistent.

newspaper column but probably with less than a book. Similarly, a conversation may, depending on how it was recorded, prove to be less convincing than a manuscript.

Footnote Form and Forms

The variety of documents is distinguished by the typographical form of the note. If a manuscript is being cited the footnote begins with the abbreviation "MS" (or "MSS" for the plural):

MS Diary of Edmund Ruffin, February 17, 1857.

If the manuscript has a title it appears in quotation marks without the label "MS":

"Big Me," William Herndon's autobiography.

A magazine article is always cited in quotation marks followed by the title of the magazine in italics:

Mrs. Kermit Roosevelt, "F. D. R., Lady Churchill, and the Brussels Sprouts" (*Harper's Magazine,* 213, August 1956, 62–64).

As mentioned earlier, an absolute rule in modern research is that *any printed volume is referred to in italics.*

The second use of quotation marks around a title in roman type is to tell us that here is a portion of the source that follows—

a printed source, since *its* title is italicized.[9] Thus it comes about that we cite articles published in magazines as we do. Note that chapter and book bear the same typographical relation as article and periodical.

Because footnotes are for convenience, the most important datum is generally put first. Most often it is the author's name:

George F. Will, *Men at Work: The Craft of Baseball* (New York, 1990).

The title of the work may come first if it is deemed more important than the author or the editor. This is true, for instance, of encyclopedias, dictionaries, anthologies, annuals, and the like:

Political Handbook of the World: 1982–1983 (eds. Arthur S. Banks and William Overstreet, New York, 1983).

Sometimes the name of the editor of a work, rather than the author, should come first. This is especially to be observed when two or more collections of an author's writings are being used and must be quickly distinguishable:

Worthington C. Ford, ed., *The Writings of George Washington* (14 vols., New York, 1889–1893).
John C. Fitzpatrick, ed., *The Writings of George Washington* (39 vols., Washington, DC, 1931–1944).
W. W. Abbot, et al., *The Papers of George Washington* (43 vols. to date, Charlottesville, VA, 1983–).

Since reference notes are strictly for the reader's purposes, they should never be used as ornamentation or ballast for the text. The quality and extent of your scholarship are not measured by the number of notes or their elaborateness. They should be as terse as possible. Thus, it has become common practice, when an author and his book are named in the text, to write a "split footnote." It completes at the bottom of the page

---

[9]In learning these conventions, be sure not to confuse "printed" with "published." Many printed works found in libraries were never published, but were circulated privately.

the information given above, as in the footnote on page 269. Instead of repeating "James G. Randall" and *Lincoln the President,* it merely adds where and when the book was published and the number of volumes, saving space and time.

Take note of a few more conventions: do not forget to separate title and subtitle by punctuation, comma or colon:

Lou Cannon, *President Reagan: The Role of a Lifetime* (New York, 1991).

Give the volume number of a magazine in Arabic numerals even if it appears in Roman numerals on the publication itself:

Notes and Queries (9th Series, 8, July–December 1901), 97–98.

Italicize the name of a newspaper but not the city; it is not considered part of the title:

Cleveland *Plain Dealer* (August 11, 1990).

True, you will find:

New York Times (January 21, 2001).

but this is to avoid confusion with *The Times* of London. For American newspapers, the state is given in parentheses when the town is obscure:

Thibodaux (LA) *Minerva* (March 1, 1856).

Put in brackets the name of an anonymous or pseudonymous author when you know it:

"Strix" [Peter Fleming], *My Aunt's Rhinoceros and Other Reflections* (London, 1956).

You may omit the date and place of publication, and certainly the publisher's name, when you plan to furnish them in your bibliography or when they do not help to identify and find the work or edition.

Gustavus Myers, *History of Bigotry in the United States,* 18.

FIGURE 22   *ROMAN NUMERALS AND THEIR USE*

I =	1	A smaller number in front of another is			
II =	2	subtracted:			
III =	3	IV =	4	XC =	90
V =	5	IX =	9	CD =	400
X =	10	XL =	40	CM =	900
L =	50	Number(s) following another is (are) added:			
C =	100	XII =	12	LXX =	70
D =	500	XIV =	14	MD =	1500
M =	1000	XVI =	16	MDCCC =	1800
		XXX =	30	MM =	2000

Roman numerals are less often used than formerly, but they must be learned because they are still found in Tables, Plates, and similar "extra" matter. On periodicals, the volume number is often in Roman numerals, and in books the front matter (preface, acknowledgments, etc.) that comes before page 1 is in Roman numerals printed in lower case (small letters), not caps: *i, vi, xiii,* etc. In old books that use Roman numerals to give the date of publication on the title page, the figure *IIII* may appear instead of *IV,* as on clock faces to this day.

Thanks to uniform scholarly texts, the citation of ancient authors can be given in condensed form, by name (and work if more than one is extant), followed by two numbers—those of the "book" (chapter or canto) and "chapter" (paragraph):

Herodotus, 3. 14.[10]

Equally systematic are the footnotes that refer to books cited earlier in the same piece of writing. Certain Latin words, abbreviated or in full, indicate these connections; such repeating symbols, being in a foreign tongue, they are often italicized, and the letters are pronounced as written: "e.g." is *ee gee;* "op. cit." is *opp sit;* and so on.[11]

[10]In citing poets the second set of numbers indicates the line(s): Lucretius, 2, 121.

[11]The English equivalents are sometimes preferable but do not imitate the writer in whose book one continually reads "See me above"; "See me below."

Some publishers prefer repeating the short title to the use of these Latin abbreviations, or Anglicize them. But since thousands of books use the system that dates back to the seventeenth century, the researcher must learn the classic symbols and usages. The most commonly used is ibid. (abbreviation of *ibidem*) meaning "in the same place." The "place" is, and can only be, the book cited in the footnote *immediately preceding*. For example:

²Hajo Holborn, *A History of Modern Germany, 1840–1945* (1969), 795.
³Ibid., 675.

If the next footnote (number 4) refers to a different book, and footnote 5 harks back once more to Holborn's volume, you must write "Holborn, op. cit.," short for *opere citato*, and meaning "in the work cited." What we have, then, is this:

²Hajo Holborn, *A History of Modern Germany, 1840–1945* (1969), 795.
³Ibid., 675.
⁴George F. Kennan, *Memoirs, 1925–1950* (1967), 130.
⁵Holborn, op. cit., 799.

The perfect clarity of this arrangement will not be affected by the fact that a page may be turned between notes 2 and 3, and several pages between notes 3 and 5. But you must guard against using *op. cit.* when you cite more than one book by the same author. Each citation must unmistakably tell the reader which is meant. But suppose that you switch back and forth between Beard's *An Economic Interpretation of the Constitution of the United States* and his *Economic Origins of Jeffersonian Democracy*. These long titles will clutter your page if you refer to them each time in full. The remedy is to use a "short title":

Beard, *Economic Interpretation*, 6;

and later:

Beard, *Economic Origins*, 302.

Occasionally it is necessary to tell the reader that in a certain work he will find almost anywhere, and not on one page rather

FIGURE **23**   *COMMON ABBREVIATIONS*

A.D. in the year of our Lord
(precedes the date)
A.L.S. autograph letter signed
anon. anonymous
B.C. before Christ (follows the date)
B.C.E. alternative to B.C.—Before the
Common Era
bk. book
c., ca. about (in dating)
cap. capital letter
ce. common error
cf. compare or see
ch., chap. chapter
col. column
ed. editor, edition, edited, edited by
(plural: eds.)
e.g. for example
et al. and others (of persons)
etc. and so forth (of things)
et seq. and the following
f., ff. and the following page(s)
fl. flourished (of persons)
ibid. in the same place
id., idem the same as before
i.e. that is
infra below
ital. Italics

l., ll. line(s)
l.c. lowercase (small) letter
loc. cit. in the place cited
MS, MSS manuscript(s)
n. note, footnote
N.B. please note
n.d. no date
N.S. New Series; New Style (of
dating, since 1752)
op. cit. in the work cited
O.S. Old Style (of dating, before 1752)
p., pp. page(s)
passim here and there
q.v. which (or whom) see
rev. revised, revised by, revision
rom. roman letter or type
sc. scilicet to wit, namely
sic thus (to show that an obvious
error is an exact reproduction of
the original)
supra above
TK data still to come (in a typescript)
tr. translation, translator, translated
(by)
v., vide see
v., vol. volume
viz. (videlicet) namely

Some abbreviations used in books can be readily understood from the context, but a writer has to know their exact meaning before he can use them accurately.

than another, the attitude or opinion in question. This signal is given by the word *passim,* meaning "here and there":

[1]For the development of the antebellum political cleavage, cf. Allan Nevins, *Ordeal of the Union* (1945, vol. 2, passim).

Be sure to learn the meaning of abbreviations that are obsolescent, such as "cf." for "see" as employed in our last example, or *supra* (above) and *infra* (below), and the rest (see Figure 23). Learn all the current forms by heart and treat them as technical terms. You will want to find out that "e.g." stands for *exempli gratia* and means "for example"; whereas "i.e.," which stands for *id est,* means "that is." The one offers an illustration; the other states an identity.

Footnoting: When, Where, How Much?

Though the researcher accounts for his findings through footnotes, their number will vary with the subject treated and the presumable audience. Quotations, novel or startling assertions, successive elements in a demonstration or argument—all obviously require footnoting, but do not write as if the reader were convinced that you are a liar. Beyond this, a good rule is to write a note whenever you think an alert person might feel curiosity about the source of your remarks. Do not in any case document notorious facts, such as the date of Columbus's arrival in America, or identify Martin Luther as having set off the Protestant Reformation.

A new subject consequently requires more footnotes than a familiar one. When Walter Prescott Webb wrote *The Great Plains,* he was attempting to show a correlation between the development of the Plains and certain inventions. Accordingly, he supplied footnotes for such things as arms manufacturing and barbed-wire design. His materials and the pattern he wove out of them were both original. Writers on the same subject now can do with fewer notes: they can now cite Webb.

His pioneering work shows that anything may be a source—an ad in a newspaper, an old theater program, a throw-away in a political campaign. But once scholarship has begun to work upon such materials and publishes the results, these *must* be used and cited along with others that are still original. As for citing from the great classics, go to the scholarly edition. Refer to Thoreau's *Works,* not the casual reprint of *Walden* that you can buy at the airport. This is both for the convenience of the reader (who can more easily find the standard edition than to lay his hands on that same cheap reprint) and for the advantage you

yourself will derive from the textual perfection and critical elu-
cidations of the *Works.* But observe that when you cite:

Hazlitt, *Works,* 6:114

you should show whose of the five editions is cited and moreover let the reader know which work is being referred to; write
in full:

Hazlitt, *Table Talk, Works* (Waller and Glover), 6:114

The lesson here is that the likely reader plays a part in deciding the kind and amount of documentation required. In a history
of Italian fascism, for example, the writer will cite and explain
references differently if he is addressing fellow scholars and if
he is writing a popular work. In the latter, he cannot assume
knowledge of Mussolini's career, the theory of the corporate
state, or the outcome of the war in Ethiopia. His footnotes will
be of the commenting and amplifying kind, and will suggest
sources only as additional readings. Logically, the scholar
should write fewer footnotes than the popularizer; but usually
the proportion is reversed.

This excess is a legacy from the 1870s and 1880s, when historians tried to become "scientific" and preferred being thorough to
being thought "literary." Now, better judgment prevails. Footnotes
are necessary but need not be obsessive. As we said earlier, they
have wormed their way into popular writing and become familiar
to all who can read. In "trade" books (for the general public), the
footnote has come into its own by recapturing the bottom of the
page after a time of exile to the back of the book.

Sometimes the commentary notes are printed at the foot of
the page and the reference notes at the back. In any case, the
several sections of backnotes should not be divided by a mere
heading "Chapter 4," "Chapter 5," followed by twenty or thirty
numbered notes. The reader has no idea in what numbered
chapter he is. Repeat the chapter heading over each page (a running head) for he does know that he is reading the part entitled
"Rolling Down to Rio."

A still better way to help the reader find his way through back-notes is to provide either page numbers ahead of each note or catch phrases or both. The page number shows that on that page a word is marked with an asterisk (*) or dagger (†) or superior number (^{23}); the catch phrase connects the note with the words the reader has just arrived at. Figure 24 illustrates the two arrangements.

In essays, articles, or reports, separating explanatory from reference footnotes is seldom done, though if the piece is over fifteen or twenty pages long there is no reason not to do so. The notes in a shorter paper are normally so few that it would be a nuisance to leaf back and forth. The one exception to these allowable choices is the scientific or technical paper, in which the custom is to do without explanatory footnotes. Reference to sources is made in the text by name and year, e.g., (Bohr, 1949). The item is listed at the back where the citations (particularly in medicine, physics, chemistry, and mathematics) are brief. Last name and initials, journal title (often abbreviated), and volume and page numbers suffice.

The Bibliography: Varieties and Forms

"Bibliography" is a rather loose term, but there is no other to cover "information about books." A list of titles, grouped together at the end of a chapter or volume, after the text and before the index, is the commonest meaning of the word.[12] Since a bibliography in this sense cites a number of books, it may be looked upon as a collection of footnotes separated from the passages that they confirm. In fact, some writers make up their bibliographies—or at least fill them out—by picking up the titles out of their own footnotes. Even when padding is

---

[12]It was pointed out in Chapter 3 that volumes containing lists of books organized by subject and flanked by criticism were also "bibliographies." But there are still other bibliographies, which consist of detailed descriptions and collations of rare or famous books, or which list and describe an author's complete works in all their printed forms. These bibliographies help to identify editions, establish dates, prove authorship, and the like.

FIGURE 24   BACKNOTES USING THE CATCH PHRASE

The Masterpiece

"**What do we do now?**" Glenn Weaver interview. Weaver to Humphrey, Oct. 31, 1967, PFPA, HP.
"**Both are determined to move . . .**": Humphrey to Johnson, Oct. 30, 1967, Box 937, HP. Herbert Beckington interview. Beckington to Van Dyk, Nov. 6 and 8, 1967, M u / p HP.

312. "**Our business is to make history . . .**": Transcript of Saigon speech, Oct. 31, 1967, Vietnam box 1965–71, M u / p, HP.
"**our great adventure**": Ibid. UPI bulletin, Saigon, Oct. 31, 1967.
"**obscene, truthless, swine, totally dishonest . . .**": *Ramparts*, Sept. 1968; *Rolling Stone*, Mar. 1972; New York *Post*, May 10, 1971.
"**Our military progress is clear**": Humphrey to Johnson, Nov. 7, 1967, Box 936, HP. Andreas to Humphrey, Nov. 6, 1967, CF68, HP. Watson to Johnson, Nov. 2, and 4, 1967, WHCF CF Exec, FG 440, Box 349, JL.

313. "**very much upset**": Humphrey to Johnson, Nov. 28, 1967, Vietnam box, 1965–71, M u / p, HP. McCarthy press release, n.d., Nov. 1967, Box 1064, HP. Humphrey to Miles Lord, Feb. 5, 1968, CF68 u / p, HP.
"**I guess I have no influence . . .**": Humphrey to Johnson, Nov. 28, 1967, Vietnam box 1965–71, M u / p, HP.
"**Johnson's Baby Powder**": *NYT*, Dec. 8, 1967. Douglas Bennet interview. Nov. 21, 1980.
"**My dad was a grocer . . .**": Humphrey memo for record, Nov. 21, 1967, WHM u / p, Box 48, HP.
"**If the war in Vietnam is a failure . . .**": Eisele, 255.

page

34   buzzing confusion. Pr. Psych., I, **488**.

35   would be produced. Ibid., I, **24**.
suggesters of these. Ibid., I, **20**.

36   connected with it. Ibid., I, **347**.
which they "know." Ibid., I, vi.

37   is metaphysics. Ibid.
in this book. Ibid., I, vii.
our farther knowledge. Ibid., **192**.

38   is conscious of it. Ibid., **197**; II, **171 n**.
two things, not one. Ibid., I, **278–79**.

39   it knows nothing. Ibid., I, **220**.
mysterious sort . . . yet in sight. Ibid., I, **687**.
systems, involve it. Ibid.
hypnotic trance. Ibid., II, **596**.

41   individual minds. Ibid., I, **183**.
in the brains of monkeys. See José M. R. Delgado, *Evolution of the Physical Control of the Brain*, American Museum of Natural History, New York, 1965.

The indicative words may come from the beginning of the sentence (or paragraph), from the middle if they are the dominating ones, or from the end. Words taken from the end are more easily remembered by the seeker of the source; they are the last he has read. The example on the left is from Carl Solberg, *Hubert Humphrey: A Biography* (1984); the one on the right is from Jacques Barzun, *A Stroll with William James* (1983).

not the aim, bibliographies contain much the same information as reference notes, but arranged in a different way for a different purpose. The points of difference are plain when the two forms are juxtaposed:

Murder for Pleasure: The Life and Times of the Detective Story by Howard Haycraft (New York, 1941), 139.

Haycraft, Howard, *Murder for Pleasure: The Life and Times of the Detective Story* (New York, Appleton-Century, 1941, 1969).

The first is a footnote; the second a bibliographical entry. In the second, the last name always begins, so that the eye can quickly find it in its alphabetical place; the publisher is given as a help to finding or buying the book; a second date denotes a revised edition, and there is of course no page number. Some writers give the total number of pages, but this, though sometimes helpful, is no longer usual.

What then determines the amount of information to be given and the arrangement of the collection of titles? As before, as always, it is the particular use that determines these choices. To cause admiration by quantity is not a legitimate use. The scholar's reason for appending a bibliography to a book is to enable readers to verify and learn more. Short or long, a bibliography should second the intention of the work. It may be one of three kinds.

The first and most frequently found in books for the general public is a single list arranged alphabetically by authors' names. It is a catch-all for books, articles, manuals, pamphlets, newspapers, and so on, all side by side. Such a roster is solid information if the author has avoided listing items that he has barely looked into.

In this first class or type, the "select bibliography" is more valuable. It offers the serious student a group of works that have been assessed for merit and brought together so as to cover the subject. One drawback is that the researcher who comes across a work not among the "select" does not know whether it has been rejected or simply overlooked.

Bibliographies of the second type are arranged by the kinds of materials; they are "classified bibliographies." The division may be simply between primary and secondary sources, or between manuscript and printed works, or between books and periodicals. The subdivisions depend on the author's subject or purpose in writing and on the variety of sources used. Keith Sward's *The Legend of Henry Ford* contains a bibliography broken down into four groups: books; magazine and newspaper articles; public documents; and legal and quasi-legal actions. This division fits the needs of most readers. The last category was dictated by the contents of the biography, which narrates numerous important patent suits.

Biographies raise special problems because their subjects, so to speak, force the biographer's hand; the author must follow where they lead. When C. Vann Woodward composed *Tom Watson, Agrarian Rebel,* he was portraying a Populist leader from Georgia whose career was full of puzzles. The bibliography matches the career by distinguishing eight categories (all but numbers 5 and 6 in Figure 25). Compare such an arrangement with that in the life of Admiral Mahan by William E. Livezey, where the subject's writings are listed not alphabetically but in the chronological order of publication between 1879 and 1931. Again, book and bibliography are in parallel, for the study traces the development of the naval officer's thought about the role of sea power in history.

A third type of bibliography is the critical, which may take the form of an essay. It is best suited to a subject on which a whole library of books and articles already exists. The author's critical remarks about each book mentioned enable future students to have the considered opinion of a scholar who has examined the literature and composed a comprehensive annotated reading list. This kind of bibliography is usually divided by chapter. But if the judgments are appended to each title in an alphabetical list, they should be brief and "telling." There is little use in saying: "A thorough scholarly treatment, generally considered definitive." Say rather: "The only book that treats fully his career before his governorship."

FIGURE 25   *COMPONENTS OF A BIBLIOGRAPHY*

---

1. Private Papers and Manuscripts (including unpublished letters)
2. Books and Ephemeral Publications (including books edited by ——)
3. Contributions to Books and Periodicals
4. Published Correspondence
5. Broadcasts and Recordings (including taped conversations)
6. Misattributions
7. Biographies
8. Biographical Articles
9. Relevant Writings of Contemporaries
10. Special Studies and Unpublished Monographs

Occasionally a biographer will add an Iconography—the portraits and photographs of his subject. Only rarely will a work of scholarship (other than a bibliography itself) make use of all the categories. Any category may be subdivided. For instance, the first above might be split among Private Papers; Unpublished Manuscripts; and Unpublished Letters; and the last, if large, could list the two kinds of study separately. Number 5 reminds us that today, in place of the traditional *Life and Letters,* an author might write the *Life and E-mails* of Senator X. Occasionally, there may be on the Internet an "e-book" worth consulting and therefore listing.

Of late years the essay form of critical bibliography has sometimes been used as a substitute for footnotes, and has turned into a chatty interlude. Unless marked by critical acumen, its value to other researchers is small. Here is a serviceable one from Richard Hofstadter, *The American Political Tradition and The Men Who Made It.*[13]

There is no satisfactory biography of Roscoe Conkling, but Donald Barr Chidsey: *The Gentleman from New York* (New Haven, 1935) is helpful, and the older eulogistic work by Alfred R. Conkling: *The Life and Times of Roscoe Conkling* (New York, 1889) has significant material. David Saville Muzzey's sympathetic *James G. Blaine* (New York, 1934) is the best study of the Plumed Knight; Charles Edward Russell's *Blaine of Maine* (New York, 1931) is more critical. . . .

The essay-bibliography is not suited to a subject on which the facts must be dug out of a quantity of scattered books and

[13] 1948, 365.

articles not readily found in libraries, or out of family papers and other manuscripts. Take for example the instructive work by Jeannette Mirsky and Allan Nevins, *The World of Eli Whitney*.[14] The printed sources on which it draws range from a history of Connecticut dated 1840 to a study of cotton processing published in 1944. Again and again these authors consulted only a page or so in one of a miscellaneous group of books: they were seeking or verifying but a single fact and had no need to read the entire work.

Deciding what type of bibliography one ought to draw up cannot be done before one is well past the midpoint of research. A writer is called on to decide so many questions in the course of work that it should come as a relief to know that the form of the bibliography will be virtually dictated by the subject, the sources, and to a lesser extent by the audience.

Taken together, footnotes and bibliography signalize our relation to the fragments of the written record that we have dredged up out of the sea of books, made our own, and reshaped in answer to our fresh questions.

[14]New York, 1952.

CHAPTER 13

REVISING FOR PRINTER AND PUBLIC

Errors and Their Ways

to revise, means to rev isit, notin order to see thee sights again but to tidy thme up

The sentence you have just read stands in obvious need of grooming. Its grammatical form will pass, but its graphic form is faulty and annoying. It stops you, the meaning dimmed because letters are transposed, words run together, and the punctuation is at odds with sense and syntax. Making presentable what you have to say is revision in the second degree. The first has brought your words and sentences to a high point of clarity, ease, and force. Now you have a script or disk that is perhaps less full of blemishes than the example above, but no matter how careful your typing, there will be some errors to scrub out. This is equivalent to washing your face and combing your hair before appearing in public—common courtesy to whoever looks at you.

You cannot be sure, even at this stage, that all the errors will be small and readily detected. Before you send in your report to the board, your paper to your teacher, your article to the editor, your book to the publisher, you re-read once more for the errors of fact and sense that have stayed hidden. Blunders, illogicalities, Irish bulls, contradictions between one page and the next, probably still lurk stubbornly. How can you unblind yourself to them? Errors are of several kinds, distinct in origin and worth regarding theoretically. It is elementary, of course, that you look over your citations to confirm titles, dates, and other figures, and over your quotations for the correct wording and punctuation. It is hard to copy a long passage with absolute fidelity, and the more intelligent and quick of perception you are, the more likely to make a slip.

The most infuriating, often comical, type of error is the Blunder. It may be defined as a whopper that makes the reader howl with laughter—hence a howler. Blunders, too, are generally due to misplaced quickness of mind rather than to ignorance. As a student of the genre has remarked,[1] they presuppose some knowledge that has unfortunately been hooked to the wrong idea. For example, when Victor Hugo in exile was beginning to learn English and also writing a novel laid in the British Isles, he had occasion to refer to the Firth of Forth. This he felt impelled to translate for his French readers as *le premier des quatre*—"the first of the four." It is clear that if he had known no English whatever he would have been incapable of producing this jewel.

The remedy is never to trust your first intuition of meanings, explanations, allusions, and references without checking it with the aid of reference work. Do this especially for *what you "know as well as your own name."* For example, you are sure that the saying "God tempers the wind to the shorn lamb" is from the Bible and therefore you quote it with the label "in the biblical phrase . . . ." The misfortune is that the saying is not from the Bible; it was written by Laurence Sterne.[2] In short, what we have long misknown wears for us an air of certainty that leads to blundering.

More mysterious is the occurrence of blind spots that prevent our seeing the blunders that we could detect at sight in the works of another. Some years ago, for instance, a biography of Haydn appeared with a portrait of the composer bearing the

[1]H. B. Wheatley, *Literary Blunders* (London, 1893), 2.

[2]In "Maria," *A Sentimental Journey through France and Italy* (first published 1768), paraphrased from Henri Estienne, *Prémices* (1594).

caption: "Haydn in his Eightieth Decade." One can see how the confusion of ideas came about, but when one thinks of the number of times these ridiculous words were read by author, editor, printer, proofreader, and publisher's helpers before issuing in print, one is struck with wonder. An experienced author will *not* wonder. There is about the texts that one is producing a sort of glare that blinds one at the very time when one is toiling toward perfection. This resembles the facility with which one keep saying "Tuesday" for "Thursday" when one is most eager to make an appointment.

An error at times reveals something other than these usual causes. Suppose that a book refers to "General Pershing, Chief of Staff in the Second World War," and suppose again that it is not a slip of the mind as in the Tuesday-Thursday mix-up. A howler, yes, you may say, but after all, he *was* a military hero—and only one word is wrong. On the contrary, much more than that is wrong: to place Pershing in the Second World War means that the author lacks any kind of mental image of the man in his accoutrements and the aura of his generation. The figure to him is a name, not a presence in his historical time and place. The error *resembles* that of making Alexander Hamilton's birthplace Jamaica instead of Nevis—an "intelligent" error that links two islands of the British West Indies—but it is radically different. One's work should by its very errors convince the reader that, as Sydney Smith put it, they have come "not in consequence of neglect but in spite of attention."[3]

Judging the Merits of a Work

In scholarly reviews the critic often devotes valuable space to listing small errors and thinks he has struck a blow for truth, while some readers mark down the book as untrustworthy. The matter is more complicated. Experience shows that all the best books, whether original monographs or reference books, attain

[3]Letter to Francis Jeffrey, August 1802.

their perfection of detail only in later revised editions. The mighty Gibbon, when edited by J. B. Bury, was found to have stumbled repeatedly through his eight volumes. He would take a place name for that of a person and he made other slips that Bury corrects in his notes without losing respect for the author and his masterpiece. A good many errors are trivial. Albert Jay Nock in his *Jefferson* has made the point in words that cannot be bettered:

There are qualities that outweigh occasional and trivial inaccuracy, and Parton[4] has them, while the other biographers of Mr. Jefferson, as far as I can see, have not; and the worth of his book should be assessed accordingly. Indeed, if one were condemning books on the strength of minor inaccuracies, Hirst himself[5] would get off badly. I noticed more inaccuracies in one very casual reading of his book than I ever saw in my close readings of Parton. But Mr. Hirst's errors of fact, like Parton's, are not important enough that one should think of them. The thing to think of is that a foreigner and an Englishman should have done as well as Mr. Hirst has done with a subject of uncommon difficulty, even for a native critic. His book should be judged on the scale of its major qualities, and so, I think, should Parton's.[6]

Judging a work "by its major qualities" is the lesson every researcher must learn if he or she is to make the best of the available literature. It would be a waste of time to go back to every indicated source to see if it had been misquoted or given a wrong page reference. To do so would negate the very aim of scholarship, which assumes, as does science, that every worker helps another by contributing one more fragment to knowledge. If nobody relies on previous work and starts afresh from the sources, the word contribution has no meaning.

But how to judge "major qualities"? That is an expertness which comes as one reads and compares. Clarity and precision of prose form is the outermost criterion. It proves nothing but promises a good deal, since important errors can reside in single

[4]James Parton, whose "life" had appeared in 1874.
[5]Francis Wrigley Hirst, whose biography had recently been published.
[6]Albert Jay Nock, *Jefferson* (Washington, DC, 1926), 333.

words. Biographers can produce a caricature instead of a portrait by errors of vocabulary, saying (for instance) that their subject *admitted* something when in fact he *declared* or *volunteered* it; that he *resented* something else when he only *objected* to it; that he *interfered* in a situation in which he *intervened,* and so on. Such misusage goes unnoticed, while reviewers who will pounce on a wrong initial will let pass these innuendos of careless wording.

A second criterion of quality is a certain fullness of treatment. On any given matter the author leaves no reasonable questions hanging. He is alive to doubts and possibilities and discusses or settles them; and he is adept at making his conclusions hinge on significant details.

In judging reference books, quality is easier to gauge. The format, print, paper, binding of the work allow us to form a first estimate: is it a quickie fashioned from other, larger works, or is it a well-conceived and well-edited performance? Reliable compilations list editors and advisors to the editor-in-chief, all of them with stated scholarly or scientific affiliations.[7] Then one turns to entries one knows something about and finds out whether they are compact, clear, and full of details well organized. Here dates, names, spellings, relationships must all be correct; they are equally significant, since the author cannot know what use may be made of any part. Some errors will be found, as we said earlier, but only a few. Finally, inclusiveness is essential.

Revision: Maxims and Pointers

With experience in judging the many components of accurate writing and reporting, the task of revising becomes more and more pleasurable, even though its purpose is the discovery of one's own failings. The ultimate effort is the stage that some artists find peculiarly satisfying: the "fixing" of a pastel or the final polishing of a precious gem or the casting of a piece of

---

[7]Kenneth T. Jackson, the editor-in-chief of the superb one-volume *Encyclopedia of New York City* (1995) drew on the talents of 68 associate editors, an advisory team of 19, and a project staff at the Yale University Press of 42.

sculpture. It is exhilarating and exhausting and one should be prepared for both sensations.

The first thing needful is to allow enough time for thoroughness at a deliberate pace. This will depend on the length of your article, or book, and your own habits of work. The penalty of frantic, last-minute patching is no secret. Many a gifted piece of writing has been lost in the flood of print because it was hastily revised and its imperfections caused annoyance and distrust.

If your work is a book, revise it chapter by chapter; if an article, part by part. Dividing the task compels you to see the work in its small aspects. Although you scan every word, sentence, and paragraph for their rightness, you must also see single letters, or you will miss typographical errors and misspellings. The rewriting stage is over, but you will seize any chance to improve your diction or syntax or transitions. More than once, probably, you have been from the outset dissatisfied with a certain word or phrase. It is there plaguing you still, because you have not found the right replacement. But now you must decide: *stet* or—what? If uninspired you may opt for the least undesirable alternative.

If you discover that you have conveyed a quite wrong impression, or seemingly contradicted yourself, or left ambiguous what you are very sure about—all this due to "not seeing" and now caught by re-seeing or revision—you may have to make rather sizable changes. That revision in form calls for a survey of the surrounding passages to prevent further troubles— repetition, inconsistency, and so forth.

In revising, it is helpful to have the assistance of someone as attentive to details as yourself and who, because of friendship or dedication to your subject, is willing to devote time to your script. Enlist this Jonathan in collating quotations (comparing with the original) or in verifying the statistics in your tables. He reads aloud; you follow and correct.

Revision: Marks and Symbols

In making changes you must write neatly, legibly; otherwise your copy editor will overlook some or mistake the indication. To insert a word or phrase, be sure that the point of insertion is clearly shown by a caret.[8] Do not sprawl over the margins or distract the eye by too heavy handwriting. Long inserts, of a paragraph or more, should be typed and entered where they belong—what is called cutting and pasting. On a computer the operation is easy; for a piece of work that someone will make a clean copy of for you, the inserts can be on separate sheets and their place shown by a marginal note. The margins are also used for instructions to the printer by means of the conventional marks in Figure 26 (caret, slash, dots, etc.) and abbreviated words ("cap," "lc," "tr," and the like). Do *not* draw guidelines from the error in the center of your text to the comment in the margin.

The Professional Touch

The minor virtue of a reviser is consistency. Every sort of correction must be shown in identical fashion. The conventional symbols were devised to insure it. They constitute an international language of symbols of printing and publishing. Here are a few directions for their use:

1. To change (or delete) words, draw a horizontal line across it with a loop at the end. To change a letter you are altering, draw a vertical line through it. It should project at top and bottom. The new wording or the new letter is entered in the nearest margin.

    ~~She greeted the crowd withoutstretched arms.~~

    # She greeted the crowd with/outstretched arms.

2. If you regret your change, you restore the former text by writing the word "stet" in the margin and putting a series of dots under the word. *Stet* is Latin for "let it stand."

3. Your editor expects your typescript to be marked up. An altogether clean one suggests that you have neglected to proofread.

[8]For the caret and other conventional signs, see Figure 26, p. 282.

FIGURE **26** *THE PROOFREADER'S MARKS*

MESSAGE TO PRINTER	MARK	INDICATION IN TEXT	CORRECTED TEXT
Remove letter or word.	*ȹ*	He read the boopk.	He read the book.
Insert letter.	*t*	She wrote a leter.	She wrote a letter.
Insert space.	#	We wenttogether.	We went together.
Change to capital letter.	*cap*	Pam asked bill.	Pam asked Bill.
Change to lower-case.	*lc*	Do You know him?	Do you know him?
Wrong font (type face).	*wf*	He mixed them up.	He mixed them up.
Broken letter. Replace.	X	Clear your type.	Clean your type.
Inverted letter. Turn.	*Ɔ*	It mnst be wrong.	It must be wrong.
Reset in italic type.	*ital*	Don't do that!	*Don't do that!*
Reset in roman (regular).	*rom*	What can it be?	What can it be?
Reset in bold-face (dark).	*bf*	The word was nor.	The word was **nor.**
Reset in small capitals.	*sc*	The sign said Stop!	The sign said STOP!
Transpose.	*tr*	but enough world and	but world enough and
Insert period.	⊙	Such is life	Such is life.
Insert hyphen.	/=/	Mr. Wycliffe Jones	Mr. Wycliffe-Jones
Insert comma.	⌃	That's all folks.	That's all, folks.
Insert apostrophe.	⌄	Dont look now.	Don't look now.
Insert quotation marks.	⌄ ⌄	Eureka, he said.	"Eureka," he said.
Insert inferior figure.	⌃	Water is HO.	Water is H$_2$O.
Insert superior figure.	⌄	E = MC	E = MC^2
Insert question mark.	?	What's going on here	What's going on here?
Paragraph.	*¶*	done? Now we must	done? Now we must
No paragraph.	*no ¶*	decided. Then they	decided. Then they
One em space.	□ □	Call me Ishmael.	Call me Ishmael.
One-em dash.	/L/M/	had if only because	had—if only because
Move as indicated.	⊏	⊏ Move left.	Move left.
	⊐	⊐ Move right.	Move right.
Close up space.	⌒	They had a break up.	They had a breakup.
Let stand as is.	*stet*	Which one did it?	Which one did it?
Straighten type.	=	Type can shift a bit.	Type can shift a bit.
Query to author.	⦵	A word overlooked.	A word was overlooked.

4. If your handwriting is uncertain, use print letters, shaping and spacing them carefully. Never try to patch up a type-written word by writing over its constituent letters.

5. Being edited before printing means that several hands decorate your copy with a quantity of pencil marks. Often it is your punctuation that suffers, because people differ about it (see p. 282). To prevent confusion, put a circle around a period, thus: ⊙ ; and a caret over or reversed under other common marks: ⌃⌃ ⌃⌃ " " 6 ⌄.

Critical last-minute changes usually concern paragraph-ing. Even the best of writers discover late a sentence that seemed appropriate to end a paragraph and now looks rather like an excellent topic sentence for the next. When you want

```
    . . . If we think of the colonies as advance

    outposts of the European powers, we come closer to

    understanding how Europeans looked upon them: they

   ⌃ represented their sovereign's strength and prestige⌃

    and

    lc/No ¶  The ensuing rivalry had repercussions in the
                ¶
    colonies overseas. Nothing illustrates this fact

    better than the story of English-Dutch relations in

    America.

    No ¶   Holland occupied little territory but it was

    located at the mouth of the Rhine. Like a watchdog,
                                            the
    she sat astride the trade routes that led out of ⌃
          ies
    Germany ⊙ ⊙ ⊙ ⊙
```

no paragraph break, write "No ¶" in the blank space in front of the indention and draw a "run on" line from the last word of the previous paragraph. Here is a set of markings for such a change of mind.

If in typing, two words have been run together, draw a vertical line between them:

Conversely, the pieces of a word must sometimes be brought together. Here is the way:

```
The author's chief qualification was in sight.
```

To change the capitalization, that is, from upper case (capital) to lower case (small letter), draw a line through the capital.[9] For the reverse, draw three small lines under the letter:

```
l.c. Not a cowboy, he thought Life on

     the range was harsh.
```

To reduce a capital to a small letter, draw a slanting line (slash) through it:

```
Feudalism put the big landowners, who

were also the leaders in war, at the

top of the pyramid.
```

For transposing letters, words, or larger units, mark the text as follows:

```
tr. pSecial
```

---

[9]In using a word processor, remember not to use capital I for *1* in any series of Arabic numbers, and especially not to combine the two styles in one number. Lacking the Arabic 1, use the lower case letter l. In referring to part of an outline write *I 2 a,* spacing the figures and letters to avoid confusion with *12a.*

For two words in the wrong order, draw a zigzag line to enclose as well as separate the parts and put "tr" in the margin:

```
tr  |Praz, /Mario\ Machiavelli in Inghilterra,℘

    =(Rome, 1943)÷
     ∧           ∧
```

When a couple of sentences or one paragraph (no more) must be moved to a new place, circle it entirely and connect it by a line in the margin with the caret that shows where to insert it. In a grafting operation of this kind, make sure that the broken edges fit when brought together. Sometimes verb forms have to be changed; sometimes words repeat too near each other for euphony. Do not hesitate to mark up your page.

The revising once done, go through the typescript and see to it that the pages are all in sequence, including charts, graphs, and other illustrations, which should be numbered or marked A, B, C, etc. to ensure the right placing. You have, of course, made an exact copy of your work showing every correction, insertion, and instruction from start to finish. If the main copy goes astray or is damaged, you can replace it immediately. Few of us could take calmly what happened to Carlyle when he entrusted the manuscript of the first volume of *The French Revolution* to John Stuart Mill, whose housemaid used it to light the fire. No typewriter, carbon copy, or copying machine existed, and Carlyle had to start afresh from his notes—an act of fortitude one shudders to think of.

At a book publisher's a script is usually edited by two people in two different ways: the editor goes over it for sense, organization, and literary style; the copy editor goes over it for spelling, grammatical niceties, and consistency forms. These first readers' fresh eye and good judgment can be very useful. But their suggestions must be returned to you for approval, because editors can become so possessive about your work that some of the changes proposed do violence to your meaning and intent. Do not let anyone write his or her book over your name. This principle

FIGURE **27** *AN AUTHOR AND HIS PROOFS*

For seekers after perfection there is no end to revising. Here is a proof-sheet of Balzac's famous novel *Eugénie Grandet,* which is a typical "revise" not only of this author's but of many others' in the nineteenth century: printing was cheap and printers were trained to follow scarred copy such as this. Today all extensive revisions must be made on the script—and much more clearly—long before it is turned in.

applies to friends or colleagues who help by reading and offering criticisms. You must interpret them in the light of *your* purpose, *your* plan, and *your* style. Almost always, the word or passage that is questioned does need some attention: it is where the intelligent reader stumbled or jibbed. What he or she suggests is not necessarily the best improvement.

The Handle to a Writer's Works

One of the last acts of revision in preparation for the press is the putting of a title to the piece. The common experience is that the right title is found at or after the end of the writing. You may have referred to your work in a descriptive phrase that fitted it. But a description is not a title; it may be a good label; it is not a handle.

Modern titles are less and less explicit. Publishers do not want a *A History of the United States*—the title has been used for too many previous books. You must propose *Freedom's Land* with the subtitle in a smaller type, "A History of the United States." In this allusive style there are fashions and it is well not to follow them too closely if one wants to avoid embarrassment when they are passé. For example, *So Fell the Angels* was a serious life of Salmon P. Chase and his daughter Kate; *A Time for Angels*—angels were popular—was a history of the League of Nations. Both tags now sound flossy and pretentious. More durable is an image such as *The Better Half*, which suggests its subject, and is confirmed by the subtitle, "The Emancipation of the American Woman." A title should indicate what realm of thought or action the work treats of, and possibly also what contribution or assertion it makes. *Born Under Saturn* fails on both counts and is rather hackneyed besides.[10]

The titles of chapters can be more descriptive than those of a book, and are best when all are in keeping with one another. The attempt to create a sense of drama or revelation is futile and

---

[10]Two excellent works hide under this designation—one a biography of William Hazlitt by Catherine Maclean and the other a study of the character and conduct of artists by Rudolf and Margaret Wittkower.

displeasing. Readers browse and judge (as we saw) by outward features. An excellent book can be misrepresented by its poor chapter titles. For example, Stewart H. Holbrook's *Story of the American Railroads*[11] fails to present itself justly, because its chapter headings lack harmony and attempt sensationalism. The first five are acceptable: 1. Panorama, 2. The Prophets, 3. Primeval Railroading, 4. Railroad Fever, 5. "The Work of the Age." But then we fall on: 6. Forgotten Genius (a few pages about one man and not a phase as in 1 to 5); 7. The Pennsy and the Central (sounds like a jump in chronology within a book of thirty-seven chapters).

From then on the sense of progression and unity of tone is broken by such headings as "War Comes to a 'Neutral' Line," "Locating the Route," "Out in the Wild and Woolly," "Up in the Cold and Icy," "The Carriers Are Harassed," "Through the Dark Ages—and After," "The Fast Mail," "Spotters," "The Little Fellers," "News Butchers," and—unexpectedly sedate for the last one—"The Railroad in the Drama." After the jazziness of the middle chapters, one expects the last to be something like "The Footplate and the Footlights"—deplorable, but at least in keeping with those just preceding.

One aspect of the desirable harmony is length. If you start out laconic with (1) "Hope"; (2) "Effort"; (3) "Power"; you cannot very well suitably follow with (4) "There's Many a Slip Twixt the Cup and the Lip." A striking device repeated is monotonous. Instead, name your chapters in the same voice, form, or construction. If you have (1) "The Outbreak of Revolution," and continue "The . . . of . . ." through (4) "The Consulate and Empire," you ought not to switch to (5) "Napoleon Falls"; you have bound yourself to "The Fall of Napoleon."

Essay titles differ somewhat from chapter titles in that they do alone the work of catching the eye. But like chapter titles, they may be explicit yet not give the point away. A good example is the title of an essay Meyer Schapiro gave to an article on Lewis Mumford's *The Culture of Cities*. It is called "Looking Forward to Looking Backward," the allusion being to Edward Bellamy's

[11]1947.

utopia, *Looking Backward* (1888). Standard combinations such as "Machiavelli's Politics," "The Education of Engineers in Russia," or "T. E. Lawrence on Leaders in the Middle East" do not enable the reader to keep the memory of one such essay clear from another on the same theme; they are not sufficiently *telling*. For successful titling, make lists of possibles as you write and the ideal phrase may flash on your mind before it is time to part with your script.

Revision: The Printer and You

At last you are going to be published. You face a fresh set of problems, most of them mechanical. It is work at a distance; you will never see those who query you and ask for your revises. Your next duty is to correct page proofs. The former practice of sending the author, first, unpaged "galleys" is obsolete, to the detriment of printing accuracy in small matters.[12]

As you reread your words for perhaps the twentieth time, you will experience the feeling that they are both familiar and somehow new, because they now look clean, black, and definitive. Your old landmarks have vanished. You associated a certain phrase with the top of page 8, and a certain paragraph seemed sprawling. Now the phrase is lost somewhere and the paragraphs looks shrunk. This change of perspective enables you to read your text again with a fresh eye.

The changes you make in page proofs are charged to you unless they are PE's: "Printer's errors." With increasing cost as printing becomes ever more facilitated by machinery, changes become more expensive and the author more restricted, because disturbing one or two words calls for rearranging the whole paragraph. On page proofs, enter any change in erasable pencil.

---

[12]When printer or proofreader or nowadays the publisher's copy editor is in doubt, he or she will "query" ("?" "Qy" in the margin). When you have answered, the change is made and a new page printed, a "revise." This sequence may also be called "first pass" and "second pass."

The Final Pages: The Index

The author's ultimate duty before launching his work is the preparation of an index. Some few books do not require any—a collection of literary essays, the casual anthology, and of course all fiction. But work for study or consultation needs an index. By it usefulness to the public is vastly increased, particularly if the index is well made. Many a writer who is wanting in patience and energy will turn the tedious task over to a professional index-maker or to a research assistant. This is regrettable, for however competent the assistant or professional may be, the author has a special understanding of the book and its contribution to knowledge; only he can accurately reflect it in the index. The index is the book reduced to its themes and topics in detail. Sorting out these so that the reader is promptly led to the fact or idea he seeks is a task even a beginner can learn. To do so, use Hans H. Wellisch's manual; it also warns about the pitfalls of computer indexing.[13]

The general principles are simple enough: with the page proof in hand, you take slips or cards of convenient size—3×5 will do—and you write on each the name or word that you think the reader will look for. These entries on your card are followed by the number of the page or pages where the subject occurs. Subentries should be made in order to break up every large topic and tell what aspect of it is treated on a given page. Alphabetize the slips or cards as you go along to facilitate the steady addition of later page numbers. When complete, the set of cards is pasted on sheets, or transcribed in pages on your word processor, and returned to your publisher with the corrected page proofs.

The degree of detail in an index varies not with your inclination but with your subject matter. A biography, for example, must contain, besides the names of persons and places, entries for the principal activities of the subject's life. But a collection of edited letters needs an even finer sorting of topics, because in the biography the table of contents leads to groups of related

---

[13]*Indexing from A to Z* (1991). Also helpful is Donald B. and Ana D. Cleveland, *Introduction to Indexing and Abstracting* (2nd ed., Englewood, CO, 1990).

facts, whereas the letters are in most cases arranged chronologically, and this tells us nothing about their contents. *The New
Letters of Abigail Adams: 1788–1801,* for instance, contains entries
for "Bathing machine," "Bleeding and blistering," "Conechigo
wagons," "Lyons: cloaks from," "Measles," "Newspapers: malice
of," "Theophilanthropy," "Wine cellar: at Quincy."

The most meager of indexes must supply proper names; the
fullest provides a clue to every item of interest, from a total
eclipse of the sun to a trivial anecdote.[14] In this regard, the
indexes that Samuel Butler prepared for his works are models.
One finds, for example, in *Evolution, Old and New,* "Day, Portrait
of Mr." and also "Portrait, of Mr. Day." By the care of its preparation, the index shows the author's pride in his work and his
regard for other researchers.

It may be that after all the pains you and others have taken,
you will open your first author's copy and immediately fall
upon a typographical error. You will grieve and feel indignant
for a day or so, while you are imagining that every reader sees
nothing but that misspelled word. Take comfort: in the six centuries of printing hardly any works have been letter perfect.
Before Gutenberg, it was the copyists who provided the absurd
errors, one at a time, by hand.

Copyright: To Protect and Defend

Your labors have brought forth a piece of property. It is yours
and it deserves as much protection as any other valuable. Since
the Copyright Act of 1976, "original works of authorship" are
copyrighted from the moment of their creation. Before your article or book leaves your hands for submission to a publisher or
to circulate for critical reading, you should therefore mark
the bottom of the first page thus: copyright ©—the letter *c* in a

---

[14]Indexes often tempt their makers to mild eccentricities and even jokes.
In a work on economics privately printed in the 1890s, one finds under
"Price": "of this book and where to obtain it." For other curiosities of indexing
see H. B. Wheatley, *How to Make an Index* (London, 1902).

circle—followed by the year and your name. Since March 1, 1989, this copyright line is not a legal requirement, but it is recommended as a deterrent to unauthorized use of your work as a whole or in part. Technically, it is "notice," a warning that the work is not in the public domain. Works published on or after January 1, 1978, are protected from the day they are produced until the end of the author's life, plus fifty years.

What about your broadcast talk, which someone tapes, transcribes, duplicates, and sells to students for classroom use? The answer is that you must enter your prohibition ahead of time, when you sign the usual agreement with the radio or television station, especially if the station is that of a college or university: allow as many rebroadcasts as you wish, but no transcripts of your words without your permission in writing, and even then with the notice of your copyright as shown above.

When your work is a book, the publisher will usually be committed by contract to obtaining the copyright either in your name or in the firm's, without either choice implying any rights as to payment for the use of the material. This registration is performed by applying to the Register of Copyrights in Washington, D.C. It should be done in the first three months of the book's existence. If there is an infringement of its contents, the perpetrator is liable for statutory damages and attorneys' fees. If registering is done later, only actual damages and profits may be claimed.

If your work is for a magazine, it is protected by the publisher's getting a copyright on the entire issue. Unless otherwise specified and agreed to, you have granted the publisher only "first publication rights."[15] Once out in that form, absent an agreement to the contrary, it belongs to you again and in full, just as if it were fresh from the mint. Later, in collecting your articles into a book, it is a usual courtesy to thank and name for each item the original publisher: it is also customary, not mandatory, to obtain permission to reprint.[16]

---

[15]Sometimes called "first serial rights."

[16]For full details, see *Perle and Williams on Publishing Law* (revised by Mark A. Fischer, 2 vols., 3rd ed., 1999).

CHAPTER 14

MODES OF PRESENTATION

Composing: By Hand or by Machine?

More professional writers than one might suppose continue to use pen or pencil. They would tell you that the speed and rhythm and unconscious ease of handwriting exactly match the flow of their ideas. If they use a keyboard, some still prefer a typewriter. If the composers by hand own a computer, it is to copy manuscript. For all such people it would be foolish to revolutionize their tested practice. The popularity of computers should not overawe and force them out of their productive groove. And using a computer does revolutionize mental and physical habits.[1]

Advantages versus *Drawbacks*

What is gained by learning a large number of new and arbitrary moves? One's re-education gives the power to do many more things mechanically. One can correct and revise ("edit") text without erasing; one can insert and move and delete text without

---

[1]Writers who compose or used to compose at a typewriter find the change to a computer a shorter leap to make, but it is still a leap. The typewriter responds simply and in plain sight to a few sure-fire commands.

cutting and pasting; one can type in footnotes and endnotes with little effort and perfect regularity; one can get pages numbered automatically; one can make as many copies of the finished product as desired; and one can store ("save") the original in the machine for further revision and the printing of copies at a later time; one can sort research notes quickly and in several different ways; one can even index a book; and with access to the Internet (as we saw) one can get information in abundance.

These are the main advantages of the computer. There are others, such as automatic alphabetizing, checking for typos and spelling, counting words, entering running heads, changing spacing and layout, inserting drawings and tables, as well as not having to take thought or action for the words to run on from the end of the line to the next ("wordwrap").

But there are constraints. One should be a touch typist and capable of fingering two dozen additional keys, as well as a "mouse" with three functions. For revising, too, the screen shows only half a page at a time. The beginner must also be prepared for at least three weeks of maddening resistance from the device. It seems not to perform a second time what it readily did the first. This is not altogether an illusion, but for most purposes one need only respect the computer's demand for the strict repetition of moves. It is not a mathematical device; but a logical one, as indicated by the better name by which it is known in some Continental languages: "ordinator." It puts in order the successive steps of any operation and will not respond to a sequence that differs.

Other drawbacks include possible effects on the user's health. Much has been written on the subject, and as a result California has passed a law requiring businesses to observe certain precautions. To be safe from the screen's low-frequency magnetic radiation, the viewer is urged to sit twenty-eight inches away. And to avoid painful conditions affecting the neck, back, wrist, and lower arm, rest periods of fifteen minutes every two hours have been mandated. Less likely afflictions are esophoria (overconverging of the eyes) and hypophoria (seeing an object higher with one eye than with the other).

A Few Rudiments for Beginners

Supposing that you have made up your mind and bought a computer, one of the first difficulties you will find is that the manuals for the various programs are unsatisfactory.[2] They are very thick books, full of illustrations, but they leave almost as many mysteries as they clear up. The vocabulary devised by the engineers for the parts and functions of the device is poorly designed for communication; it is now set and must be learned, and besides, the manuals overlook important terms and operations. The smaller books that come with the machine are still less adequate; they disclose only some of the functions it can perform. One comes across the other uses by chance or by conversation with friends or instructors. In fact, most beginners are well advised to take a one- or two-day course in the use of the program they choose. It may therefore help the prospective user if we mention a few of the working principles behind the detailed functions. Practiced users can skip to the next section p. 297.

The digital computer relies on a simple device: the switch—not of course an ordinary switch, but a complex form to do a simple thing: it controls the transfer of current or resistance—hence the name "trans-sistor." In alternating this flow of power at amazing speed it creates two "states" that can be made to carry significance: "on" represents the figure 1, "off" is zero. The pulsing is arranged so as to create permutations of these digits within a block of eight called a *byte,* for example, 01101010. Each byte thus represents a letter, number, or control symbol, which is magnetically recorded on a suitable surface. Reversing the process is what is meant by "reading" that record in the computer's "memory," namely that same surface. To manage the various recording disks and reading "heads" is the role of the central unit—the

---

[2]Some experts are aware of its awkwardness; one writes: "The people who created computerese are far less intelligent than you. Considering the mishmash of acronyms, fractured conjunctions and tortured idioms they have jumbled together, it's obvious they are far less intelligent than anyone" (G. McWilliams, quoted in the *New York Times,* Oct. 2, 1990).

FIGURE **28** *IT WON'T EVEN BARK*

"Somebody's having a bad day."

"microprocessor," the heart of the machine. The storage capacity or "memory" of any model is expressed in thousands or millions of bytes (kilobyte, megabyte). One megabyte of memory holds more than one million characters (letters or numbers).

A computer's ability to perform consists of three powers: first, what the computer is built to do; next, what the "operating system" organizes in one part of the memory. Think of the former power as the nature of the unit and of the latter as its acquired habits. Third and last is the ability of the system to record whatever the user wishes and to handle it as he ordains.[3]

[3]Another analogy, for musicians: the computer is the instrument, with its particular range and timbre. The operating system is the clef marked on the staff, and the program is the key signature—the sharps and flats appear there. The composer then sets down whatever he wants within the three sets of conditions.

This last capacity goes by the misleading name of Random Access Memory (RAM). Far from random, access is precisely directed. Suppose you are working on page 10 of your project and want to refer to an earlier passage. By clicking the mouse you "scroll back" (a good clear term) to page 6, which contains what you need. You find there cause to recall something else, say in the chapter you wrote last week. You summon it up without losing your current place, and can compare statements by splitting the screen into two "windows" that display the passages together.

Inquiring spirits will want to know more about the structure of the computer, the ways of programming (telling it all it must do), and the conclusions of those who design it, when they are inclined to reflect on the consequences of its role. All this can be found in *The Philosophical Programmer,* by Daniel Kohansky (1998). For a convenient travel guide to the digital world, read *The Internet Handbook* by McGuire, Stilborne, McAdams, and Hyatt (1997). Word processing, i.e., composing text, is but one of a choice of functions. Others are: the making of *spreadsheets* (tables, statistics, financial statements, and the like); of *databases* (filing systems, as for notecards); and of *graphics* (drawings and diagrams). So much by way of introduction to digital composition.

The Whole Circle of Work: Editing a Classic

The quality of your writing gives the general reader a fair idea of your mind at work. But to a professional judge the test of skill is *editing* a source or a classic. It is the application of all the components of research; it calls for intellect and not mere attention to detail. The editor of a well-known work has a double obligation, to his author and to his readers. The author's text must be presented faithfully and also intelligibly. This means recording variants from different editions, explaining allusions, identifying names, and clearing up apparent or real errors and contradictions. An able editor may also want to indicate sources and influences and offer a judgment on points that over the years have created controversies. The latest editor settles everything for his author's benefit and the public's, and produces a readable text. A modern practice tends to make the apparatus overwhelm the text. Variants are stuck between brackets in the middle of a sentence, and a blizzard of notes and symbols blankets the comments. The good scholarly editor explains only what needs explanation and disposes his remarks artfully, so that the reader who does not need a particular identification can ignore it easily and the reader who does can find it just as easily. Variants should not pop up where they distract.

Framing explanatory footnotes is by no means easy. It calls for combining scattered facts to throw light on a particular point. For example, identifying an obscure name: "Claude Ruggieri (fl. 1630) was descended from a large family of pyrotechnic experts who came to France under Louis XIV and who maintained their specialty through the ensuing regimes." Or again, about a source: "This supplement, dated 1867, does not occur in the National Edition of Mazzini's works, but only in the six-volume English selection from the writings. It is therefore given in the words of the English translator of that edition, who presumably worked from the Italian original." Conciseness is imperative; for the editor has invariably turned up more information than was needed; he must not be tempted to unload it all on the reader. For a model of intelligent editing see Roy P. Basler's *Collected Works of Abraham Lincoln*.

Speaking What You Have Learned

The researcher no doubt looks to the printed word as the means by which his findings will reach others. But latterly, thanks to talk shows, the public already used to the Sunday sermon willingly attends innumerable lectures. So a few words on giving a talk will suggest attitudes and habits that are desirable for lecturing. The two facts to ascertain before preparing any sort of talk are: "how long am I expected to speak?" and "who and how many are expected to attend?" The first determines the amount and kind of material to present; the second, the vocabulary, tone, and degree of complexity that are appropriate. Knowing the characteristics of your audience, you can pitch your remarks at the right level. If, for example, you are addressing the League of Women Voters you can count on a degree of political sophistication that allows you to present your ideas on a public issue with confidence that it will be listened to with a ready grasp. The requirements of a freshman class at the beginning of the year or of a mixed public audience seeking diversion will naturally be different. You must supply more detail and proceed step-by-step.

An academic lecture usually lasts fifty minutes, and a practiced lecturer will find that on any subject he knows well he can deliver, without looking at the clock, fifty minutes' worth of coherent information. To prepare a lecture of any sort means carving out a subject that has unity; assembling and organizing the material; writing out a text or notes; and measuring the time of delivery. You measure by rehearsing the speech with an eye on the clock, or by writing out every word and counting. A good rate of delivery is 125 words a minute. It allows for variations of speed as well as pauses for rest or emphasis.[4]

All lecturers should limit themselves to a few points—six at most. These ideas, conclusions, issues, questions form the invisible structure of the performance. One may announce them near the beginning, refer to any later on to show relationships, and restate them in conclusion. This device makes up for the uncertainties and elusiveness of communication by word of mouth: the listener cannot turn back the page or request "please say that again" and cannot stop and think over a new idea or interpretation. On his side, the lecturer cannot help forging ahead. When the listener is taking notes, a gap of time and thought will quickly widen between them. Hence the lecturer repeats main points in different words; the auditor gets a second chance to follow what all parties hope is consecutive thought.

---

[4]The English advocate Marshall Hall spoke, in at least one famous case, at the rate of 158 words a minute. His opponent, Rufus Isaacs, spoke 120 words a minute (Edward Marjoribanks, *The Life of Sir Edward Marshall Hall,* London, 1929, 307–308). These are perhaps the two extremes.

The speaker must be equipped with an aid to memory. It is all too easy to forget Point 3 when its time comes or to anticipate it at the wrong place through association of ideas. On formal occasions lecturers bring a text fully written out.[5] Improvisation is a sign of disrespect. Among risks entailed by speaking without text, the worst is waste of time: stumbling, backtracking, and repeating tediously. With a complete text the speaker says more in the same number of minutes and says it more exactly.

On informal occasions, or on subjects frequently treated, one lectures from notes, brief or full. Full notes, such as a set of selected paragraphs or of heads and subheads when the thoughts between, are sure to come, or often in the outline style, should be clearly typed so that the lecturer seizes on the clue at a glance. Brief notes will fit on a 3×5 card that lists the four or five main heads; five or six cards accommodate a group of key words under each heading. Old-time after-dinner speakers used to jot down the hints on their starched cuffs, from which grew the expression "to speak off the cuff." The impromptu, off-the-cuff speaker can give himself and his hearers a special pleasure, but only if he is fluent, clear, witty, and coherent. He seems like a friend addressing each listener intimately. He sounds spontaneous, unprepared, even his cuff is not in sight. Such artistry is the fruit of much preparation and long practice.

Whoever wants a grateful audience should learn to enunciate properly and pay attention to his words, not mumbling, halting, or dropping his voice at the end of every sentence.[6] That terminal swallow, which sometimes comes at a joke or ironic

---

[5]The sponsors of the lecture are likely to ask for the full text a week or more before the lecture, in order to give it to the press, and they often want it also for printing or excerpting afterwards.

[6]A study has been made of speakers' hesitation in the form of *ums, ers,* and *ahs,* which shows that these fill-ins depend for their frequency on what is being talked about. Scientific subjects offer fewer choices of wording than literature or art and prompt fewer hesitations. See Stanley Schachter et al., "Speech Disfluency and the Structure of Knowledge" (*Journal of Personality and Social Psychology,* 60, March, 1991, 362–367).

comment, is tiresome. To be avoided for the same reason are tricks of the hand, head, and limbs—fiddling with objects, rocking on your feet; or clutching your chair, lectern, or elbows.

Most important, the lecturer must always imply that he and his listeners are on the same plane of intellect, equals in their concern with the subject and in their mutual courtesy. Lecturers who intend to read their text need a warning about their prose: the essay style is not suited to oral delivery. It is difficult to follow and it sounds authoritative in the wrong way. The mind when listening cannot immediately grasp the thought as it unfolds, because the periodic structure recommended for good order and conciseness in silent reading (see Chapter 10), puts a burden on the memory when spoken. If a statement begins: "Although the conditions of . . ., even when . . . it remains in most cases undoubtedly true that . . .," the ideas that come between *although* and the close are quickly forgotten and the sense of something lost is unsettling. So keep sentences short and put modifiers and explanations after the main assertion.

An audience for the same reason likes an occasional signpost about the progress of the journey; for example: "At this point we have seen . . . now we go on to . . ." Or: These three reasons are perhaps enough to show that . . ., but let me assure you that a few more could be given." The you-and-I attitude of friendly talk is appropriate for lecturing, formal and informal. And however formal, the tone should be modest. True, as lecturer you know more than "they", but collectively they know more than you. In a question period you should readily admit errors of fact or expression that are brought to your notice. But this does not mean that you should be patient under heckling or insults. In that event the speaker with a word of apology to the civil part of the audience, retires from the place of turmoil.

Heading Committees and Seminars

Besides writing and lecturing, the researcher loaded with relevant information may be asked to act in a capacity that some quite

FIGURE **29** *MARKING A SPEECH FOR DELIVERY*

AT OUR LAST MEETING, ‖ MY PURPOSE ׀ WAS TO GIVE YOU AN *acc't*

~~ACCOUNT~~ OF THE RISE OF ART AS A RELIGION IN THE NINETEENTH

CENTURY. ‖ BY SHOWING HOW ÁRT CAME TO BE REGARDED ׀ AS THE

SUPREME EXPRESSION OF MAN'S SPIRITUAL POWERS, ‖ I WAS ABLE TO

EXPLAIN HOW ׀ AT THE SAME TIME ׀ ÁRT NECESSARILY BECAME THE

(2)   (1)
ULTIMATE CRITIC OF LIFE AND THE MORAL CENSOR OF SOCIETY. ‖׀

AT THE END OF MY LECTURE ׀ I SAID I WOULD NEXT DISCUSS THE *final*

               (2)   (1)
~~FINAL~~ PHASE OF THIS CLAIM AND THIS DUEL, ‖→ THE PHASE OF

   (2)   (1)   ‖
ESTHETICISM AND OF ABOLITIONISM WHICH FILLS THE QUARTER– *century*

A lecture to be read is typed triple-spaced in a large and legible font. It is then marked. Any convenient signs will do, provided they are used consistently. The vertical line(s), short or long, suggest pauses of corresponding length—for emphasis or the separation of ideas. The dotted horizontal indicate that the voice must hold up to the end, which is often not visible to the right. Numbers in reverse order over a series of terms show how many equal and matching parts are to come. The curved arrows point when necessary to the next phrase or line as needing utterance without pause.

able persons fail at entirely: directing a group. The modern world is a mass of committees; nothing gets done without a meeting. A seminar, a professional association that presents its work in sections, an editorial conference, a discussion class at any level—all these are in essence committees: such groups do not lead themselves. An agenda no doubt has been prepared, but a leader is needed to run the show. Too often, he or she is present but missing; the meeting drags on pointlessly; everybody is restless and bored and goes away grumbling. Hence the complaint: "Another meeting?—Oh no!" To run a meeting efficiently and fairly is an acquired skill, because obstacles to transacting business are to be expected. So general advice about dealing with them is needed.

The point to settle first is whether the kind and size of the meeting call for an impartial arbiter, a chairman properly so called, or for a moderator who is allowed to contribute ideas on an equal footing with the other members. If the person in the chair is to lead a large group, he or she must master the Rules of Order set down by the indispensable Robert.[7] Most of them have a commonsense reason that is not hard to guess. For example, nominations may be debated but need not be seconded, because everybody should have an equal chance to gain office— no need to have *two* friends, or even one, to put one's name in the hopper.

Meetings usually can be run informally, because the membership of ten or twelve develops conversational ease. Still, someone must keep order, while drawing out individual opinion. As it comes out haphazardly, he helps to organize it into collective wisdom. To do so, a leader should hold in mind the stated subject and insist on pursuing it. Failure to guide the speakers from point to point is the cause of futile palaver. Not that the moderator aims at a particular outcome, he aims at *some* outcome or other.

---

[7]The latest version is *Robert's Rules of Order* (10th ed., 2000). A useful abridgement is *Webster's New World Robert's Rules of Order, Simplified and Applied* (2nd ed., 2001).

If the leader knows where he is along the way, he can afford to let the group digress occasionally (and briefly) into interesting sidelines. For if pressed too hard forward, some participants will feel regimented or manipulated. But if not hauled back, the talkers will wander far afield and the clock will tick on and on to no purpose. To maintain interest in the proceedings the chair limits repetition. It cannot be prevented, but it can be cut off diplomatically and with an even hand. To move ahead, each speaker should be nudged into adding his or her thought to the previous point, not start a hare half a mile off. Nor should two or three members be allowed to monopolize the time. Nothing alienates the less vocal sooner than this abuse; it is the leader's duty to involve as many people as possible in the work. Then no complaint is heard later that "my" or "her" useful ideas were neglected. Unless the "meeting manager" is forearmed in these ways against the muddle that occurs whenever a group comes together, the transaction of business will be slow and painful, or will not take place at all.

The Etiquette of Leadership

But in what manner, with what words, to exert firm control, on the one hand, and arousal on the other? Holding down the garrulous takes tactful timing and phrasing. After a reasonable stretch of some member's monologue, the chairman breaks into the flood with a soothing remark, such as: "Good way of looking at it, but I wonder what others think of the idea." A particular person may even be called on. To elicit still more suggestions, put a question about the topic: "I hear no views expressed on this proposal, the last one, by the way, on our agenda." Again, the prodding may refer to the inanimate state of the group itself: "Come now, I know it's late and we're all tired, but we must get done; we surely don't want another meeting." In teaching (since until the final week of the term "another meeting" is inevitable), let all questioning bear on subject matter, not individuals. Young people are tender-skinned; they respond best to the firm hand in the kid glove.[8] Such are the main features of life when one is leading a group.

Making the Most of Time

You have now reached the end of a long course of instruction, exhortation, and advice. It may seem as if there were too many things to observe at once to enhance your research, writing or speaking. You have been made aware of traps and have been given many useful pointers, but not the blueprint for your present project. Quite so: your reading has not been in vain; you have been made to reflect on the talents you must exert and the responsibilities you must fulfill, but you remain free agents.

You and only you can adapt and transfer the suggestions to your work. Do not worry: no new knowledge can ever be grasped and made use of in one sweep of the mind. Time is needed to assimilate it and form new habits. If necessary, go back to one or another topic and refresh your memory about what was actually said. In short, begin to use this book as a reference work.

One matter not mentioned before calls for your decision, the matter of when and how to work. Chapter 2 gave some hints about the division of tasks in research, and we may repeat them here: keep your clearest stretches of time for the uninterrupted study of your main sources. Verifying dates, hunting down references, and, generally, all broken-field running should be reserved for occasions when you have a shorter time at your disposal or when you are feeling less alert or energetic than usual. Your best mind should go to what takes thought, not simply attention.

The same principle applies to writing, with variations and additions. Faced with the need to write, most people (including practiced writers) experience a strong and strange impulse to

[8]An elaborate treatment of the discussion method will be found in *Education for Judgment: The Artistry of Discussion Leadership,* eds. C. Roland Christensen, David A. Garvin, and Ann Sweet (Boston, 1991).

put off beginning. To confront that blank screen or sheet of paper is like facing a firing squad. Why not turn aside, look up another source, reconsider the organization of the paper, refresh the memory by another look at the notes; or ultimate cowardice— you think of some shopping that cannot wait. *There is no cure for the urge to escape.* But there are palliatives, and some good enough to turn the struggle into a game.

The palliative principle is that only a regular force can overcome a recurrent inertia. Arrange to write regularly, never missing a date with yourself, regardless of mood, and you have won half the battle. Start on the dot. What you produce at first may not please you, nor should you expect a set amount, but *some* writing you must do from the hour that is kept sacred for the purpose. The writer's problem is the inverse of the reformed drunkard's. The latter must never touch a drop; the former must always do his stint. Skip but one writing period and you are set back for days.

Of course these writing periods must be close enough together to create a rhythm of work, and they must be truly convenient given your present mode of life. If possible, choose a time with no other fixed obligation at the end; that will keep you from looking at the clock halfway through the session. Use the same common sense as to the place. Do not try to write at home if you can hear your brother's DVD or the symphony of kitchen and nursery noises. A private office is ideal if the phone is cut off and your associates are cooperative.

What causes the distaste for beginning to write is that it is an act of self-exposure. When we plan to publish—in print or vocally—our aim is to show our thought to the outside world; everybody is given a look inside our mind. Self-protection and shyness combine with a sense of our mental confusion or uncertainty to make us postpone the exhibition. Hence the value of being alone when writing. In silence our thoughts become more settled and coherent, and as soon as a few of them are satisfactorily on paper, they draw out the rest. They gather momentum until after a time the sheer bulk of work sets up a desire to keep adding to it. One may even find oneself waiting for the set time or day the work being truly *in progress.*

In the light of this analysis, other rules of thumb follow as corollaries:

1. Do not wait until you have gathered all your material before starting to write. Nothing adds to inertia like a mass of notes, the earliest of which recede in the mists of time. Rather, begin drafting your ideas as soon as some portion of the topic appears to hang together in your mind.

2. Do not be afraid of writing down something that you think may have to be changed. A first draft is malleable substance to be molded and remolded as many times as needed.

3. Do not hesitate to write in any order the sections of your work that have grown ripe in your mind. There is a moment in any research where details come together naturally, despite small gaps and doubts. Seize that moment whether or not the portions that result are consecutive.

4. Once started, keep going. Resist the temptation to get up and verify a fact. Leave a blank or put in a question mark in the margin. Do the same for the word or phrase that refuses to come to mind. It will do so by itself on revision. This economy of time also serves momentum.

5. When you get stuck in the middle of a passage, reread the last two or three pages and see if that will not propel you past dead center. Many writers begin the day's work by reading over the previous day's accumulation. Some prefer to warm up by answering one or two letters, transcribing a few notes, making a diary entry, and the like—in short, *writing.* But ignore this type of running start if it distracts you from the main task.

6. When you come toward the end of your writing session, break off in the middle of a topic, not at the end of any natural division. The next day you take up the story in midstream, instead of having to begin the day *and* the new section together. Some writers make a point to break off the day's work before they run down and while they still have ideas in mind. They

scribble two or three in shorthand phrases to jump-start the next day's labors.

7. Since the right openings for chapters or sections are difficult (see Chapter 8), special attention must be paid to them. They require bearing in mind throughout your work. Be on the watch for ideas or facts or words that would make a good beginning and jot them down.[9]

8. It may happen that the opening sentences of the piece (or a part) will on rereading seem unrelated to what follows. That first portion was but the warming-up, and the true beginning is a few lines down. This "false beginning" is comforting, because it proves that a sluggish start on Saturday morning is no reason for discouragement.

9. To write with a sense of freedom, any preferences and peculiarities as to the mechanics of composing had best be humored. You use a pen better than a machine; favor a certain size or color of paper; want to arrange the books and notes on your desk just so; may prefer certain clothing, posture, or lighting. In all these matters one is entitled to complete self-indulgence. One has thus no excuse for putting off the task. And stick to your choices, so that the very sight of your working environment will trigger all your good habits.

With the first draft done, the back of the job is broken. It is then a pleasure—or it should be—to carve, cut, add, and polish until the script conveys what you have learned. Earlier chapters (2, 9, 10) have described the big and the small operations to perform in Revision. With the best will in the world, your work will not be free from error. But the bulk of it that is sound, clear, readily grasped and remembered will be a contribution, no matter how limited its scope, to that explicit order among facts and ideas that is called knowledge. For as Francis Bacon wisely observed in his *New Method,* "Truth will sooner come out from error than from confusion."

[9]See again p. 267.

A Few More Recommendations

On Research Methods

Beasley, David R., *Beasley's Guide to Library Research* (Toronto and Buffalo, University of Toronto Press, 2000).

Brady, John, *The Craft of Interviewing* (New York, Vintage Books, 1977).

Collins, Donald, Dianne Catlett, and Bobbie L. Collins, *Libraries and Research: A Practical Approach* (3rd ed., Dubuque, IA, Kendall/Hunt, 1994).

Mauch, James E., and Jack W. Birch, *Guide to the Successful Thesis and Dissertation: Conception to Publication: A Handbook for Students and Faculty* (4th ed., New York, M. Dekker, 1998).

Smith, Robert V., *Graduate Research: A Guide for Students in the Sciences* (3rd ed., Seattle, University of Washington Press, 1998).

On Leads to Information

Berkman, Robert I., *Find It Fast: How to Uncover Expert Information on Any Subject* (5th ed., New York, HarperResource, 2000).

Glossbrenner, Alfred, and Emily Glossbrenner, *Search Engines on the World Wide Web* (2nd ed., Berkeley, Peachpit Press, 1999).

Hillard, James M., with Bethany J. Easter, *Where to Find What: A Handbook to Reference Service* (4th ed., Lanham, MD, Scarecrow Press, 2000).

On Writing

Barzun, Jacques, *On Writing, Editing and Publishing* (2nd ed., Chicago, University of Chicago Press, 1986).

Bowen, Fredson, *Principles of Bibliographical Description* (New Castle, DE, Old Knoll Press, 1994).

Brower, Reuben, ed., *On Translation* (Cambridge, MA, Harvard University Press, 1959).

Neumann, Richard K., Jr., *Legal Reasoning and Legal Writing: Structure, Strategy, and Style* (4th ed., Gaithersburg, MD, Aspen Law and Business, 2001).

Spatt, Brenda, *Writing from Sources* (6th ed., Boston, Bedford/St. Martin's Press, 2003).

Stainton, Elsie Myers, *The Fine Art of Copyreading* (2nd ed., New York, Columbia University Press, 2002).

Wingell, Richard J., *Writing About Music: An Introductory Guide* (3rd ed., Upper Saddle River, NJ, Prentice Hall, 2002).

InfoTrac® College Edition Terms

Chapter 1
research
interpretation
accuracy
logic
honesty

Chapter 2
subject
material
compose
note-taking
reader

Chapter 3
facts
library
internet
database
catalogues

Chapter 4
verification
identification
evidence
falsification
attribution

Chapter 5
idea
terms
fallacy
tautology
scholar

Chapter 6
evidence
probability
subjective
causation
pragmatic

Chapter 7
pattern
period
bias
revisionism
"laws" of history

Chapter 8
chronological order
topical order
chapter
outline
book review

Chapter 9
revision
jargon
image
omnibus words
idiom

Chapter 10
style
sentence
construction
tone
rhythm

Chapter 11
quoting
citing
fair use
copyright
translate

Chapter 12
footnote
ibid
passim
bibliography
catch phrase

Chapter 13
revision
titles
blunder
index
consistency

Chapter 14
computer
spreadsheets
graphics
editing
palliative principle

Index